# PowerNomics®

# PowerNomics®

## *The National Plan to Empower Black America*

*Claud Anderson, Ed. D.*

*PowerNomics Corporation of America, Inc.*
*Publisher*

PowerNomics Corporation of America,
P.O. Box 30536
Bethesda, Maryland, 20814
(301) 564-6075 phone (301) 564-1997 fax
www.powernomics.com

This book contains information gathered from many sources. It is published for reference and not as a substitute for independent verification by users when circumstances warrant. It is sold with the understanding that neither the author nor the publisher is engaged in rendering any legal, psychological, accounting or business advice. The publisher and author disclaim any personal liability, either directly or indirectly, for advice for information presented within. Although the author and publisher have used care and diligence in the preparation, and made every effort to ensure the accuracy and completeness of information contained in this book, we assume no responsibility for errors, inaccuracies, omissions, or any inconsistency herein. Any slights of people, places, publishers, books or organizations are unintentional.

We gratefully acknowledge permission to reprint the following: *The Daily News* for the cartoon on page 2, originally entitled "Flesh Has Changed But The Spirit is The Same," and the *Washington Post* for the map of the "Number of People Living with HIV or AIDS."

Editors: Kevin Briscoe and Sara Reese; Book cover design: Laura Gaines Illustrator: Rene Toussaint

PowerNomics is a trademark of PowerNomics Corporation of America.

Library of Congress Card Number: 00-108185
1. African-American history 2. American history 3. Slavery 4. Blacks, economic empowerment of 5 Race relations, economic aspects of 6 Race relations, political aspects of

ISBN: 0-9661702-2-9

*Other Books and Educational Materials by the Author*

**Books**
*Black Labor, White Wealth: The Search for Power and Economic Justice*
*Dirty Little Secrets about Black History, Its Heroes and other Troublemakers*
*More Dirty Little Secrets about Black History, Its Heroes and other Troublemakers*

**DVDs**
*A Vision Beyond the Dream*
*Inappropriate Behavior: Road Blocks to Empowerment*
*On the Firing Line: Questions and Answers with Dr. Claud Anderson*
*Reparations: Now or Never*

Contact your local bookstore or PowerNomics Corporation of America for any of the above products. PowerNomics Corporation of America is the exclusive publisher of Dr. Claud Anderson's books and producer of his multimedia material.

## The PowerNomics Vision for Black America

*The PowerNomics vision is a Black America that is politically and economically self-sufficient and competitive by the year 2005.*

# Dedication

*In memory of my loving Mother and Father and to those very special people who are helping me build projects to make my vision for Black America a reality.*

# Acknowledgements

I am deeply indebted to those individuals who over the centuries have challenged American slavery, and Jim Crow semi-slavery, and decried the wealth inequalities between Blacks and Whites that racism produced. I am also indebted to two Black heroes who called attention to the inappropriate behavior patterns of Black people. My writings are infused with their observations and efforts.

Wealth inequity and inappropriate behavior are the two most fundamental problems facing Black Americans. Though it is not unusual to address the question of economic inequity, it is highly unusual to focus attention on the self-destructive behavior of Black people as a whole or Black individuals who mislead. In respect to self-destructive behavior among Blacks, the words of two historical figures, Harriet Tubman and Dr. Carter G. Woodson, stand out. Their words cut to the core of inappropriate behavior and compel us to accept the reality that many Blacks are more concerned about getting along than getting ahead. Well over a century ago, Harriet Tubman spoke her memorable lines at a public event in her honor. In response to the praise heaped on her as the "Black Moses" who inspired and led more than 300 slaves to the freedom of the "Promised Land" of the North, she reportedly said, "But I could have saved thousands, if they had only known they were slaves."

The words of Dr. Carter G. Woodson, noted Black author and historian, a century later, also moved me. Woodson said, "No people can go forward when the majority of those who should know better have chosen to go backward, but this is exactly what most of our [Black] misleaders do."[1]

These two outspoken Black champions from our past taught and inspired me. I want also to thank and acknowledge several other people in my life who worked directly with me to make this book possible. First, this book could not have been written without the support and loving assistance of my wife, Joann Anderson, Ph.D. I thank her for her review, comments and for her invaluable support in so many ways. She made this book possible by keeping my life calm, peaceful and happy. I thank the supporters of the Harvest Institute. A special thanks to Edward D. Sargent for his commitment to this project and for his encouragement and assistance in shaping Issues. I thank Kevin

M. Briscoe and Sara Lomax Reese for their editing and moral support and Rene Toussaint for his illustrations. I want to particularly acknowledge and thank Laura L. Gaines for the book cover layout and design. Her enthusiasm and creativity were incentives to the entire book team. Thank you to Derrick Humphries, Esq. for his friendship and legal review and to Shawna Jones and the many other people who supported me as I wrote this book and started a number of *PowerNomics* projects for Black America.

# CONTENTS

## Part I
## How Winners and Losers are Predetermined

## Part II
## Organizing for Empowerment

## Part III
## Empowerment Principles and Practices

# CONTENTS

# Introduction

Despite the fact that integration began 50 years ago, Black Americans remain the primary targets of conservative hate groups, police brutality and abusive government actions. According to a Federal Bureau of Investigation (FBI) annual report, Blacks are the victims of approximately 67 percent of hate crimes, though they are only 12.4 percent of the nation's total population. With recent incidents such as 170 church burnings, Black men dragged to their death behind pickup trucks in Texas and Illinois, or shot 41 times in New York while reaching for a wallet, it is not difficult to understand how the tally quickly reaches 67 percent. The FBI's hate crime list does not even include soft crimes like denying Black people home mortgages, jobs, or the right to use the highways without being pulled over for "driving while Black." Within every category of socioeconomic deprivation, Blacks represent six to eight times their proportionate number of the general population. The fact that Blacks are over-represented on this nation's welfare, poverty, unemployment, homeless, drug addiction and crime rolls is no accident and should come as no surprise. The function of racism is to marginalize Black people.

Racism is an undeniable factor in American society. It is distinct from and plays a greater role in life prospects than any form of gender, class, ethnic, language or religious discrimination. Contrary to prevailing myths, America has never been a color-blind society. Yet, racism continues to be ignored at all levels of government while the nation's attention and resources are focused on less contentious issues. White society has an out-of-sight, out-of-mind attitude about racism and avoids any substantive discussions of, let alone action against, racism. The callous indifference, disrespect and sometimes actual hatred that the majority society feels toward Black people are creating conditions that are dangerously parallel to those in Germany prior to the Jewish Holocaust of the 1930s and 1940s. Daniel J. Goldhagen, author of *Hitler's Willing Executioners*, writes about the Holocaust and the perils that can be expected when any national government permits hatred of an identifiable minority group to fester without efforts to mitigate or diffuse the hatred. When such widespread hatred goes unchecked in society, the targeted minority group is at risk.[1] The racial problem in America continues to exist because some ignore the problem and others simply do not know what to do. It is to the latter group that I address this book.

In 1994, in my first book, *Black Labor, White Wealth: The Search for Power and Economic Justice*, I wrote about the structural inequities that became part of our society during slavery and Jim Crow segregation. Seven years after that book was published, these structural inequalities remain unaddressed. *Black Labor, White Wealth* analyzed the historical relationship between Whites and Blacks, then tracked how the Western world used laws, policies, and social customs to enrich itself via the unpaid labor of enslaved Black Africans. *Black Labor, White Wealth* documented how legal, political and economic advantages were passed on to succeeding generations of White Americans. These legacies of White preference effectively mal-distributed nearly 100 percent of this nation's wealth and resources into the hands of the majority society and relegated Blacks to a permanently dependent, non-competitive, loser status.

In our social democracy, many have forgotten or simply do not know that the Federalist Papers, the foundation of the Constitution, laid out the responsibility of the majority to protect the rights of the minority in a majority-rules social democracy. Thus, it is the responsibility of the White majority to protect the rights of the Black minority. Not surprisingly, that protection has not occurred. Instead, the White majority has made the Black race a permanent, involuntary minority and has systematically denied generations of Blacks sufficient means to protect their own rights and compete in mainstream society.

*PowerNomics: The National Plan to Empower Black America* proposes a plan of action for Blacks to create a new, prosperous and empowered community that builds upon the yet unrealized competitive advantages of Black America.

The economic, political and educational action steps, principles, strategies and models that are offered in this book are based on analysis of the complex web of racial monopolies and other structural impediments that continue to drive Blacks deeper into an underclass structure. They also come from a comparative study of wealthy and powerful minority groups that have lifted themselves into competitive positions within the majority society. This book is a plan specifically intended for Black America, because no other group will support the elevation of Blacks to a position of group prosperity, respect and competitiveness. It is not in the best interest of others to help Blacks become more competitive. Thus, it is up to Black America to pull itself up by its bootstraps. Empowerment will not happen by chance, accident or wishes. It will require purposeful planning.

*PowerNomics: The National Plan to Empower Black America* picks up where *Black Labor, White Wealth* left off. It presents a conceptual framework and a plan to lead Black America to political and economic self-sufficiency and competitiveness by the year 2005. The term *PowerNomics* combines the concepts of power and economics. Power is the ability to get things done despite the resistance and opposition of others. Economics is the production, distribution and consumption of goods and wealth. *PowerNomics* then is the ability of Blacks to pool resources and power to produce, distribute and consume in a way that creates goods and wealth that Black people control. The facts and recommendations presented in this book are sometimes stark, bitter medicine, because *PowerNomics* is like a strong tonic intended to stir to action and guide those people who are motivated to help Black America in fundamental ways.

Much of my personal inspiration for writing *PowerNomics* came from the readers of *Black Labor, White Wealth* and people who attended lectures and workshops I have presented. Many of them thanked me for explaining the problems and presenting principles that should be used in crafting solutions. They then asked me to take one more step and blend my experiences and research into a program of action that individuals and groups can follow to empower their communities. *PowerNomics* provides that missing link between the historical analysis of the problems facing Blacks and the strategies needed to correct those problems.

This is not a book on how to succeed in White corporate America or how to invest one's personal funds for retirement. Nor is it a volume of warm and fuzzy motivational stories about personal triumphs and successes and how to improve one's relationships with the opposite sex. This book is about a people surviving and prospering. The tone is direct and simple. I make no pretense of being objective. This book makes moral judgments and predicts that racial disasters will occur unless this nation seriously addresses the historical injustice imposed on Black Americans. This book has two premises: first, those who desire to create effective solutions to a problem must understand the nature and history of the problem. Second, Black America needs a national plan with how-to strategies in order to move into political and economic competitiveness with America's mainstream society and its various ethnic sub-groups.

Admittedly, *PowerNomics* runs counter to the conventional thinking of visible and successful Blacks in America today. Though the wealth and power gap between Blacks and non-Blacks is widening, visible and successful Blacks remain committed to protecting their own personal comfort zone by avoiding association with anything that is identifiably Black. Today's Black leaders in many cases display some of the inappropriate behavior discussed in this book. And, while many of these leaders are personal acquaintances and friends, it has been their choice to give top priority to working, not for Black people, but for minorities, women, poor people, people of color, the handicapped and newly arriving immigrants. The failure of visible and successful Blacks to appropriately lead the race leaves 36 million Black Americans in a leadership crisis.

The PowerNomics plan is offered to the nation in hopes of saving Black America. It is a synthesis of my experiences in government, business, research and academia. It is necessarily subjective, contains few citations and frequently uses first person references. It is not intended to be an academic recitation of facts or of other authors' opinions. It is offered more informally as a road map with clearly marked milestones. It will not answer all your questions.

Once you have finished this book, if you are not motivated to use this plan to help build a more competitive and independent Black America, then simply lay it down and continue doing what you would normally do. However, for those who want to help an unjustly treated and forgotten people, welcome aboard. Accept the reality that the legacies of slavery and Jim Crow semi-slavery still exist in various forms of structural racism, then try some of the countermeasures this book recommends.

The probability is high, even at this late hour, that with deliberate actions, Black people can still become a competitive and self-sufficient group in America. It was in the spirit of that possibility that this national plan was written. The following section provides summaries of the eight chapters of this book.

**Chapter One** paints a picture of the depth and magnitude of Black Americans' socioeconomic predicament. It examines the collective inherited advantages of being White and the collective inherited disadvantages of being Black. It describes how four centuries of slavery, Jim Crow segregation, and benign neglect locked Blacks into the lowest societal strata, while mal-distributing nearly 100 percent of this nation's wealth and resource power into the hands of a pecking order of European and other ethnic groups.

The socioeconomic disparities between the races have evolved into modern-day monopolies protected by structural racism, inheritance laws, immigration and other public policies. These established monopolies not only guarantee White society an advantaged lifestyle, but they also *predetermine* racial winners and losers in a supposedly open and competitive society. Instead of being truly open and competitive, American marketplaces are dominated by powerful political and economic racial forces.

**Chapter Two** introduces the rationale for the *PowerNomics* empowerment culture, group vision and related enabling paradigms: **ethno-aggregation** and **vertical integration**. This chapter discusses the importance of having group self-interest and a sense of group competition. The paradigms of ethno-aggregation and vertical integration provide Blacks with tools to alter their mind-set and transform their traditional way of seeing, thinking and behaving in regard to racial matters. Clearly understanding the empowerment vision of *PowerNomics* and its paradigms can help Black Americans make decisions that are in the group's best interest. This chapter also explains how the application of these paradigms as conceptual templates can increase consistency and efficiency in race-related decision making. Ethno-aggregation and vertical integration can serve as conceptual cookie-cutters that can be used to build racial unity, and replace outdated, passive civil rights and integration ideologies.

**Chapter Three** focuses on the importance of community, and the role that communities play in fostering competitive group politics and group economics. It identifies three important elements that Black people need in order to transform their residential neighborhoods from mere geographical groupings into functional communities. Once Blacks form real communities, they can then use them as repositories for storing their history, culture, wealth, income, businesses, security and sense of "people-hood." This chapter lists the steps to build real Black communities, and discusses how a community builds its radius of trust, cooperation, and accountability. It also stresses the importance of "marking and closing" Black communities.

A major part of this chapter examines two of the most pernicious social systems devised to control human beings and destroy their sense of community. The first system of meritorious manumission (often called Willie Lynchism) was imposed on Blacks in the early 1700s. This social conditioning process is compared with a system of brainwashing that was imposed on American soldiers in Korean prisoners of war camps during the early 1950s. The techniques and results of both systems were nearly identical and engineered behaviors into the target populations that destroyed group unity and reduced the communities to groups of people who functioned as individuals.

**Chapter Four** urges change in the traditional role of schools in educating Black children. Specifically, this chapter advises Black Americans to take control of the governance of their neighborhood schools and redesign them around the needs, interests and goals of Black America. The premise of this chapter is that schools are producing exactly what they were designed to produce—a marginally trained Black laborer capable of taking orders and using his or her physical strength to entertain, enrich, protect, and comfort the majority White society. Since schools were never intended to educate Black children to be self-sufficient, independent and competitive, this chapter argues that they must begin to receive an education that is reality based and teaches them to live, work and compete in a pluralistic society. Implementation of the *PowerNomics* national plan requires that Black Americans educate their youth to use their intellectual resources to help the group. To accomplish this end, schools in Black communities must close down, like an automobile assembly factory getting ready to produce new models, retool and reopen only after they are ready to accept a new role in which educational goals, curricula, teaching methods, governance and funding have been crafted in alignment with the national empowerment plan for Black America. Black communities must also inspire and demand political changes on a local level regarding the methods of school governance and funding. Thus, this chapter discusses the role that education should play to free new generations of Black minds from the old social conditioning, so that

Black children can gain the skills, social unity, and human resources to compete with children from all other groups.

**Chapter Five** offers a new economic model to convert Black neighborhoods into core economic engines for building wealth and practicing group economics. It highlights how Blacks have remained outside of this nation's economic booms and prosperity for centuries. An endless influx of European ethnic immigrants have entered this nation as first class citizens and joined the majority White society in the economic suppression and exploitation of Black Americans. This chapter points out: how Black Americans are violating every known principle of group economics; the growing wealth and income inequalities between Blacks and Whites; how ethnic groups build niche businesses; how Whites and ethnic groups boycott Black businesses; the capital and brain drain from Black communities; racism in our immigration policies; and the self-inflicted damage of non-economic integration and civil rights.

**Chapter Six** is a how-to chapter. It serves as a user's guide to empower Black communities by industrializing them. With America downsizing its industrial capacity, this chapter stresses the importance of Black America building and operating its own industries to capture and control technology rather than continuing to be its primary victim. Though Black people are the only population group denied the cultural economic and technological benefits of participating in any of the world's industrial revolutions, it is still not too late for us to build our own. Based upon our consumer spending patterns, cultural assets and market advantages, we can create vertical industries within our own business communities. This chapter identifies some of the industries that Blacks should pursue. Moreover, it suggests ways in which Blacks can amass capital and control consumer markets. Using the basic *PowerNomics* empowerment tools of ethno-aggregation and vertical integration, this chapter describes how to construct industries by vertically linking every process, from supplying raw materials at the bottom of the chain to selling the product to the retail consumer markets at the top.

**Chapter Seven** looks at politics through the framework of the *PowerNomics* vision and offers 12 principles Blacks can use to win group-based political benefits. It questions the historical practice of Black Americans ritualistically electing political candidates to public office without receiving reciprocal benefits, voting simply to exercise the right, and failing to hold those they elect accountable for delivering benefits to Black communities. The political principles presented in this chapter show Black Americans how to play and win as a group in competitive politics.

**Chapter Eight** proposes a theology of economics. It issues a call for Black religious organizations to use their vast resources to enhance the earthly quality of life for Black people—just as churches do for every other ethnic or racial population. Nearly every known organized religion has developed a theological doctrine to morally justify and in some cases, even to support exploitation of Black people. To counter the effects of centuries of spiritual and economic abuse, this chapter recommends expanding the traditional role of Black churches to encompass specific economic and political activities that are needed to improve the immediate quality of life for Black people.

In these eight chapters and the appendices, *PowerNomics* presents a national plan that analyzes the racial dynamics within our society and prescribes new political, education, economic and social remedies designed to bring about true equality between the races. The analysis and recommendations within this book are designed to stimulate soul-searching discussions among all segments of our society, particularly within the Black community. Since Black America stands to benefit or lose the most, Black Americans must lead the way.

On an editorial note, the Black community in the United States is divided over whether to identify its members as "Black" or "African-American." In this book the two terms are used interchangeably. Similarly, there is debate regarding whether the terms "White" and "Black" should be capitalized. It is illogical to capitalize American Indian, Hispanic, Arab or Asian yet not capitalize the terms used to describe the two largest racial populations in the United States. Accordingly, I have chosen to capitalize both "White" and "Black." In addition, as a writer who is Black, my perspective shifts between the first and third person when writing about Black people. Finally, a major premise of this text is that Black people lack communities and have yet to build communities, but I frequently use the term "Black community" to refer to Black people simply as a population. Now, for those readers who are ready to shift into a reality mode and begin a new road to Black prosperity and true equality, let us begin our journey.

# Part I

# How Winners and Losers are Predetermined

# CHAPTER ONE

## *Racism, Monopolies and Inappropriate Behavior*

> *Alice: Which road do I take?*
> *Cheshire Cat: Where do you want to go?*
> *Alice: I don't know!*
> *Cheshire Cat: Then it doesn't matter which road you take!*

— Lewis Carroll, *Alice in Wonderland*

### *The Challenges We Face*

As the Cheshire Cat said to Alice, who was lost in a Wonderland fantasy, it doesn't matter much which road you take if you don't know where you are going. It is time for Black Americans to take a good hard look at where they have come from and where they are going. Are they moving forward or standing still? After centuries of participating in protest marches, race riots and demonstrations, and pushing for integration and passage of an endless number of civil rights laws, Black Americans are increasingly sensing that something is wrong. They question whether or not they are on the right road. A comparative analysis of our socio-economic conditions shows that Black Americans have entered the new millennium much the same way they entered the previous four centuries—as an impoverished, powerless and neglected people. Since there have yet to be any programs and public policies specifically offered to eliminate the plight of the Black masses, their future, like their past, looks bleak.

Amidst a rising tide of White conservatism, the wealth and income gaps between majority White society and Blacks are widening. Nearly a half a century after the Supreme Court ordered racial desegregation, Black Americans still bear six to eight times their proportional share of poverty, broken homes, homelessness, criminal incarceration, unemployment and other social pathologies. Desegregation should have been about redistribution, wealth, power and resources, not social integration. Social integration has only addressed the symptoms of our

1

dilemma rather than the causes. As indicated in Figure 1, it is extremely difficult for Black people to progress when the same hands that held the whip still hold almost all of the wealth and power.

New York Daily News, 1937, artist unknown. Reprinted with permission.

Figure 1. Same Overclass, Same Underclass

During centuries of Black enslavement and Jim Crow semi-slavery, the majority society secured and retained its inherited advantages.

While a Black minority inherited a legacy of disadvantage in this race-based society, Whites acquired ownership and control of nearly everything of value as well as a system for keeping Blacks non-competitive and powerless. The sheer existence and size of a growing Black underclass is prima facie evidence of institutionalized racism that manipulates symbols, resources and power to advantage Whites over Blacks. The reality of Black America's dilemma is that they are predestined to become a permanent underclass, if they do not break free of the numerous disadvantages they have inherited.

Blacks should get off of the social road to nowhere. There are no yellow brick roads to the future, nor will Blacks simply stumble into wealth and power in a competitive society. To find a better road requires Blacks to unlearn old behavior models, strategies and "learned helplessness" in race matters. Blacks must understand the nature of the "competitive race" and make a radical metamorphosis. They must decide where they want to go, get out front of their competitors, and work hard to get there first. If Blacks compete, they can expect to succeed and survive in the race for wealth and power.

## *Race, Racism and Wealth*

Although slavery and Jim Crow semi-slavery ended generations ago, their legacies live on in various forms of structural racism. Contrary to popular notions about the concept of race, it is more than a biological grouping. Race is about financial, political and social currencies. It is a form of stored wealth and power. Whiteness has monetary value. Knowing the origin and nature of the value of race is essential to any analysis of Black America's dilemma. It is important that Blacks know why the race problem refuses to die and how it is used to keep them a non-competitive and powerless group. The word "race" first appeared with the emergence of the slave practice in the 16th century.[1] Records indicate the word race was selected because the various European slave-trading nations were in a contest, competing to profit from the mineral and human wealth of Africa. The prize for winning the race was the power to develop Western civilization, using the wealth extracted out of Africa. Black people were non-competitors in the race. They *were* the prizes, so they could neither play nor win,

All the competing slave trading nations, religions, and ethnic groups benefited and were advantaged by Black slavery.

Slavery is most often approached in social and moral terms. It is seldom discussed in terms of the primary incentive that undergirded the slave trade—wealth building. Slavery must always be explained in monetary terms. Throughout the 16th, 17th and 18th centuries, organized religion used doctrines to justify slave trading. During this same period, botanists and others in the biological sciences were studying and attempting to stratify plants and animals based upon their biological similarities and differences. They ordered plants and animals by "species." Though it took nearly 300 years, the concept of race eventually merged with the concept of biological species. By that time, White Europeans had secured nearly total control of the world's wealth and resource powers. Their new concept of race established superiority on the basis of who controlled the wealth, power and resources at that particular time in history. Wealth, power and privileges became the prerogatives of non-Blacks. Through intellectual sleight-of-hand, race became synonymous with the term *species* in the mid-1800s. At that time, Charles Darwin developed the concept of biological race, in his *Origin of the Species* and it quickly became popular. Often called the "survival of the fittest," Darwin's theories as well as a number of other quasi-scientific concepts were used by educators, politicians, and religious leaders to justify Black slavery and establish a qualitative ranking of inherited genes and human fitness.

Naturally, those controlling the wealth and power put their cultural values and biological characteristics at the top of the racial order and Blacks at the bottom, beneath Caucasians and Mongols (Asians). All the major European religious denominations at the time used the Bible to teach racial ranking with implicit Black "inferiority."

During the Black civil rights movement of the 1950s and 1960s, the concept of biological races was intentionally expanded to include cultural, religious, ethnic and all Spanish-speaking language groups, which were competing with Black people for rights, space and privileges.[2] The concept of race was then diluted to an attitudinal level, and the term racism was used interchangeably with such terms as bias, prejudice, bigotry and discrimination. Now, the term "racism" has become so amorphous that it has little meaning and is applied to all so-called minorities. If Black Americans are to resolve and reverse the legacies of slavery, they must view and treat racism based upon its original meaning and intent.

## *Racism: A Race Without a Finish Line*

Racism is a wealth- and power-based competitive relationship between Blacks and non-Blacks. The sole purpose of racism is to support and ensure that the White majority and its ethnic subgroups continue to dominate and use Blacks as a means to produce wealth and power. Centuries of Black enslavement and Jim Crow semi-slavery resulted in the majority society becoming 99-foot giants and Blacks one-foot midgets. This massive inequality in wealth and resources made Blacks non-competitive and totally dependent upon Whites for the necessities of life. True racism exists only when one group holds a disproportionate share of wealth and power over another group then uses those resources to marginalize, exploit, exclude and subordinate the weaker group. In America, it is Whites who use wealth and power to marginalize, exploit, and subordinate Blacks. Whites can deny Blacks employment, educational opportunities, business resources, a place to live or the right to vote. Therefore, according to this definition, Black people cannot be racists. No group of Blacks has the power or exclusive control of resources to the degree that they can educationally, politically, economically and socially exploit and marginalize the White race.[3] Blacks can only react to racism and try to alter the conditions that racism creates. Despite the realities, there are numerous conservative Blacks who act as apologists for White racism and confuse the issue. A conservative Black radio talk show host in Los Angeles, for example, charges that Blacks are as racist as Whites. His desire for White approval as well as his ignorance of history impedes him from understanding that White racism and Black prejudice are not the same thing. Blacks have a reason for their feelings about Whites based on how they have been treated by Whites. The White race, on the other hand, has never been marginalized by the Black race. Racism reinforces the legacies of slavery and Jim Crow semi-slavery. Blacks have been unable to escape from those legacies because the majority society acknowledges the operation of racism in the distant past, but minimizes its present significance.

## *The Burdens of Inequality*

The concept of race has progressed from the international competition for wealth and power, to religious doctrine, to biological classification to a personal attitude. Yet, conditions and opportunities are unequal between competing minority groups. There has been no equal sharing of burdens in our equal opportunity society. Members of ethnic, class, gender, disabled, religious, Spanish language and sexual orientation groups have not been treated in a manner equal to Blacks. This nation has never enacted and supported public policies and laws that have denied non-Blacks access to this nation's educational, political, social and economic systems. These groups have not been customarily lynched, castrated, exploited and denied the fruits of their labor. Blacks are the only group of people forced to practice capitalism without capital in the richest and most capitalistic nation on earth. These facts, coupled with the majority society's total unwillingness to approve corrective action and reparations for descendants of Black slaves reveal the true nature of racism against Black people.

Racism and other legacies of slavery predetermine the success of Black Americans as a group. One of the most glaring examples of inherited inequalities is wealth distribution. Black America's percentage of ownership of the nation's wealth remains where it was in the 1860s on the eve of the Civil War. At that time, when nearly every Black person in America was either in full slavery or semi-slavery, Blacks owned one-half of one percent of this nation's wealth. The emancipation of enslaved Blacks in no sense rendered social justice and economic recompense.

Today, more than 140 years later, we are "100 percent" free, yet Black Americans still own only one-half of one percent of this nation's wealth. Today, the income of Blacks as compared to Whites has regressed to the level it was at the end of the 1960s. Approximately 38 percent of the Black population is beneath the poverty line and another one-third is marginal, just above the poverty line. The limited assets that Black Americans most often have, such as automobiles and personal effects, depreciate rather than appreciate in value.

Blacks even find that our homes, usually our most valuable assets, have a limited market and prices are dictated by urban renewal, expressways or gentrification. The average Black person passes on zero assets to future generations. The typical White family is more economically stable and secure. Approximately 87 percent of this nation's economic assets are now frozen within the dominant White society and are passed on from one generation to the next in such forms as stocks, bonds, land, businesses, trust accounts, endowments, foundations and insurance policies. Therefore, White children are privileged to enter the world with 87 percent of the resources that they need to succeed in life already in their families, race, communities, businesses, schools, governments or social organizations. Thus, succeeding generations of Whites can access these wealth resources over and over again.

What is wealth? Wealth refers to the net value of a person, group or community less their liabilities or debt at a given point in time. It is stored value. Income, in contrast, refers to a flow of dollars over a period of time. With rare exceptions, most Blacks are so marginalized that they own and control little wealth or resources anywhere, including their own neighborhoods.

The ancestors of enslaved Blacks were forced to concentrate simply on surviving, pursuing civil rights and integration. They had little to bequeath to their descendents. Even though they succeeded in their social and civil rights efforts, their children cannot inherit welfare, food stamps, public housing or a "good" job.

## *Three Major Impediments to Black Competitiveness*

Regardless of how fast and how high Black Americans jump, without proportional wealth ownership and control of resources, it is nearly impossible for Blacks to play the game of capitalism, and even more difficult for them to win. Why can't Blacks win? Let's examine three major impediments to Black self-sufficiency and competitiveness. Figure 2 shows that the three major impediments are:

- Mal-distribution of wealth and resource powers
- Inappropriate behavior patterns
- Lack of a national plan for empowerment

Each of these three major impediments is carefully examined and discussed in detail in the next few sections of the book.

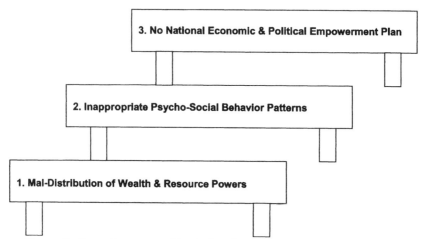

Figure 2. Impediments to Black Self-Sufficiency and Competitiveness

## *The First Impediment: Mal-distribution of Wealth*

The first impediment to Black empowerment is the structural wealth inequities between Blacks and Whites. To begin our journey to self-empowerment, we must first understand that these inequities are structural, much like the framing of a house. The frame provides the underlying support for the walls, ceilings, and floors. You cannot see the framing once the walls and flooring have been completed. As long as the house stands, the way in which the house was framed will dictate not only its shape but also the mobility of the people who live inside the house.

The structural racial inequities of wealth and resource powers function in a similar way. They are buried in the fabric of American society. They dictate life chances, rewards and opportunities and explain how people act in race matters. Whites have had such total control over wealth, power, resources and basic necessities of life that it has become the norm.

Racial myths have long promoted the belief that the conditions of Black Americans are the consequence of nature rather than the result of this nation's historical acts. The structural inequities of race can only persist if the historical origin of White control of wealth, resources and power remain either unknown or ignored. White society will not publicly admit that its powerful self-interests perpetuate the legacy of slavery and Jim Crow semi-slavery. The critical contributions of Black people to the development of this nation and the Western civilization are largely hidden. To admit Black people's contributions is to trigger White guilt and a sense of responsibility for Black people's predicament.

According to records, the majority society compiled its wealth by using a simple economic principle: the industry of slavery produced a 1500 percent return on investment without the burden of wages, employee benefits, and taxes. The lifetime profits produced by slaves were passed on to the slaveholders' heirs and their heirs' heirs. Wealth accumulated for White society while poverty accumulated for Blacks.

Our nation claims to be an equal opportunity, color-blind society, after more than a century of mal-distributing the nation's land and wealth-producing resources to everyone but Blacks. Even after Jim Crow segregation ended in the 1960s, and this nation formally became a "just society," the White society committed only $15 billion to conduct a "War on Poverty." Since this program included every group in America, it is unclear how this limited effort was supposed to correct the centuries of abuse inflicted specifically on Black people. Social conservatives argue that seven years of the Great Society programs fulfilled all responsibilities that White society had to Blacks for 400 years of slavery and Jim Crow semi-slavery.

Neither the U.S. government nor social conservatives have offered a public explanation for including gender, ethnic, class, Spanish-speaking and disabled groups in a program that supposedly paid the nation's debt to Blacks. Ironically, during the same seven-year period, this nation spent $120 billion on the war in Vietnam, which was eight times larger than the amount spent on the War on Poverty.[4] Hidden behind the façade of a color-blind society, racism in the 1970s became politically incorrect. To maintain the status quo, structural racism replaced overt racism, and the term "minorities" replaced "Blacks."

## *Our Monopolized Society*

Racism in America has gone through a number of mutations, though always retaining its inequities. It is now practically impossible for members of our society to see and prove racism against Black people. It is now hidden behind a pseudo-egalitarian smoke screen. Social conservatives and the power elite praised Martin L. King, Jr., picked up the rhetoric of the Black civil rights movement, but distorted the fundamental intent of the movement. They proclaimed that racial inequality no longer existed and all groups were starting out even. Thus, they created an illusion. Just like the drunk who took his pet alligator into a bar, cut off its tail, painted it yellow and called it a dog, social conservatives and the power elite are taking racism through similar false transformations. However, no matter how it is camouflaged, racism is still right before our eyes. Old-fashioned racism has gone legitimate again, masquerading with all of the rights and privileges of approved monopolies.

The word monopoly emanates from the word monarch. According to Charles R. Geisst, the author of *Monopolies in America*, the tradition of monopolies was inherited from English common law: "The British crown granted patent letters to merchants, giving them exclusive right to provide certain goods or services."[5] Any monopoly conveys the ultimate source of power, wealth and control to a person, group or business. When a business entity has a monopoly, it dominates and controls nearly all aspects of an industry and can use its massive power to raise barriers to control markets and bankrupt competitors.

A racial monopoly, like any other monopoly, is defined by its origin and the power it has over its competitors. On its way to becoming the essence of various White monopolies, racism has passed through three monopolistic stages. The first stage is a **natural monopoly** that protects things that are strategically vital to the government itself. In race matters, Whiteness, and all of its ramifications, was always strategically vital and invaluable, entitling its bearer to wealth, privileges, authority, power and certain inalienable rights. The United States Constitution codified Whiteness as a national asset. Various state and local governments passed anti-miscegenation laws that defined Whiteness and protected it from race mixing.

The second is a **collusive monopoly**. This monopoly exists when members of a tightly knit group of public agencies or private corporations enter into specific agreements to control the marketplaces or the wealth, power and resources of a society over their common competitor. In race matters, it is a collusive monopoly when this nation continuously expands the definition of Whiteness to include a hierarchy of ethnic groups. Today it includes a succession of immigrants from Europe, the Middle-East, Spanish speaking countries and Asia. All of these groups are unified as members of the Caucasian race with the exception of Blacks and Asians. And, according to Andrew Hacker, Asians are on probation to be classified as White.[6] Immigration laws are examples of specific agreements that control marketplaces, wealth and power. These laws established new priorities for admissions: country of origin, family members who are already here, possession of needed skills and the financial ability to purchase entry. This criteria is biased toward immigrants with skin color that is more acceptable than Black.

The third stage is a **shared monopoly**. This is a popular term used in the business world today. A shared monopoly is a composite of a collusive and natural monopoly. It reaches its maximum effectiveness when members of a group work together to control or drive competition out of the marketplace. Small businesses have federal anti-trust laws to protect them from the power of large corporate monopolies. But, there are no constitutional or government provisions that prevent the White society and its feeder immigrant groups from shutting Blacks out of political and economic marketplaces.

## *A Brief History of Monopoly Building in America*

Over the course of this nation's history, there have been at least three major phases of monopoly building for wealth and power. The first monopoly-building phase in American history occurred during the colonization of America when Europeans, in general, and the English, in particular, formed and held natural monopolies in land ownership, slave trading and slavery-supported industries. England exerted the power of its newly found slavery-based wealth by instituting the Navigation Act in the 1760s and other laws and tariffs that mandated that American colonists ship their slave-produced raw products and goods to England for processing, manufacturing, and marketing. The colonists then had to purchase back the finished products at higher and inflated prices.

This system effectively allowed England to exercise full economic and political control and to economically exploit its colonies as well as other nations. England became the king of slave trading and held a natural monopoly on constructing slave-based economies. The English crown established the first franchising system that built plantations, financed the slaveholders, supplied the slaves and shipped and processed the slave-produced goods. It took a full century for the American colonists to recognize that they were locked into an English monopoly. Once the reality set in, they began calling those monopolies, "tyranny." The American colonies rejected England's plans to expropriate the fruits of slave labor and to control the politics of the colonies. The colonists knew from the English history of serfdom that any system that politically subordinates, economically exploits and socially dominates a group of people is tyrannical because it reduces them to slaves. The colonists did not want to be England's serfs. They preferred to fight and when they did they ignited and fought the Revolutionary War for their independence.

The second phase of monopoly building began shortly after the Revolutionary War. The American colonists immediately drafted the United States Constitution, which imposed on Black people the same government-sponsored tyranny, that the colonialists rejected under the English rule. The "founding fathers" of this nation, most of whom were slaveholders and sympathetic to other slaveholders, drafted and ratified the United States Constitution. That document gave the colonial slaveholders a collusive monopoly, the same monopolistic controls that England had over the colonists before the war.[7]

Just as slave labor had made England wealthy, it allowed Southern slaveholders to operate in their own best interest rather than the best interest of Northern Whites or enslaved Blacks. The North eventually concluded that it could not acquire competitive wealth and political power until it broke the South's monopoly on Black labor. In 1861, the Civil War broke out between the North and the South over wealth and political power.

The third phase of monopoly building occurred after the North won the Civil War. The war effectively destroyed legalized slavery and transferred the South's monopolies on wealth and political power to the North. The North focused its newly acquired wealth and power on industrializing the North and the West. The massive amounts of money previously invested in the slavery industry and Civil War military production was used to build bridges, canals, railroads, ships and factories. However, in achieving the political and economic defeat of the South, the North had ignored the five million ex-slaves. Major political organizations in the North went on record opposing emancipation of enslaved Blacks unless they were shipped out of the country in order that they not compete against White men's labor, Stephen Steinberg[8] wrote. The North abandoned Black ex-slaves. The South got the message and commandeered Blacks into semi-slavery while the North looked the other way. According to a *Memorandum of Proceedings in the United States Senate*, "The Southern states by their situation and climate require Black labor and must have it or the states will cease to have any value."[9]

The Southern states enacted Black codes that again gave them a shared monopoly control on land, economic systems, governments, education systems, and Black labor for another 100 years. Both the North and the South used various levels of government to create White-only business and political, intellectual and social monopolies.[10] These advantages of property, technology, political participation and major business opportunities were passed on to succeeding generations of White males.

## *Racial Monopolies in America*

Racial monopolies predetermine winners and losers and are considered a normal part of our politico-economic structure. Through these monopolies, White society maintains a lock on the essential elements of Black people's lives and makes Black people spectators in the democratic process. The racial monopolies discussed below are but a few of the nearly invisible structures that marginalize and justify Black America's position as this nation's permanent minority loser.

### *Monopolies Established in the Constitution:*

As indicated earlier, the United States Constitution is not and has never been color-blind. It is race-specific and color-conscious. For all intents and purposes, the Constitution remains unchanged. The founding fathers were the first ones to "play the race card." In fact, they were the original card dealers. They allocated rights, resources and power to the majority White society. America essentially has two

13

constitutions: one for Whites and one for Blacks. Constitutional amendments one through 12 are race-specific and empower the majority White society. The 13th through 15th Amendments were also color-specific. They gave citizenship and empowerment rights to Black ex-slaves. The 13$^{th}$ Amendment eliminated legal slavery. The 14$^{th}$ Amendment gave Blacks equal protection and due process rights. The 15$^{th}$ Amendment extended voting and other social rights to Blacks. Majority society has co-opted these Amendments. During Reconstruction in the 1860s, major social and economic forces began to make these Amendments color-blind, even though they were originally specific to Blacks. The term color-blind was not formally used until 1896 when Chief Justice John M. Harlan of the Supreme Court issued a dissenting opinion in the Plessy v. Ferguson decision. The Supreme Court held that there was nothing wrong with "separate but equal" accommodations for Blacks and Whites as a public policy. But, Justice Harlan said the Constitution was color-blind. He was the first to say it, but he was wrong. The Constitution is and always has been color specific.

The color consciousness of the Constitution was no accident. The Constitution codified the racial inequalities that existed initially in our society. James Madison, a major author of the Constitution and a slaveholder, knew he was not including Black people when he spoke of how the country would always be divided between those who held property and those who were themselves property. When he spoke of "owning property," he meant items such as household furnishings, livestock and land. He also clearly included ownership of slaves. When the Constitution was finally ratified in 1789, however, it used broad, ambiguous, and inoffensive public relations type words such as "all" and "everyone" rather than to refer directly to Black slaves. Still, it established a system in which the racial group defined as "White" could hold monopolies of wealth and political power over the subordinate Black group that was classified as personal property and only "three-fifths" of a human.

The Constitution also included an affirmative action provision for the South that eventually led to a Civil War between the North and South. The Constitution made White Southerners a protected "minority" with the privilege of holding a monopoly on slavery. More specifically, provisions in the U.S. Constitution gave the Southern minority political rights, preferential treatment in the Fugitive Slave Act, favorable quotas on the export and import of slave-related products, and set-aside advantages on elected representation in Congress. This revered document declared freedom and justice for everyone but Blacks, while giving special status, privileges, and rights to the South. The Constitution continues to be used as the basis to deny preferences, affirmative action and reparations for Black Americans.

Citizenship and the benefits of Whiteness were constitutionally denied to Blacks. Ironically, like Blacks, Indians were also specifically identified in the Constitution, but they were excluded from "official" abuse because they were categorized as free inhabitants and encouraged to assimilate into White society. By the end of the 19th century, American Indians had the option to leave the reservations or remain protected wards of the government. Yet, throughout their relationship, White leaders and various institutions have recognized Indians as an acceptable extension of White society that ranked higher in the biological order than Blacks.

When the U.S. Constitution was modified in the 1860s through the addition of the 13th, 14th, and 15th Amendments, the Black Constitution, after numerous rewrites the final language contained ambiguous words such as "all persons," "any person," and "everyone," although it was commonly understood that the Constitutional Amendments were for Black ex-slaves. The initial Congressional enabling language hinted that these civil rights laws bound the U.S. Congress to take care of Black ex-slaves until they could take care of themselves. To this day, however, Congress has never abided by their own laws in this regard, and members have sat by silently while the dominant society has boldly undermined the economic rights awarded to Black people. They allowed the majority White society to co-opt the Black Constitution and promote the myth that the United States Constitution was color-blind. The Constitution was conceived as a socioeconomic covenant for those who already had power, wealth and nearly unlimited rights. To be a truly democratic society, this nation would have to redistribute and share some of its wealth and power with Black America. The Black Constitution was passed following the Civil War because of the efforts of a small group of radical liberal Republican Congressmen who succeeded in amending the Constitution by including color-specific amendments for Blacks. These amendments gave

Blacks a minimum level of rights that certain Congressmen hoped would offset some of the tyranny of the White majority society.

## Population Monopolies:

One of the first acts of the U.S. Congress following the ratification of the Constitution was the enactment of this nation's first naturalization and immigration law in 1790. This law declared America to be a "White nation" and set a zero quota on Black immigrants, except as slaves. A quota of approximately zero remained in effect until 1965 when it was increased to its current level of one-half of one percent.[11] Throughout most of this nation's history, peoples of African descent have been nearly shut out of the immigration and refugee programs of the United States. Blacks have competed in this nation's "majority wins" population game almost exclusively from birth rates rather than immigration. Though they could never win as a national majority, they also have never won as a local majority. The Black civil rights movement's quest for integration ensured that Blacks would always be a minority population in White schools, businesses, jobs, communities, or entertainment centers.

The census is conducted every decade and establishes the official population count of the country. Efforts to create a "multicultural category" in the 2000 census will most likely dilute and, in reality, distort downward the number of Blacks in America. Dilution of population numbers assures that Blacks will lose status as the numerical majority minority. Government efforts to change racial definitions will retain the White population majority (monopoly) and inflate the numbers of Hispanics in the population.

In his book, *Uprooting Racism*,[11] Paul Kivel says, "Whiteness is a many faceted phenomenon, slowly and constantly shifting its emphasis, all the time maintaining a racial hierarchy and protecting the power that accrues to White people . . . Although there are no natural or essential qualities or characteristics of Whiteness, or of White people, it is not an easy fiction to let go of."[12] By constantly enlarging the ethnic boundaries of Whiteness (all Europeans, Middle-Easterners, Hispanics, and soon Asians), Whites separate people who are entitled to privileges and wealth from people who are exploited and violated. In a group-based society, constant efforts to enlarge the majority

White population ensure that a shared racial population monopoly will continue to exist far into the future. The 2000 Census form offers Blacks 54 sub-categories to opt out of their race and further atomize their population numbers. The Census will not dilute Whiteness. On the contrary, it further expands the definition of Whiteness.

Let's look at how a shared White monopoly impacts Black America's life chances. Whites are a planned majority. Blacks, on the other hand, are a planned permanent minority. Limited by immigration policies, Blacks are only 12.4 percent of the general population. They are out numbered seven to one by a shared White majority that is 87 percent of the population. This means that Whites can override Blacks at least seven times, making it impossible for Blacks to "take over" anything. Moreover, with the exception of entertainment, Blacks do not exceed one percent of ownership, control or representation of anything positive in American society. In critical skill professions, such as doctors, lawyers, architects, engineers, scientists judges, physicists, business owners, wealth holders and elective officials, Blacks never exceed 1/2 of one percent.

If every Black professional was hired in public sector or private sector jobs, Whites would still hold approximately 99.5 percent of the professional positions. If all of the 36 million Black people in the entire country were employed—the educated, the uneducated, senior citizens, those in prison, children, infants, teenagers—their total numbers could never exceed 12 percent of the workforce. When Blacks try to even marginally increase their percentage in the workforce, Whites are threatened and initiate a backlash.

## *Wealth Monopolies*:

Slavery and Jim Crow semi-slavery did not just make Whites a little bit richer than Blacks. Whites are vastly richer. They have deprived Black people of nearly the whole economic pie. It is the proportion of the pie that a group owns that determines its access to functional schools, competitive businesses, equal justice, essential health care, personal comfort and the length and quality of their lives. The nature of White wealth has cut Blacks off from nearly all of these fundamentals of life. White society not only owns or controls most of the nation's wealth and power resources, but most of it is passed on from one generation of Whites to the next. This is one reason why there is a lower proportion of Whites who are poor compared to the number of poor Blacks, and why the children of affluent White parents are less likely than Blacks to ever become poor. Wealth is frozen and stored inside the White race—in its families, culture, businesses, churches, communities, education systems and organizations in the form of stocks, bonds, land, insurance policies, trust accounts and foundations. It is inconceivable that Blacks could cross racial boundaries and successfully displace these frozen forms of wealth.

As indicated in Table 1, Whites own nearly 100 percent of all corporate bonds and stocks, which amounts to approximately $13 trillion. In 1986, the 256th largest company of the Fortune 500, a White corporation, had sales equal to the $16 billion total combined sales of the nation's 100 largest Black-owned businesses as listed in the August 2000 edition of *Black Enterprise Magazine*. While the wealth gap continues to widen between Blacks and Whites, the number of millionaires and billionaires increases. During the 1980s, for example, the number of millionaires and billionaires also increased by 300 and 500 percent respectively.[13] Although a handful of Black entertainers and sports figures are included in the millionaire category, their standing is most often a result of increased income, which is not the same as increased wealth. Moreover, none of the wealthiest Black entertainers and athletes appear on the *Forbes* list of the wealthiest 500.

Table 1:  White Wealth Ownership Compared to Black Wealth Ownership

| | Aggregate | | % Greater Than Black |
|---|---|---|---|
| | **Black** | **White** | |
| Total Net Worth | 268,568 | 8,863,993 | 3300% |
| Interest/Earnings in: | | | |
| Financial Institutions | 21,979 | 1,265,262 | 5,700% |
| Regular Checking | 2,452 | 48,048 | 1900% |
| Stocks and Mutual Funds | 2,901 | 592,180 | 20,400% |
| Equity in Business | 10,496 | 789,781 | 7,500% |
| Equity in Motor Vehicle | 29,127 | 499,781 | 1,700% |
| Equity in Home | 181,458 | 3,744,453 | 2,000% |
| Equity in Rental Property | 21,052 | 700,596 | 3,300% |

Table 1:  White Wealth Ownership Compared to Black Wealth Ownership

| | Aggregate | | % Greater Than Black |
| | Black | White | |
|---|---|---|---|
| Other Real Estate | 8,134 | 381,919 | 4,700% |
| U.S. Savings Bonds | 1,256 | 50,307 | 4,000% |
| IRA or Keoghs | 4,336 | 381,714 | 8,800% |

Source: Extracted from National Urban League's *The State of Black America Report* (1993), as taken from U.S. Department of Commerce, Bureau of the Census, *Household Wealth and Asset Ownership* (measured in millions of dollars, 1988).

Obtaining wealth equality in America is a rigged game. There is no equal opportunity to gain wealth. Such opportunities typically depend on four factors:

• Inborn capacity,
• Cultural and educational opportunities,
• Ownership and control of resources,
• The power of racism.

In summary, this means a White person of normal talents, who lives in an enriched culture with parents who can afford the best, has an excellent chance to become rich and live well. Economic Darwinism tracks both parental and racial bloodlines. Structural racism enables Whites to acquire wealth, while capital gains and inheritance laws ensure they will keep and control wealth. Steve Brouwer[14] stated in his book, *Sharing the Pie*, that in 1996, Charles Darrance, of the Campbell Soup family, inherited a great deal of wealth. He traded in nine million shares of company stock and earned $740 million. Warren Buffet, a Wall Street investor, profited $10.6 billion over a period of 24 months for a total fortune of $21 billion. In comparison, nearly 50 percent of Black America has a net worth approaching zero because its debts negate any property or assets they can pass on to their offspring. The White economic stronghold on essential empowerment resources is also reflected in business ownership and management, which is nearly 100 percent White and mostly male.

When White economic monopolies open up, White females get in the door first, followed by those ethnic minorities classified as White. As Brouwer writes, "White men are in no danger of losing or even sharing control of management of the nation's top 500 corporations for at least 25 years."[15] America's top 104 corporations have an average of one Black in senior positions.

## Media Monopolies:

Commercial media create a virtual reality of our society. Not only are the owners of media responsible for the information that we see and hear, but they create images of Blacks and define us and our sense of community. This is troublesome for Blacks because Whites hold ownership monopolies over this nation's print and electronic media. Media ownership is a source of control over power, wealth, *and* information. Media power is political power. Whites control nearly 100 percent of this nation's 1,500 daily newspapers, 11,000 radio stations, 11,800 cable systems, 1,500 television stations and the major Internet businesses. These monopolies ensure that Blacks will never have an effective mass communication system of their own. It means that Blacks will always have to ask permission to use White-owned mass communication vehicles to reach out to other Blacks or discuss sensitive racial issues. Members of the public who desire to be exposed to the perspective of Blacks are deprived of that information and do not have access to that type of unfiltered programming.

White society constructs monopolies inside of monopolies. Clear Channel Communications provides a good example of media owner-ship as an important racial monopoly that is also a major source of wealth and power. According to the company's 1999 annual report, it owns 900 radio stations, 19 television stations and 700,000 outdoor advertising units in the United States. It has equity interest in 240 radio stations internationally. The company's gross revenue in 1999 was $3 billion which was up 97 percent from 1998. White media protects White interests. Without wealth to own media outlets, Blacks will always be in the position of complaining about the images others present of them, but they will never have sufficient means to change or fashion appropriate images of themselves.

In 1999, the National Association for the Advancement of Colored People (NAACP) led a complaint and threatened a boycott against all the networks for a television season that lacked "minority" characters in the program lineup. The network owners did not *forget* that Blacks existed. They *chose* not to include them. In matters like this, Blacks negotiate from a position of weakness because they own no networks and few television stations.

In the case of the complaint, the NAACP would have come closer to addressing a core Black problem, if it had challenged the Federal Communications Commission (FCC) and the Executive Branch of government to demand greater Black ownership of television outlets. Without ownership, Blacks are unable to communicate with their own people without passing through and having the approval of non-Black media owners. And, since Black issues tend to make Whites feel guilty or threatened, White media only give Blacks access to their media when the issues are race neutral or relevant to the majority society.

Even when Blacks own media, they have impediments to programming and economic success. The few broadcast and print properties that are Black-owned are so dependent upon White advertisers for revenue that programming from a Black perspective is often muted to avoid disapproval as "too Black." Anything that is "all Black" is "too Black." There are not enough Black advertisers to support Black media companies which are an afterthought with White advertisers. If they do elect to purchase advertising from Black-owned media outlets, it will be safe programming. They avoid supporting Black media when it reflects racial controversy. No other group has such social prohibitions. Nearly 99 percent of all White Americans live in all White communities, work in all White offices, conduct business with White customers, and send their children to all White schools. White print and broadcast media outlets target nearly 100 percent White audiences but, they are not criticized for being "too White."

Even national political parties spend less with Black media than they spend to reach other groups. According to the May 18-May 24, 2000 issue of *The Challenger* magazine, the Republican National Committee indicated it would spend $10 million in advertising with Hispanic media and zero dollars with Black media in its 2000 presidential campaign. As late as two months before the polls opened, unofficial reports indicated that the National Democratic Party had yet to commit money to Black media.

White media monopolies go unchallenged, regardless of how frequently and unjustly Black people are treated. The control of images we see by media and the corporations who buy advertising was demonstrated in Detroit, Michigan at the premiere showing of *The Tulsa*

*Oklahoma Massacre: The Hidden Story* in Spring 2000. The movie, produced for Home Box Office, tells the story of the 1921 racial assault that claimed the lives of approximately 600 Blacks. Their homes and businesses were robbed, bombed and burned by Whites who admitted in the program that they were jealous of Black people's economic successes. Although this film is a poignant and important historical documentary, White businesses in the Detroit area refused to financially support its airing on the Wayne State University campus.

Government resources have always been used to develop and maintain majority monopolies. Government policies allow media and communication monopolies such as the telephone and broadcast industries. The Internet, developed largely with government funds, is now owned by private companies and is becoming another White-owned media monopoly.

## *Political and Judicial Monopolies:*

The nation's political and judicial systems are racial monopolies that form the superstructure of society. Those monopolies make nearly every political and legal issue about race a foregone conclusion. Politics and the court system tend to be more anti-Black than the larger society. Legal justice has come to mean ensuring that Blacks do not break the law while forcing them to cheerfully submit to Whites breaking the law. Though their population monopolies ensure that Whites will always dominate and rule, racism within the political and legal systems guarantee Blacks will rarely win. Thurgood Marshall, by his acts and omissions, was probably the only U.S. Supreme Court Justice prejudiced in favor of Black people. However, outnumbered eight to one, his legal opinions had little real impact on race rulings.

Conversely, Marshall's replacement on the U.S. Supreme Court, Clarence Thomas, seems most concerned about his acceptance by White society. In fairness to Clarence Thomas, even if he were to begin acting as a responsible Black man, his vote would not change the way the U.S. Supreme Court works and rules. He too is outnumbered. Several justices were appointed when there were two litmus tests for any appointment to the Supreme Court: credible conservative views and willingness to avoid using the court to correct historical injustices, especially those committed against Blacks. Michael Lind in his book, *Up From Conservatism,* shares a story that illustrates how bias against Blacks is institutionalized in the judicial monopoly. Lind says, "William Rehnquist, the Chief Justice of the Supreme Court, was ordered away from a polling place in Arizona in the 1950s, because he was demanding that Black voters be forced to prove they could read by reading the Constitution before being allowed to mark their ballots."[16] Rehnquist passed the litmus tests of President Reagan, who appointed him, along with his racial attitudes, chief justice of the highest court in the nation. In this position, his racial bias could infect court decisions throughout the nation. Any counter-bias for Blacks was nullified with Thomas' appointment to the U.S. Supreme Court. Consequently, judicial monopolies control the fate of Blacks in ways that are rarely beneficial. Research supports this premise. As late as the 1990s, nearly 60 percent of Whites, Hispanics and Asian-Americans continued to perceive Black people as inferior, undeserving of justice, and innately criminal. Justice for Blacks in a system that reflects such bias and indifference is virtually impossible.[17]

Whites maintain a monopoly on holding political office whether Blacks vote or not. For example, increases in Black voter registration and participation resulted in a 9,000 percent increase in the number of Black elected officials within the last two generations. Yet, Black public office holders still represent less than one percent of this nation's elected officials. The political and judicial systems are cornerstone institutions that Whites monopolize even as most people espouse belief in the color-blind myth.

A monopoly on the elective and appointment process for public office will continue to place White males in control of 99 percent of all levels of government and legal systems. Whites in positions of power and authority have been conditioned by their experiences in American society to protect the status quo and the advantages of their own group's self-interest. They instinctively reflect the mores of structural racism in the normal course of behaving.

The majority of Whites who hold high positions in the political and judicial systems are descendants of White immigrants who entered this nation centuries after the ancestors of Black Americans. Though their ancestors were not in this country when Blacks were enslaved and segregated, special admission status reserved seats of power for them in the judicial and political systems.

This nation's fundamental democratic values of inalienable rights and principles of fair play have yet to apply fully to Blacks. There is no credible evidence that Whites understand the true nature of racism and its monopolies or are concerned about the negative impact of them on the life chances of Blacks. Whiteness, as a monopoly, is a subconscious construct that promotes aversion to any form of Blackness, especially within the political-legal system. Whites tend to equate Blackness to liberalism, which has the effect of moving all the nation's political parties to racial selfishness. They stack the law enforcement and court systems with conservative officers and judges who are predisposed to anti-Black feelings. The 14th Amendment of the U.S. Constitution, which was enacted solely for the equal protection of Blacks, is co-opted and used by the political system to maintain White dominance. By the virtue of Black peoples' inherited disadvantages and Whites' inherited life advantages, the races are locked into conflict and competition.

These racial conflicts and the accompanying racial disparities cannot be eliminated by indifference or Black leaders' accommodation. When Black leaders accommodate and compromise, they lose respect and the Black masses move no closer to the corridors of power and wealth. Moreover, Whites find it easier to pacify Blacks with symbolic rather than substantive political benefits and opportunities. This only further reinforces racial inequities.

## *The Implication of Monopolies*

The advantages that flow to White society from various monopolies—the visible manifestations of racism—have yet to be weighted and analyzed to determine how they handicap and injure Black Americans in a competitive society. White monopolies guarantee White winners, as if ordained by the gods. Few see their societal dominance as a persistent and fundamental injustice within American society. Racial monopolies adversely affect the welfare of Blacks, and further the best interest of the majority society. Within any marketplace, the majority society forces Black competitors out of existence.

This country's founders created a flawed social and political structure that only began to take on the appearance of a social democracy through the pain and suffering of the Civil War, Reconstruction, and a

Black civil rights movement. These national events were more symbolic rather than substantive for Blacks and now the likelihood of ever catching up with a majority White population is extremely remote. Blacks suffer too many wealth and resource power deficiencies. After nearly four centuries of trying to climb a greased pole, many Blacks have given up hope of ever closing the inequality gaps.

Structural racism and its monopolies have "boxed and locked" Black people. But nothing created or constructed by mankind is perfect, including structural racism and racial monopolies. Myths of a color-blind, race neutral society support racial monopolies. Public policies or programs that claim to be race neutral or color-blind will not help Black Americans, but support the status quo and prevailing inequalities. The dominant society uses its accumulated advantages to foster and provide even greater advantages for its members. However, with proper planning and preparation, Black America can compete and in some instances, beat a monopoly. Let's look at three possible options that an oppressed group might use against the tyranny of a majority monopoly. The oppressed group can:

1. Revolt and engage in civil disobedience that brings about political and economic reform or an entirely new government.
2. Petition government to intervene on its behalf and force a White monopoly to divest itself of some of wealth, resources and power.
3. Construct alternative political and economic systems and monopolies, based on its own group advantages within its own communities.

The suggestions in this book include all three options but draw most heavily from numbers two and three. With carefully planned behavioral changes, Blacks can compete and in some instances beat monopolies. The second impediment to the empowerment of Black America is just as prohibitive as the first impediment.

## *The Second Impediment: Inappropriate Behavior Patterns*

The conditions of Black Americans cannot be totally blamed on White society's structural monopolies. The second impediment to empowering Black America is inappropriate behavior among members of its group. Their inappropriate behavior patterns stem from distorted vision. They are conditioned to be color-blind. They neither see nor want to be Black.

Blackness is not just skin color. It is more so an appropriate behavior pattern based upon a rational perspective—a perspective borne out of a group's experiences and continuing dilemma. An erroneous perspective causes inappropriate behavior patterns. These behavior patterns de-empower rather than empower Black people. In a society based on White superiority, it is inappropriate behavior when Black people participate in their own subordination and exploitation. It is inappropriate behavior when their actions support the established racial hierarchy and encourage dependency on White society. The more a minority group, especially a planned Black minority, becomes dependent on the majority White society, the harder it is for the group members to differentiate who they are and behave in their own best interest. Their dependency distorts racial reality and causes many of them to live in a state of denial, tolerating and justifying why they are in an oppressed state. They are generally willing to accept their poor quality of life and avoid any form of competitiveness unless it is against members of their own group.

## *Categories of Inappropriate Behavior*

There are many types of inappropriate behavior ranging from the classic Sambo (A Sambo is a Black person who betrays his own race and gains personal profit.) to a militant with an attitude of Blacker-than-thou arrogance. Inappropriate behavior is the manifestation of the intentional softening of the competitive impulse in an individual or group to the point that everything is turned upside down and backwards. The individual or group is inclined to compete among themselves and ally with outsiders rather than allying with members of their own group to compete against outsiders. What is even more troublesome is that inappropriate behavior teaches Whites and others how to treat Black people. If Black Americans want to change how they are treated, they must change what they are teaching their competitors. Below, we will briefly discuss a few of the most common, and destructive categories of inappropriate behavior.

**Collusion with the Competition**: This type of behavior is visible in coalition building. It is without a doubt the most troubling for the race because it is a strategy used by so many members of Black America's leadership class. Although coalition building is a popular concept, coalitions almost always operate at the expense of Black Americans. Even though Blacks themselves are not organized and do not have stated group goals, coalition building encourages them to coalesce with other groups that do have articulated goals, rather than to organize their own group. Black participation gives credibility and strength to ethnic, class, gender, disabled and Spanish speaking groups, some of whom compete openly with Blacks for wealth and power and openly oppose Black gains.[17] When Blacks participate in coalitions, they allow the unique status, history and debt owed to Blacks to spread to all of the sub-groups. Race is made synonymous with minority and racism synonymous with any form of discrimination. These are gigantic distortions of reality and give fictional common ground for building coalitions between Blacks and any group that perceives itself as aggrieved. Blacks should not be against any group, but what political or economic benefits do they derive from coalitions with Asians, American Indians, Hispanics, women or gays that take Black problems, convert them into minority problems then propose non-specific universal solutions. Political coalitions created under the broad, ambiguous concepts of minorities, cultural diversity, and multi-culturalism do not benefit Blacks as a group.[18]

In Collusion with the Competition, coalitions give Black Americans a trickle-down political experience. They get what is left after gender, ethnic, religious, disabled and Spanish language groups in the coalition receive what they want and need. Black Americans lose by default, due to the inappropriate behavior of Black leaders who choose cross-group alliances, White approval, and corporate dollars at the expense of their own people.

**Social Etiquette**: Behavior patterns in this category appear to stem directly from the old social or Southern racial etiquette. Though one of the major accomplishments of the Black civil rights movement of the 1960s was to modify some of the social etiquette that traditionally existed between Blacks and Whites, many Blacks across America, especially in the South and Midwest, continue to honor old social customs. They avoid situations that make them appear free, independent and active in shaping their own lives. They are perfectly happy to go to work or to church, look at television and then go to bed. They still know their place and know how to play "git-low." To them, what happens to Black people locally or anywhere else is of little concern. They want to appear as "Good Negroes," content, happy, compromising, and non-competitive. A good Negro or "safe" Black person seeks approval of Whites. These Blacks will neither speak up nor speak out on Black issues, nor will they defend against Black injustice.

**Avoiding Blackness**: Blacks who exhibit this behavior avoid association with any form of Blackness. They want to be the first or only Black person in an integrated company, school, neighborhood, organization or political party. Like Whites, many Blacks gauge the amount of Black presence, and anything that is not integrated or is "all Black" is too Black and "politically incorrect." This phenomenon is peculiar to Blacks. There is no similar expression that someone or something is too Jewish, too Indian, too White or too Asian? Avoiding Blackness allows many to live in a state of denial until the "reality roosters" come home.

A true story illustrates how Blacks try to avoid Blackness. A woman who had grown up in a conservative mid-western town was proud of the respect and status Whites accorded her family. She was proud that she and her children were economically better off than most Blacks in town and her husband was well known in White political circles. However, her world came tumbling down one day when she was in the grocery store with her young daughter. When leaving the store, they came face to face with a White mother and daughter. The young White child pulled on her mother's dress and said, "Look Mommy, there are some Niggers!" The White mother pulled the little girl close and whispered, "Hush honey, those are Wilson Niggers!" The friend who related the story was the young Black daughter. She said that for the first time in her life she knew that regardless of her family's economic status or prominence she was not allowed to escape her skin color. While Blacks do not mind being identified with a particular sports team or political party, many reject being identified with the skin color team that God has assigned them.

Avoiding Blackness is counter to the way out-groups respond.They exhibit an increased sense of group consciousness and close their ranks. They create associations, organizations, and businesses dedicated to whatever characteristic others dislike. For instance, if Jews are persecuted because of their religion, they protect and strengthen themselves by building Jewish businesses, organizations and tight-knit communities. They build Jewish synagogues that teach Jewish culture, history, and religion. They help build and support the Jewish State of Israel.

Women who feel marginalized by the system because of their gender respond by building women's organizations and businesses to promote women's issues. The gay community builds gay organizations, businesses, and tight-knit communities. Asians respond to this type of adversity by building businesses, organizations and tight-knit communities around their Asian culture. When Whites say they despise Black people, Blacks adopt that same attitude. They imitate Whites and run from Blackness, which should serve as a rallying point around which to build defenses. When Blacks run away from themselves and avoid their own skin color, heritage, history and other members of their race, they become vulnerable and defenseless. They cannot protect themselves.

**White Ice is Colder**: Another category of inappropriate behavior is the persistent belief that "White ice is colder." Black America is conditioned by family, school and all the social institutions to believe that Whites are inherently superior. Although there have always been Blacks who tried to disabuse other Blacks of this belief, their efforts have had limited effect. The superior quality of the White man's ice remains a commonly accepted belief and expression in Black America. I am a witness. In the mid-1970s, I actually saw a real-life display of this inappropriate mind-set and behavior. Standing with a friend in front of his office building in Tallahassee, Florida, I saw a Black man drive up to a Black-owned grocery store. He got out of his car and walked over to the ice machine. He picked up several bags of ice, examined them, put them back into the ice machine, then walked across the street to a White-owned liquor store. There, he went to the ice machine and took out two bags of ice. He examined them, then went to the drive-through window to pay for them. My friend and I were so struck by the behavior that we asked him why he rejected the ice at the Black store but purchased the identical brand from the White-owned store. He said, "I don't like Mr. Brown's ice. It's too lumpy. Jax Liquor's ice is better." That day, I learned that not only was White ice colder, but apparently "smoother" to at least one Black man.

Inappropriate behavior has become deeply rooted in the psyche of Black America's dialectic type of reasoning. If Whites touch it, make it, sell it, repair it or talk about it, only then is it acceptable to Blacks. But on an even deeper level, Black inappropriate behavior seems to suggest that a significant number of Blacks place more value on being alive than the conditions under which they live. Eradicating these self-depreciating habits and learned inappropriate behavior patterns begins with offering Black people new information, new political and economic goals, new social-psychological models and new hope.

## *The Third Impediment: No Plan for Empowerment*

Through the years, Blacks and Whites alike have called for Blacks to organize and help themselves rather than depending on Whites. As early as the 1860s, Albion W. Tourgee, a visionary abolitionist, prophesied that neither the enactment of laws, nor appeals to the majority society's conscience would reverse the tide of White racism or lift Black people. Tourgee believed that the solution to the nation's race problem rested in Blacks becoming more independent, exhibiting greater militancy and self-assertion. Tourgee was so committed to those beliefs, that even as a White man, he fought the conservative philosophies of Booker T. Washington, a Black man. Tourgee tried to convince Washington that Black Americans would never gain political and economic parity in America until they organized themselves and pursued a course toward economic justice.[19] A century later, a national commitment to *economic* justice for Blacks still has not been made. Social integration and civil rights remain the foremost issues.

Black America needs a national plan and knowledgeable, committed leadership to guide it toward group empowerment and economic justice. *PowerNomics* is a national plan and requires institutional leadership to implement it. It is reverse social engineering. The sole purpose of *PowerNomics* is to unleash the economic and political potential of Black America by addressing the historical, structural economic inequalities between the races and the self-defeating inappropriate behavior patterns of Black Americans by the year 2005. Now that the need for empowerment has been established, the remaining chapters and appendices of this book explain the *PowerNomics* plan and how to achieve Black empowerment.

# CHAPTER TWO

## The Keys to Empowerment

*Any race that loves the world and hates itself
will eventually become its own oppressor.*

The first chapter discussed how slavery generated racism, which created race-based monopolies and vast wealth for Whites. These raced-based monopolies made Whites the proverbial 900 pound Gorilla and rendered Black Americans null and void as a competitive and productive group in the marketplaces. However, like any monopoly, White racial monopolies are not perfect. They can be beaten. But, Blacks will need the right combination of skills, appropriate mind-sets, clear direction, a sense of group self-interest and a competitive group spirit in order to compete and win. When these attitudes are properly mixed with our group competitive advantages, we can begin to play real life Monopoly. In this chapter, we will learn about the keys and tools that can empower Black America and make it unified, self-directed and economically stronger.

Many will ask the questions, is it possible for Black America to transform itself into a state of economic and political competitiveness? Can modern Black America do what 18 previous generations of Blacks failed or were not allowed to do?

In this chapter, you will find that the answer to both questions is, "Yes!" It can be done, but it will not be easy. It will require Black Americans to make drastic behavior changes. We will have to overcome the primary impediments to Black empowerment: a historical wealth inequality between the races, our own learned inappropriate behavior and lack of a national plan. For those who are serious about building a new foundation of group wealth and political power, the first thing we must do is examine how we see, think and behave regarding racial matters. This chapter will contain many technical concepts that are essential to understanding the action steps and principles recommended in the later chapters.

## *Distorted Perspectives*

Our experiences give us our point of view. Like Alice in Wonderland looking into the mirror, what we see is distorted. It is not reality. Yet, what we perceive we believe and what we believe eventually controls how we behave. As Black people, we tend to see ourselves and the solutions to our predicament through the eyes of non-Blacks. We have done this for so long that we do not question whether or not our perceptions of reality are accurate. When we fail to challenge what we see and believe, we allow distorted views to lead to inappropriate behaviors. It is now time for us to correct the distortions by changing rather than keeping our perspective.

## *Out-of-the-Box Thinking*

It has been said that the epitome of madness is to do the same thing over and over while fully expecting things to somehow change. We have spent centuries seeking civil rights and social acceptance while our conditions remain relatively fixed. As long as we continue to perceive and respond to our socioeconomic situation in the same old manner, we should expect to get the same old results. If we want different results or an improved lifestyle, we have to see, think and act differently. Our national empowerment plan must be based on new, collective out-of-the-box thinking. Every social, political, legal and economic policy and practice that relates to Black people must be re-thought so that we can find creative channels through which we can emerge as a competitive political and economic force.

The following line-dot puzzle illustrates what we mean by out-of-the box thinking. The problem is to connect the nine dots in Figure 3 Box A by using only four straight lines without taking the pencil or pen off the paper. Most people cannot solve the problem because they are bound and limited by their perspective. They will see the dots as boundaries and they will want to stay as close to the dots as possible. To solve the puzzle, a player must be free enough in his thinking to extend his or her perspective beyond the dots, as indicated in the set of dots in Box B.

Conventional wisdom and perspectives will neither solve the puzzle of racial justice nor empower Black America. Racial inertia and competing social and economic forces are too strong. Black Americans have been locked outside the system for so long that we need to learn a new perspective in order to connect the dots.

**(A)**          **(B)**

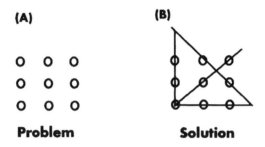

**Problem**          **Solution**

Figure 3. Out-of-the-Box Thinking

We got into our dilemma as a group and since racism is a team or group competition, we must play and win this contest as a group. Our new perspective then must be one of group solidarity. When a skin color team loses, everybody on the team loses, regardless of job, income or education. In team competition, it is the responsibility of every member of the team to be sure his or her actions result in a team win.

A perspective of group solidarity on race matters empowers us to see the world and others through our own eyes and to prioritize our interests and needs above all others. For Black America to place its own group self-interests ahead of every other group does not mean dislike for other groups. It simply means that we have matured politically and economically and will neither love nor treat any other group better than we love or treat ourselves.

## *Following the Majority*

The premise of our social democracy set the stage for a majority population to dominate and direct. But, these special rights and privileges for the majority come with some special obligations. According to the Federalist Papers, which promoted the ratification of the U.S. Constitution, the majority rules but has an inherent obligation to address the needs and interests of its losing minority population. This obligation is emphasized when the nation has a planned, permanent minority. Since the majority society has clearly failed to include the needs and interests of its Black minority population and its interests are not reflected in the nation's laws, customs and public policies, it is incumbent upon Black Americans not to blindly follow the majority society. The majority society's needs and interests cannot be placed above those of a Black minority. Playing to win as a team means Black America ought to set its own course rather than continuing to follow a game plan contrary to its own best interest. When a group is in last place within a society, if it continues to follow the pack, it will remain in last place.

Playing a game of "follow the leader" calls to mind a sled team of dogs. Only the lead dog determines direction and sees a changing view. The hind dogs see only the rear end of the dog that is ahead. As long as they stay in the harness and follow the line, the hind dogs will never see where the sled is heading, or be able to change direction. The dogs locked in the rear guarantee that the lead dog will arrive first and get the praise and the comfort of knowing that he is still leading. The hind dog only gets the satisfaction of knowing that what he sees everyday will never change. As we shift into an empowerment mode, we are shifting from the perspective of the hind dog to the mind-set of the lead dog who can choose a new way. As we wriggle out of the harness and outside the box, it must always be clear that we will no longer have to follow the lead of majority society.

## *The Empowerment Mode*

Empowerment is too frequently used interchangeably with motivation, but the two words are very different. Motivating Blacks or any other group is little more than getting them interested, creating excitement and making them feel good. For instance, Blacks as a group can be motivated to travel and see the world, but if they lack the money, time and other resources, they are little more than motivated Blacks who cannot leave home. Empowerment does not simply stimulate interest in travel. It also inspires confidence and, most importantly, it provides tools and other needed resources necessary to accomplish the goals. Without the benefit of empowerment tools such as money, transportation, hotels, passports and other personal necessities, it is highly unlikely that motivated Blacks will be doing any traveling.

Motivational and inspirational speakers, workshops and books are designed primarily to make people feel good. However, Black people have been in a socioeconomic ditch for centuries. Rather than motivating them to feel good about themselves while they remain in the ditch, they need the confidence and resources to get out.

Thus, we must begin our self-empowerment by obtaining both confidence and the tools. We need tools that give us a clear group direction and sense of togetherness. We need tools that prepare and guide us to evaluate and formulate our best interest. Our tools must always remind us of who and where we are. We are a very special people with a unique history. Therefore, rather than seeing race matters through the traditional rose-colored glasses, we must begin our solutions by looking realistically through race-colored glasses. The rest of this chapter offers Black Americans these new glasses in the context of the *PowerNomics* national plan. The four *PowerNomics* empowerment tools for Black America are: 1) an empowerment culture, 2) a group vision, 3) the paradigm of ethno-aggregation, and 4) the paradigm of vertical integration. The remainder of this book will explain the need for these tools and show how Black America can best use them.

## *The First Key to Empowerment: An Empowerment Culture*

Since humans rely on culture for survival, culture is an essential empowerment tool for Black Americans. Culture usually refers to the norms or systems of behavior and shared values that are passed on from one generation to another. Essentially, culture is a script that is never neutral in its purposes. It either empowers or de-empowers a group. What it does to a group depends in large measure upon the position the group holds in the societal pecking order of acceptability[1] and whether they are an in-group or an out-group. Culture's most important function is to promote cohesiveness and trust that bind members together through values such as group loyalty, pride and respect. It is through culture that members of a group know who and what they are, and how to behave.

The culture of America's dominant society is Euro-centric. Through its culture, it promotes its own values as the baseline against which every other group is compared. Blacks must build a foundation on the roots of their culture as illustrated in Figure 4. The dominant culture promotes negative images of Black people, expropriates their culture, then labels Blacks culturally deprived, inferior, dependent, non-producing, compromising, powerless, impoverished, politically inept and non-competitive.

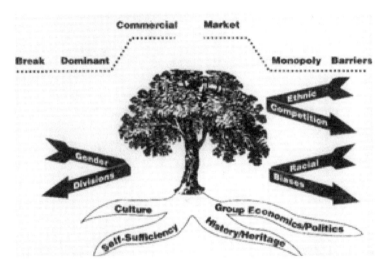

Figure 4. Break through with Group Self-Interest

Euro-centric culture incorporates the Horatio Alger myth of ethnic success and individualism. This myth asserts that individuals who are hard-working and who live exemplary, pious lives can always achieve and move up the economic and social ladder. Sociologists and politicians buy into the Horatio Alger myth then use it as a yardstick by which to rate the cultures of entering ethnic immigrants. Over the last century these authorities have systematically ranked various ethnic immigrant groups and their cultures, then granted them the option of assimilating into the majority society while retaining their respective cultures.

Black Americans remain an official out-group and are chastised as culturally deprived or lacking middle-class White values. To keep

Blacks de-empowered, the dominant society promotes the myth that all ethnic and racial groups started out even and at the bottom in America. The Horatio Alger myth gives the impression that Blacks alone are responsible for their failure in American society. The White culture script justifies the racial exclusion, exploitation and abuse of Black people as the official out-group. Those justifications are transmitted through negative images of Blacks that are imbedded in the larger culture as well as Black American culture. These images devalue Black culture and, in effect, script Blacks against themselves.

Since Jews, Asians and Cubans are the groups most often held up as the cultural models of success, let's look at them to see if and how their culture empowered them. Without a doubt, Jews have been one of the most successful immigrants to enter the country. Jewish economic success in America is usually attributed to their cultural values of being a thrifty, ambitious, commercially aggressive and close-knit group. They are also known for their business acumen and their cultural ethic of taking care of members of their own community. These are valued Euro-centric cultural characteristics too. However, historical analysis reveals other factors in the American society that empowered Jews. They came to America at the right time, just as the country was beginning to industrialize. Jews had occupational skills that were centuries old that allowed them to capture certain industries and move immediately into semi-skilled and skilled positions in factories in this country. The American economy provided a place for them to build shops and do contract labor that produced products that did not require a lot of capital. Jews then became rich and powerful in America, in part because of their cultural values, but more because they were accepted and allowed to become empowered by America's culture. They built a new culture around their economic base, which empowered them even more.

Similarly, Asians and Cubans are held up as models because their cultures promote education, patience, determination, hard work, discipline and family ties. These ethnic groups ranked higher in the pecking order than Black people even before they placed a foot on American soil. Both Asians and Cubans came to this country as well educated immigrants. During the 1960s and early 1970s, more than 50 percent of the Cuban refugees entering South Florida were professional people. Similarly, a study of 52 Korean businesses in four cities found that 70 percent of the owners had a college education. This nation unfairly compares some of the brightest Asian and Cuban immigrants against the whole of Black America.[2]

This country's political overclass knows that Blacks have not had the same educational training and business experiences that maturing ethnic immigrant groups have had. If middle-class cultural values are so important to success in our competitive society, then it is White society itself that must accept the blame for "culturally depriving" Blacks for centuries. Whites have combined the myth of biological inferiority with a notion of cultural inferiority and deprivation. Both notions promote the de-empowerment of Blacks. The mainstream society has demonstrated it has no responsibility or interest in helping put Black Americans' cultural house in order.

Therefore, we alone as Black Americans must now construct our own culture of empowerment. We cannot be empowered by reading the role others have written for us. To improve our condition and empower our team, we must rewrite our own script. We must construct and institutionalize a culture that is based on pragmatism and group strengths that generate sustained, high levels of inner-group trust and group pride. How do we do this?

Black people's culture must psychologically and emotionally elevate them and give them grounds to be a confident and proud people. It should promote the ethic that Blacks are a very **special people**. Blacks are the **original people** on the earth. In this country, they are the **only non-immigrants**. Blacks should be proud of and promote the fact that they have a **natural talent for generating music, dance and language**. They have **extraordinary emotional and physical strength** that took them through 300 years of slavery and Jim Crow and allows them to dominate in nearly all the sports they are allowed to enter. Black slaves were noted for their ability to perform hard work. Blacks should adopt and inculcate a **hard work ethic** into their empowerment culture. Prior to their enslavement, Blacks were a **strong communal society** that believed in the concept and **value of an extended family**. Black Americans have made the most **spectacular educational achievement** on earth. After 300 years of slavery and forced illiteracy, they reduced their illiteracy rate by half within 30 years. And amazingly, they educated themselves during an oppressive and deprived period during Reconstruction. No other racial or ethnic group can legitimately make such a claim. These spectacular accomplishments in education must be used as bench-marks that today's Black students can reach as we endeavor to create new educational models based on our new empowerment plan. Blacks should build their empowerment culture around the character-istics listed in bold type. These cultural elements would build group confidence, self-esteem and prepare Blacks to cope with reality.

To achieve our empowerment culture, our schools, families and churches will have to mentally prepare our team to take **calculated risks**. As we travel a new road we will have many choices to make regarding economic development, politics, education and our places of worship. Our traditional institutions must accept the double respon-sibility of educating and psychologically conditioning Blacks to take calculated business risks and compete in areas other than sports and entertainment. Our institutions should help us practice the process of collecting information and assessing it through a set of principles, then making an informed decision, taking a calculated risk. The will-ingness to risk failure allows the exploration that leads to success. Needless to say, one should never take risks simply for the sake of risk. But as a noted military strategist once said, as he was preparing to do battle, "If you take risks, you may still fail. But, if you do not take risks, you will surely fail."[3]

## *Second Key to Empowerment: A Group Vision*

A group vision functions to provide a clear collective destination and a sense of how it should be achieved. Black Americans are very fortunate to have survived nearly four centuries of slavery and Jim Crow semi-slavery without a vision of where they should be going and how they should get there. We did not even have the benefit of a group dream until the end of the Black civil rights movement. The dream, however, was based on very broad and amorphous concepts of freedom, equality and justice. All of these concepts are relative and very difficult to define. On the other hand, they are palatable and excellent motivators, especially for a group whose acceptable options at the time were relegated to marching and demonstrating. Today, we need more practical, tangible and measurable racial goals and supportive activities that bear directly on resolving our wealth inequality or inappropriate behavior patterns. We should accept nothing less.

History is full of examples of how oppressed groups envisioned their escape by taking power for themselves. For those who did obtain freedom or justice, their vision was always the key that unlocked the door to their group's resources. In Biblical times, Moses had a vision for his people that drove him and thousands of poor Jews through almost insurmountable obstacles to the envisioned "Promised Land." Moses had a vision, not a dream. A vision means the mind's eye is wide open. A dream implies the mind is asleep. Jews today remain committed to Moses' vision of a powerful self-sufficient minority religious group. Thousands of years after their Exodus, Jews and Israel are politically and economically powerful. There are more recent examples here in the United States of a minority group with a group vision. Generations of poor European immigrants came to the country with a vision of expropriating Indian land and using free Black labor to shape a new world. This vision resulted in the building of the United States of America, the world's greatest superpower.

Spanish-speaking people, now called Hispanics, are another example. They have a vision. Not only are they coming to America for an improved quality of life, but according to William V. Flores and Rina Benmayor, in their book *Latino Cultural Citizenship,* and public statements by the Council of LaRaza, Hispanics are coming to America with a vision of becoming the majority-minority over Blacks.[4] While Black Americans are fighting the battles of civil rights for everybody, these two authors explain that Hispanics are working to have cultural rights equated to Blacks' legal rights. Geoffrey Fox, in his book, *Hispanic Nation,* proclaimed that a new ethnic identity is being constructed in the United States, made up of Mexicans, Puerto Ricans, Cubans and all other Spanish-speaking groups that will surpass Blacks in population and change the political focus from Black and White to White and Hispanic.[5] Their vision is to achieve economic and political power over major geographic areas of the United States, especially the Southwestern and Southeastern states.

Whether Jews, European Whites or Hispanics, all of these groups have used their group vision to move their people. The collective vision is in the mind's eye of the group and it plays a vital role in guiding the group's behavior. Our national empowerment vision will function the same way. It will be used to focus our attention, give us a single-minded purpose, serve as a template for decision making and establish group direction. For example, when Black America is asked then, "Which way is North?", they will not all point in different directions. Their direction will be anchored in reality. Black America must have a vision that describes what Black people need and what they are capable of becoming by a specific year in the future. In order not to be "pie in the sky," the vision must be linked to a realistic plan.

## *The PowerNomics Vision for Black America*

> *The PowerNomics vision is a Black America that is politically and economically self-sufficient and competitive by the year 2005.*

The *PowerNomics* group vision is crafted to do a number of things. First, it is called the *"PowerNomics* vision" to lock into Black America's mind a concept that defines the solution for our racial predicament. We need economic power. This newly coined phrase and vision will keep us from wandering back into the pursuit of limited social goals. Secondly, this vision is very specific. It tells us what we are seeking: political and economic self-sufficiency and competitiveness. Any acts or issues that do not result in greater ownership and control of economic and political resources for Black Americans do not fit the *PowerNomics* template and should be given a low priority. Third, the group vision sets a timetable, the year 2005. This is a short, but workable, timetable if we commit ourselves to the task. Any shorter period is unrealistic. Any longer period and we would be much too far into a permanent underclass status for any actions to make a real difference.

The *PowerNomics* vision is offered as a beginning point, but Black America is free to use it as a guide and build on it as required. The *PowerNomics* vision reduces confusion about issues and makes it more difficult to mislead the group into focusing time and resources on symbolism rather than substance. The *PowerNomics* vision, founded on an empowerment culture, prioritizes and directs our energy and resources into activities that result in Black people becoming more self-sufficient and competitive.

There are many examples of activities that are at odds with Black empowerment such as including Blacks in the concept of minority. For example, major American corporations are again pushing Congress to increase the immigration quota on the number of highly trained foreign nationals who could immigrate into this country to fill high tech jobs. This practice has a direct impact on Black Americans. Trained in their country of origin, these immigrants represent a free ride for American corporations. They do not have to pay for the training of the immigrants, and they also avoid paying taxes to educate under-educated Americans, especially Black Americans, for these high-tech jobs. They do not feel any political obligation to hire Black Americans, even though there are also many Black scientists and engineers already qualified for these high-tech positions. A group of Black engineers, physicists and other scientists formed a coalition to fight corporate efforts to bring in more immigrants over Blacks. These immigrants are rarely if ever from a Black country. Unfortunately, the coalition of Black engineers and physicists made the mistake of framing the issue as a *minority* issue rather than a Black issue.

The group solicited support from the Congressional Black Caucus. The response of the Congressional Black Caucus was to ask that measures be taken to boost minority employment. The response of the White House further mis-focused the issue. Rather than aiding the Black scientists and engineers, the White House recommended legislation to provide training programs to all Americans, with a special emphasis on minorities, women, poor students and the disabled. These Black engineers got what they asked for. The immigrating technical workers are non-Black minorities.

The problem? Nobody wants to propose Black solutions for Black problems. Society is more comfortable recommending broad minority solutions for problems that are actually unique to Black people alone. The recommendations of the Black scientists, the Congressional Black Caucus, and the White House will help Hispanics, women, and a myriad of other groups, but not one will help the Black scientists who raised the issue. Hispanics and all of the imported foreign workers will be direct competitors to Blacks because of their minority status. Requesting assistance for minorities is actually requesting assistance for competing groups. The solution fashioned did not solve the problem of Black scientists. In contrast, the *PowerNomics* vision is designed to give a sense of direction based on group self-interest; to economically and politically empower Black people by the year 2005.

## *The Third Key to Empowerment*

The third key to empowerment is two supportive *PowerNomics* paradigms that can function as windows through which Black America's view of the world is further refined. We must not underestimate the importance of having paradigms that guide us to see, think and behave as a group, based upon our own self-interest. These two paradigms are **ethno-aggregation** and **vertical integration**. They align with the *PowerNomics* vision for Black America and shore up inter-group deficiencies and counter the most insidious aspects of structural racism and inappropriate behavior. These *PowerNomics* paradigms are very important tools in our empowerment chest. They are specifically formulated, designed and engineered to further shape and guide Black people's behavior in the 21st Century. The old civil rights paradigms no longer make sense in a competitive pseudo color-blind society. They are not grounded in reality. They have encouraged and prepared Blacks to compromise rather than to compete. Jeff Gates, in his book *Ownership Solution,* helped define the role of a paradigm. He stated the word paradigm came from the Greek word for pattern and it was used by Plato to describe a basic form or image encompassing one's fate and fortune and determining one's destiny.[6] In other words, paradigms are deeply held assumptions or values that operate like models, templates or patterns. They shape what we see in a cultural and racial context.

In practical applications, using the *PowerNomics* vision and paradigms is comparable to dressmaking. The process begins with the dressmaker's vision of the garment he or she wants to create. In the vision, it is clear whether the garment will be a dress or a blouse. After the dressmaker has decided on the nature of the garment, he or she needs a pattern (or paradigm) to ensure that the pieces cut for the garment are identical to the pattern. The pattern will determine whether the dress will be long or short, have sleeves, a gathered waist or flared skirt. The pattern ensures that all the dresses made from the pattern are the same. Likewise, the *PowerNomics* paradigms will shape our group thinking and behavior, establish a consistent group mind-set and guide Black America's collective decision-making. They will reduce conflicts, and establish a stage upon which we can act out our respective roles.

As much as we would like to believe this nation is a melting pot and that we are indivisible, that is not and never has been the case. We are a collection of groups bound together by one national government, but we still have different histories, agendas, cultures and needs. Black Americans remain outside of the mainstream society because Whiteness is non-porous to Blackness. Is Black success totally dependent on acceptance into the White mainstream society? No, it is not. The two paradigms that follow are the next two empowerment keys. They will help Black America to own and control resources so that they can compete inside or outside of the mainstream society.

## Paradigm #1: Ethno-aggregation

Ethno-aggregation is best defined as the voluntary concentration of individuals and their resources around their ethnic or language commonalties for the purpose of improving their economic and political competitiveness. The term ethno-aggregation may be new but the concept is not. It is a behavior pattern used everyday by religious, gender, ethnic and Spanish speaking groups. The culture of these groups emphasizes that members rally around common characteristics or attributes (ethno) in order to pool their collective resources (aggregation) and compete with non-group members.

According to the *PowerNomics* plan, the primary purpose for ethno-aggregation is to convert dis-aggregated Black individuals and groups into a national team and to concentrate their resources. The more concentrated their resources, the greater their impact and competitive advantage will be. For Black Americans, this paradigm is important because it can directly reverse past conditioning and is the antidote for Willie Lynchism (a slaveholder plan to divide and conquer Black slaves). Ethno-aggregation encourages Blacks to unify as a people as an alternative to seeking to unite with others. It encourages Blacks to pool their resources. A fist has greater impact than five separate fingers, but a scattered group is like separate fingers. The impact of the five fingers working together as a fist has an even stronger impact if directed towards the weakest part of a competitive force. An aggregated group has a competitive advantage over a group whose resources are scattered. Likewise, ethno-aggregation is most effective when the resources are organized and directed.

Blacks already ethno-aggregate every time they attend all-Black churches and participate in a Million Man March. In politics, we have voted as a bloc within both the Republican or Democratic Party and, although we have seldom received direct benefits, our collective voting has testified to our political strength and our ability to ethno-aggregate. We must now learn to be more strategic with our ability to ethno-aggregate in politics and learn how to *unite* and *concentrate* our *financial* resources to achieve group economic goals, just as Whites and ethnic immigrants have done for centuries.

## *Examples of Ethno-aggregation*

Our society is replete with examples of how Whites and ethnic groups aggregate for political and economic competitive advantages in the marketplace. Organizing begets group power. Before the Black civil rights movement, Europeans (English, Jews, Irish, Germans and Italians) used their togetherness as a social and economic foundation. American Indians have been successful in using their ethnic image and treaty rights to hold onto reservation lands and government subsidies. In recent years, they have enjoyed windfall wealth from their approximately 257 gambling casino permits. Newly arrived ethnic and language groups aggregate their resources to build political and economic communities such as Chinatowns, Little Koreas, Little Cambodias, Little Saigons, Little Vietnams and Little Havanas.

Of all of the above, Miami's Cuban community in South Florida represents probably the most visible model of ethno-aggregation in the country. Cubans control the political and economic activities of South Florida, which has become their home turf. As they came into the country, they first rallied around their common language characteristics then they voluntarily aggregated into the same neighborhoods and established businesses. Next, they began to compete with non-members of their group. They took control of the politics, the schools and dominated the language. They take pride in being a closed society. They are very nationalistic and sometimes even push the rule of law. In political and economic terms, Cubans have placed a flag in the ground around Little Havana, Hialeah and South Florida. From behind their Latin culture and Spanish language, they aggressively intervene in international affairs. They play a key role in Radio Marti, radio programming beamed directly at Cuba via satellite for the sole purpose of erasing or interfering with Cuba's regular radio broadcasting. They have flown airplanes into Cuban air space to drop leaflets and interfere with the Castro government. They have rallied around common characteristics, pooled their resources, and improved their economic and political standing. Cubans in South Florida require those who come into their area to play their game by their rules. Within one generation, Cuban immigrants economically and politically subordinated Black Miamians and became a political challenge to Whites throughout the state of Florida.

Arab immigrants in and around Detroit are probably the second best example of ethno-aggregation. They began coming into this country about the same time as Cubans, in the late 1960s. And, like Cubans, they ethno-aggregated to such an extent that, within a 30-year period, they totally subordinated Blacks in selected cities and have begun to challenge the majority White society for both wealth and power. Approximately 275,000 Arabs immigrated into the Dearborn, Michigan and Detroit areas initially. In that short time period, Arabs built the largest, wealthiest and most powerful political base outside of the Middle East. They invest their profits to build more businesses in Black communities. They almost exclusively hire their own people and refuse to buy from Black businesses. Black Detroiters serve as a large concentrated consumer pool that Arabs use to enrich themselves and their countries of origin. Detroit is an 82 percent Black city. According to an article in the *Detroit News* (Metro Edition, July 8, 1999), Arabs, who constitute less than one percent of the city's metropolitan area population, have taken control of 90 percent of the city's gas stations, grocery stores, party stores, discount strip malls, and medical supply businesses. According to the article, Arab businesses were so profitable last year that their owners sent $69 million back to their homelands to help Arabs who were fighting with Israel in the Middle East. This drain of capital weakened Black Detroit, but it strengthened the developing Arab communities.

Once Arab immigrants aggregated and concentrated their resources in and around Detroit, they increasingly used their acquired economic power to obtain local political power. Arabs know that politics follows the money. In this regard, it was reported that when Al Gore, the vice-president of the United States, visited Detroit in the summer of 1999, he chose to meet with the top 100 Arab businessmen, not the Black political leadership. Arabs pledged heavy financial support to Gore and in return for their financial pledges they asked for greater business opportunities in Black Detroit. Arabs are now in the phase of ethno-aggregation where they are beginning to use the wealth and power they acquired from Blacks to politically and economically subordinate Blacks. To shore up, protect and give credibility to their ethno-aggregation, Detroit Arabs hold street festivals and encourage Blacks and Whites to attend. They engender pride in their own people by promoting their culture, religion and language, while masking over the economic competitiveness that they are conducting against Blacks in Detroit.

It is their ethno-aggregation that gives Arab immigrants their competitive advantages over Black Americans. They use their cultural togetherness to compete for economic and political resources. Even though Arabs may have religious differences with Jews and some Christians, they are still classified as Whites and receive the advantage of a higher level of social acceptability than Blacks. Arab immigrants use their ethnic advantages by remaining an identifiable, non-assimilated group politically and economically linked into a national and international network.

### The Implications for Black America

Arab immigrants, in limited ways, can be a powerful example to Blacks who have integrated out of Black neighborhoods. Arab immigrants see clearly why they ought to ethno-aggregate and remain culturally and financially connected to their own people and their own power base. Blacks, on the other hand, have been continuously weakened by events from the Diaspora, slavery, Jim Crow segregation and integration, all of which have made Blacks a scattered group. The ethno-aggregation paradigm is specifically designed to shore up the weaknesses created by the involuntary and voluntary scattering of Black people.

Power itself always exists in concentrated forms. The application of ethno-aggregation will create mind-sets that provide incentives for Black people to learn to pull together, to concentrate our power resources, and compete with various ethnic minorities as well as the majority monopolies identified in Chapter One.

With the mind-set of ethno-aggregation, we will begin to have more control over our own fate, regardless of what the majority society decides. One way to explain ethno-aggregation, is to view it as a form of voluntary separation just like Little Italy and Greek Town are separate ethnic enclaves. More specifically, ethno-aggregation signals that we as Black people have gone the full route of integration and have found it wanting. Now we want to pull back a little and to voluntarily interact with members of our own race. Actually, our greatest competitive advantage rests in being neither integrated nor forcefully segregated. Jews, American Indians, Hispanics, Asians and Arabs have the option to assimilate, but have chosen instead to maintain separate institutions, organizations and communities. Like them, we as Black people want the same option, to have, own, and control our own institutions, organizations and communities.

Our first step to group empowerment is to develop communities in which to practice ethno-aggregation. Blacks are the only group in America that do not have communities. We have residential neighborhoods. (Chapter Three discusses community building in detail and the difference between communities and neighborhoods.) Decades of integration caused an exodus of middle- and upper-middle-class professional Blacks—the backbone of our community—into the White suburbs, thus weakening the cohesiveness of earlier Black neighborhoods and making it difficult physically and psychologically to identify and amass our group resources. We are still stymied. Under racial segregation, White indifference to Black communities allowed Blacks to have Black businesses and a sense of community, but while we could aggregate our resources, we were never allowed to use those resources to achieve a group goal or to function as fully independent and competitive communities.

## *Pooling Group Resources*

The ethno-aggregation paradigm creates a context within which Blacks can come together and share. In ethno-aggregation within Black communities, every individual contributes to the group's pool of resources. Individually, Blacks may be poor, but even poor Blacks can contribute to resources that collectively benefit individual group members as well as the group as a whole. One may have only a cupful of beans, another may have only a few strips of bacon, another only carrots. Yet, when the individual ingredients are collected, the group can make soup to feed itself or sell to others. This is the competitive advantage of a group. Black leadership, politicians, government officials, corporations and marketing firms do a disservice to us when they support and recommend policies that disperse our resources and make us vulnerable to others as a passive consumer market.

## *A Move Towards Voluntary Separation*

Re-grouping Blacks through ethno-aggregation is necessary to counter the effects of individualism which teaches Blacks to oppose each other rather than pool resources and cooperate with one another. Ethno-aggregation would give Blacks a powerful political and economic base.

To this end, while serving as the education advisor to then Florida Governor Reubin Askew during integration, I always stressed the importance of Blacks retaining their communities and educational institutions, and that the State of Florida should not place the burden of integration on the shoulders of Blacks. While speaking out on the issue of school integration, I said to an audience that Black people should not have to leave their communities to find quality schools, homes or consumer products.

After my speech, a concerned Southern White gentleman approached me and said, "Dr. Anderson, after listening to you, I am more confused than ever about what Black people want. On one hand, you have Rev. Martin Luther King pushing for integration. On the other hand, you have Malcolm X pushing for separation. Which end of the stick do you Black people want?" I answered that we did not want either end of the stick. We want the same rights and privileges that every other group has—the right to choose. I asked the gentleman, "Have you ever asked Indians, Hispanics, Jews, Arabs, gays, women, or Asians which end of the stick they want?" The gentleman shook his head and said, "You are right. You all should have that right. I've just never thought about it like that."

Most Americans have probably never thought about it like that either. Black people have an *obligation* to come together as a group in their own best interest. America should be neither threatened nor puzzled by the thought that Blacks would not want to be forced into either choice. Blacks in America are the only ethnic or racial group that continues to wrestle with the philosophical debate over integration versus segregation, when, in fact, neither one has to be accepted. As long as people are not forced into separate sectors and no group has monopolistic control of the resources that are locked into their institutions and communities, there is nothing wrong with separation or integration. Groups do not have to hate and exploit each other simply because they are informally divided.

The failure of integration is tragic especially when one considers that among all the so-called minorities, only Blacks have openly pursued integration. Hispanics, Asians, Arabs and Jews, all of whom are members of the majority society, are unilaterally committed to maintaining their own separate communities and organizations, even though they have the option of assimilating.[7] Though ethnic immigrants are included in this nation's definition of minority and are eligible for affirmative action assistance, the majority society does not require them to integrate their people and resources. If they do not have to integrate to be acceptable, why do Blacks? Would not a voluntary return to some form of separation provide Black America some of the communal strength of other racial groups and ethnics?

For instance, Jews tried integration in Europe in the mid-19th century, but it did not work. Later, when they were forced into ghettos in various European cities, as horrible as the situation was, they found one advantage. Being separated from the rest of the population made Jews more self-reliant, more productive, and more zealously committed to preserving their group's unity, culture and wealth at all costs. Aggregating around our own assets and self-interest can do the same for us as Black Americans.

An ethno-aggregation paradigm has the task of recapturing and concentrating Black cultural resources scattered by the integration process. (See Figure 5.) The integration process took away our sense of community, leadership, talent and brainpower, labor, disposable income, athletes and entertainers, business and professional middle-class and cultural assets. Retrieving some of these lost assets and storing them inside of Black communities will give us competitive advantages and platforms upon which we can begin to build our own political, economic and cultural systems.

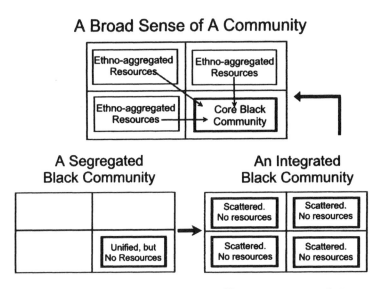

Figure 5. From Segregation to Integration/Disintegration to Cohesiveness

## *Paradigm #2: Vertical Integration*

Now that we understand the concept of ethno-aggregation and the process of pooling group resources, let us move on to the second empowerment paradigm: vertical integration. Vertical integration is a directional paradigm that comes into play after Blacks as a group have ethno-aggregated around their most common and prominent characteristics. There is a commonly accepted rule in sociology that when ethnic groups are wedged in hierarchies of wealth, power and privilege, competitive conflicts are inevitable. Vertical integration empowers Blacks to be territorial and vertically mobile. It places Black self-interest first and propels Blacks in an upward economic direction because that is where this nation's wealth and power are localized.

Wealth, income, businesses, privileges and resource powers are fixed and parallel, with Whiteness at the top of the resource ladder and Blackness at the bottom. Wealth and power resources are continuously and disproportionately distributed to those at the top first. These resources circulate horizontally among members of the White in-group before portions of the wealth and power "trickle down" to Blacks and other out-groups at the lower levels. On the bottom level, Black Americans get what those above either did not want or didn't need. Either way, the result is the same: It is always too little too late.

However, we have a choice. We can continue to wait, hoping for those at the top to have a change of heart and share some of this nation's vast fortune. But that is against the grain of history and not likely to occur. Our best remaining option is to implement a national plan with strategies for moving up the nation's pecking order and compete for wealth and power resources at every level.

## *Vertical Integration vs. Ethno-aggregation*

Vertical integration, working hand-in-hand with ethno-aggregation, is symbolized by the "Power T" illustration in Figure 6. A group aggregates and concentrates its resources at the base of the stem of the "T" for maximum strength. Once Blacks have concentrated their resources they should move them up the stem towards the cross bar at its top. As Blacks ascend the stem, they compete at each class level with each and every ethnic, religious, language and gender group.

Regardless of how high Blacks ascend, if their resources are pooled and connected, they continue to receive cultural and racial support from their base, their roots. They hold all newly captured turf so that other Blacks from below can have a clear channel through which they too can ascend.

Those Blacks who reach the top of the "T" can then capture new territory by moving horizontally into non-Black communities and pursuing political and business opportunities. As more Blacks reach the top, they too can expand horizontally to capture new political and economic resources. The earlier example of Arab Americans in Detroit exemplifies "Power T" activity.

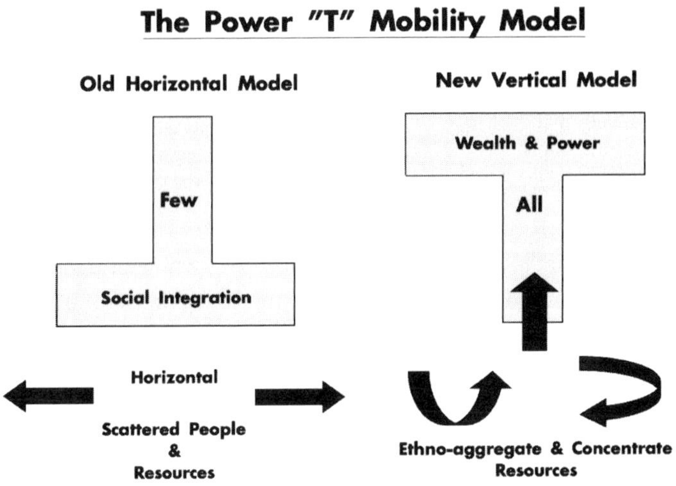

## The Power "T" Mobility Model

Figure 6. Power "T" Mobility Model

## *Social Integration and Horizontal Negatives*

Black Americans as a group cannot improve their wealth and power holdings by advancing horizontal social integration. Wealth, power and other resources are not stored horizontally in a pecking order, nor are they stored on the same level with Black Americans. Black Americans are locked into a caste system upon which this nation's class system rests. Horizontal movement places Blacks in economic competition with poor Whites who have yet to ascend the pecking order. Social integration in the Old Horizontal Model in Figure 6, has misled Blacks into believing that wealth and power resources are stored just over the next horizon or in the next suburb, all within marching distance.

Also, horizontal movement locks Blacks into competition with immigrants and other evolving minorities. Multi-culturalism, cultural diversity and a color-blind society give the illusion of progress. Blacks wore convinced into believing that aligning with ethnic immigrants who have been in this country less than 30 years is somehow progress for Black people. Aligning with these immigrant groups and their horizontal issues detoured Blacks. Moreover, it blurred the obligations that this nation's advantaged society has to its disadvantaged Black citizens. Even now, every Black initiative is burdened with a universalism that requires them to share the fruits of their victory with other horizontal groups competing against Black America.

Black Americans must not allow the vertical line of obligation between themselves and Whites to be blurred. Blacks are injured by those who do not make distinctions between them and other minority groups. Equating other minority groups with Blacks demonstrates a poor understanding of history and hides the fact that Black people remain at the bottom of the pile. Horizontal movement to align Blacks with other minority or special interest groups erases Black America's special moral claim on our society and history. Although our labor built this country, we have not been properly recognized nor compensated. Worse, we have been treated as just another aggrieved minority group. We are reduced to just another political group with outstretched palms, a special interest vying for the same affirmative action programs as Eskimos and Salvadorians. We recapture our special moral claim and status by aspiring upward.

Horizontal movement promotes the social phenomenon called "crabbing" among Black people. When the multitude of Black Americans are locked in the lowest horizontal level of our society, like crabs in a barrel, they cannot escape. Misery does love company. Social integration requires most of us to move laterally. We remain on the same horizontal or class level with most Blacks, even though we may have received a job promotion or moved into a new integrated suburb. Every Black remains in competition with every other Black for the few financial, political and social crumbs that are available. Crabbing will dissipate when we move vertically. Rather than competing with each other for crumbs, we compete with other class levels for the whole cake as we move vertically. If there is crabbing, it will be done as a group in competition with other groups who are crabbing for their respective groups.

Horizontal movement does not redistribute the ownership and control of wealth and power resources. Instead, it simply wastes time and resources. As an example, how did moving from the back to the front of the bus, from the ghetto to the suburbs, from a Black restaurant to a White restaurant or from a Black school to a White school, improve Black people's ownership and control of wealth and power? For example, before horizontal integration of the 1960s, Winston-Salem, North Carolina, had a Black city bus line, Black theaters, Black hotels, Black restaurants and Black communities. But, now all of these things are gone. We are still suffering from the waste of a horizontal movement. If we had been thinking vertically, rather than moving to the front of the bus, our concerns would have been instead about Black people manufacturing, owning, operating, repairing and chartering the city bus lines. How much tangible difference does it make where you sit on the bus if the destination and the quality of the seating is the same? This is a distinction without a difference. Social and horizontal integration played major roles in killing off Winston-Salem's only Black bus line and other Black businesses. Where is the vertical progress when Blacks are still just passengers or customers in businesses owned by others?

As indicated in Figure 7, horizontal integration is at cross-purposes with the self interest of Blacks. Racism runs up and down, from the highest point to the lowest point. It affects every member of the Black race, regardless of education, employment, class or party affiliation. The only Blacks who benefit from engaging in cross-purpose activities are those directly behind the point where the horizontal issue intersect. For example, when Black women devote their resources to the horizontal gender issue, any benefits from their efforts will not accrue to the race, but to all women. But within the gender category, benefits gained will trickle down to Black women who will still be on the bottom of the gender issue. Therefore, the horizontal issues such as gender, political affiliations and class should be secondary to racism and the structural economic inequalities that it protects. Horizontal issues that affect everybody have the potential to overshadow racism, divert resources and prolong this nation's racial inequalities. The so-called aggrieved minorities and women upon whom horizontal issues focus, together form a majority of the White population. When Black Americans participate with these groups, not only are they working at cross-purposes with their own best interest, their participation pits them against other Blacks.

## *The Advantages of Vertical Integration*

In association with the *PowerNomics* empowerment vision of economic and political reform for Black America, the vertical integration paradigm has numerous practical and important purposes. Nine purposes are listed here: 1) Vertical integration gives Black Americans access to the primary holders of the nation's wealth and resource powers; 2) It gives Black America a collective sense of direction for their collective self-interests; 3) It gives Blacks a channel for upward mobility; 4) It is a tool to capture new physical, financial and cultural territory; 6) It gives Black Americans the mechanism to control an economic industry from the raw material at the bottom, to the retail markets at the top; 7) It instills Black Americans with a mind-set that encourages them to concentrate and direct resources for maximum impact, benefit, and visibility; 8) It promotes a hierarchy of authority and respect within Black families, Black neighborhoods and Black people. 9) Finally, it reduces Black Americans' vulnerability to competitive groups by dissuading them from engaging in self-defeating horizontal integration, lateral mobility and cross-purpose issues. Vertical integration advantages Black Americans by vertically linking its authority and institutional leaders with the Black masses.

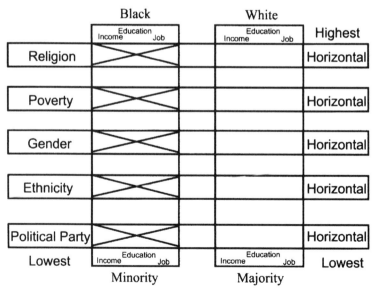

Figure 7. Vertical Cross-Purpose Categories

## *Applications of Vertical Integration*

Chapters Five through Eight contain specific applications of vertical integration, however, this paradigm applies across the board to all aspects of group empowerment. It applies especially to the business, education, and political principles of self-interest, unity and monopolistic dominance. The vertical integration concept creates an alternative structure within which Blacks can collectively compete in most aspects of our society. In those businesses in which Black entrepreneurs have competitive advantages based upon *PowerNomics* empowerment principles, the vertical integration paradigm facilitates industrialization. Once Black communities are rebuilt, industries, moreso than businesses, will provide them with greater wealth, income, employment, and power-building opportunities. Equally important, vertical integration serves as a mechanism for controlling every layer of business within an industry. For instance, if Black manufacturers of Black hair care products form a vertical industry, it will be possible for them as well as other Black entrepreneurs to move up or down in the production, distribution and retail processes. They will be able to protect themselves by establishing control over the raw materials and manufacturing, and by building their own suppliers, distributors and retail outlets. They will also be able to collectively encourage and support independent Black suppliers and retail outlets. Clearly, vertical integration holds enormous potential for Blacks.

## *Do Our Competitors Profit from Our Horizontal Orientation?*

Yes! Black Americans cannot protect their existing assets by moving horizontally. We paid a high price for horizontal social integration, including the loss of our communities, culture, colleges, professional sports teams, political leadership and businesses. As we opened our culture and communities and abandoned Blackness, our competitors came in and filled the void. While others enriched themselves playing and singing our music, many of our singers and musicians faded away. As our young people fight for admission and financial assistance at White colleges, many historically Black colleges are now predominantly White. While Black businesspersons argue for affirmative action and set-aside preferences, Black businesses that once were all Black—because they provided services and products that were unique to Blacks—are now forced out of business by the majority society and newly arriving immigrants. We left the back door open while we were busy horizontally integrating. Now, it has closed and locked us out.

Let's look again at the hair care industry to illustrate this phenomenon. Only Blacks have Black hair. Until the beginning of horizontal integration in the 1960s, Blacks not only dominated, but also had a monopoly on Black hair care. Black businesspersons attended to every aspect of Black hair care, from the manufacture, distribution, and retail sale of products, to the operation of barber shops and beauty salons. Now, all of that has changed. Asians and majority White companies have taken over and now dominate the Black hair care business. While the country was horizontally integrating, Black hair care providers were locked out at the bottom and top. Majority White retail outlets, especially drugs stores and supermarkets, did not integrate their store shelves by including Black hair care products. Once the Black hair care businesses became financially weak, White firms bought them out. Retail outlets made shelf space only after Whites acquired ownership. Blacks went through integration but business opportunities did not. Even then Blacks were the primary manufacturers until Asians took over the distributorships and effectively cut Black producers off from most retail outlets. This divide and conquer tactic forced most of the remaining Black hair care producers to sell out. Black hair care is now a vertical industry controlled by everyone but Blacks. Black hair care was left unprotected by horizontal social integration.

## Should Blacks Ever Move Horizontally?

Should Blacks ever move horizontally, in their quest of greater wealth and power? The answer is, yes. But only after they have ascended up the wealth and power pecking order as indicated in the Power "T" mobility model as shown in Figure 6.

Black businesses can move either vertically or horizontally, but the timing and the order is important. Often we get the sequence wrong. We integrated and moved horizontally first. Vertical must always come before the horizontal. The objective of a horizontal move is to expand within an existing market that Blacks dominate.

As indicated earlier, there is a point at which Blacks have ascended high enough into the wealth and power structure, that it will become OK for them to expand horizontally and seek out new turf at the higher levels of this nation's racial hierarchy. We should participate in horizontal activities only after we have monopoly control of the politics and economics of our own neighborhoods, communities and consumer markets.

## *Conclusion*

We have looked at the four keys to empowerment: an empowerment culture, a vision, an ethno-aggregation paradigm and a vertical integration paradigm. These tools are designed to frame how we think, see, and behave regarding racial matters, and to bring us together as a team. The majority society's social engineering has polarized Black Americans to the point that it is nearly impossible to get Black people to work together for any purpose, let alone to pool their financial and non-financial resources. If we remain in such a state, it will not be possible for Blacks to progress as a group. The empowerment tools presented and discussed in this chapter are interrelated but should be used in the following sequence:

1) Establish an *empowerment culture* to foster mind-sets, values and codes of conduct that prohibit members from acting in violation of their own people's best interests.

2) Acquire a *group vision* that articulates for us a clear picture of what Black America should be and what we can achieve.

3) Use the *ethno-aggregation paradigm* in order to combine the assets within our group to reach a group goal.

4) Use the *vertical integration paradigm* to point out the direction in which we should travel.

These are effective tools for creating group self-interest, competitiveness and team spirit. Also, they can function as templates to compel us to be consistent in situations where we must see, think, and make decisions on racial matters. Now that we have our tools gathered, Chapter Three focuses on the importance of communities and how we can build them to our advantage.

# Part II

# Organizing for Empowerment

# CHAPTER THREE

## Building Competitive Communities

*This nation will be color-blind when Whites proclaim their Black blood like they proclaim Indian and European lineage.*

A group's ability to compete is determined by its internal cohesiveness and self-interest. Black Americans must therefore build functional communities within which they can ethno-aggregate then practice group economics and group politics. A functional community can best be defined as a grouping of people who come together and organize for their own self-interest rather than misdirected altruistic interests. Once built, whether based upon geographical boundaries, ethnic or racial commonalties, a community cares for the collective interests of its members. Building our own communities will allow Black Americans to become economically and politically competitive, but will also give us something we have never had—a chance to compete from the vantage point of our own physical space, cultural values, resources, institutions and history. For the first time, we will be free to organize and work in our own best interest rather than the interest of a universe of ethnic and class competitors.

Historically, societies were built upon three institutions that served as pillars—the family, the church and the community. True communities are communities of mind and physical structures within a space. Both are important, but no traditional society built on land that it did not own or control, has been successful or prospered. Neither the landless European serfs nor the landless Jews, under the Pharaohs of Egypt were able to do it. For this reason, Black Americans need a solid foundation of communities upon which to begin empowering ourselves.

Like Moses, we must begin to build physical communities and maintain a strong sense of community. Moses used his vision of the promised land to mobilize his people for a 40 year journey to a land upon which Jews built functional communities families, religious institutions, commerce, schools and a strong sense of a community.

## *Boundary Lines: The New "Color Line"*

Nearly a century ago, W.E.B. Du Bois accurately proclaimed that the color line would be the problem of the 20th century. It's a new millennium now, and it is becoming clear that the problem of the 21st century will be community boundary lines. America is Balkanizing along racial, ethnic, economic and religious lines. Across America, groups are aggressively seeking territory or communities in which they can store their wealth, resources and political power to enjoy and preserve for their future generations. As noted earlier, Hispanics for example, are assembling their economic and political intentions behind their Spanish language and culture. They intend to use both to capture territory, rights, and a political base within the United States.[1]

The practice of seeking territory for communities will intensify as more and more people from around the world immigrate to America. They come to America in search of a better quality of life, not to integrate with Whites or to get along with Black Americans. They are coming to this country to get ahead economically and to find wealth and fortune. They commit themselves to competing with any and all groups economically and politically on behalf of themselves, their families and their native countries. Typically, their initial destination is close to or within Black neighborhoods. They have learned from official and unofficial sources that they can find great opportunities in Black neighborhoods. Within Black neighborhoods, ethnic immigrants expect to find the least expensive housing, lax enforcement of laws and regulation and little business competition. They also find readily accessible consumers, government assistance, easy access to elected officials and employment opportunities. Though they are aware of the crime problem in Black neighborhoods, the advantages outweigh the disadvantages. They find territory and build communities.

As ethnics fill in business voids in Black neighborhoods with a modicum of success, they begin to practice ethno-aggregation. They bring in and aggregate their families and others from their native lands. They then develop more businesses in Black neighborhoods. As they capture territory, they establish powerful economies and political organizations, using their ethnic culture, language and religion as their common ground.

Watching how these new arriving immigrants use a sense of community to build social and economic power-bases should be instructional for Black Americans. It takes a fully functional community to raise a child and to raise up a competitive race of people.

## *Neighborhoods Are Not Enough*

Neighborhoods are problematic for any group seeking empowerment. Unfortunately, most Black Americans live in neighborhoods, not communities. A community signifies commitment and the potential for power. Neighborhood does not. *Webster's New World Dictionary* defines neighborhood as a vicinity or physical place where there are "people living near one another." The concept of a neighborhood implies an area that is residential in nature, with lesser wealth, power and status than a community. The majority of Black Americans live in impoverished Black neighborhoods and spend approximately 95 percent of their annual disposable income with people who live outside of the neighborhood. They spend only five percent of their disposable income in Black neighborhoods. They spend three percent with non-Black-owned businesses that are located in Black neighborhoods, but whose owners live outside of Black neighborhoods. Thus, only two percent of Black America's disposable income is spent in Black-owned businesses in Black neighborhoods. It is impossible for any large population or neighborhood to be self-sufficient on only two percent of its income. By spending its disposable income in other groups' businesses and communities, Black America impoverishes itself and impedes the growth of functional communities.

One benefit of Jim Crow segregation was that it forced Blacks to build what could appropriately be called "quasi-communities." Unlike neighborhoods, where people simply live in the same area, during Jim Crow segregation, Black Americans were unified with a code of conduct. They lived together because they had the same interests and needs, but equally as important, they trusted and depended on each other. From the Civil War until the end of the Black civil rights movement in the 1960s, Blacks successfully built a vibrant culture, marginally competitive schools, Black churches, personal service businesses and a professional class. Though they were small in number, these community assets produced jobs as well as products and services for Black people. The desire for integration caused Blacks to abandon their businesses, communities, culture and the code of conduct. Black

Americans' need to be accepted by White society was greater than their need to be accepted by Black society.

Today's Black neighborhoods no longer qualify to even be called quasi-communities, because they no longer have a network of Black businesses or a group code of conduct. Today, Black neighborhoods are primarily where the majority of Black people eat and sleep. They do not embody the criteria for a functional community. Consequently, Black neighborhoods are typically referred to as "ghettoes," "urban areas," "inner-cities" or they are sometimes identified by terms such as the "hood." These broad, ambiguous terms signal the dependent, non-competitive nature of Black geographical areas across the country.

## Developing a True Sense of Community

What is a sense of community and why is it important? A sense of community is the collective thinking, seeing and behaving as a "we," not as a "me." Social integration has intensified our need for a strong sense of community or a sense of people-hood. Having abandoned their quasi-communities, culture, schools and businesses for the integration promised land, many Black Americans cannot easily return to physical communities that are primarily Black. Those who cannot return can exercise an option: they can identify with Black physical communities and organizations via their mind-set, actions and support. This strong identification and support is what is commonly referred to as a "sense of community" or "sense of people-hood." It is what people feel when they have a strong psychological identification with a physical community and its inhabitants. They are attracted to and desire the cultural familiarity, security and satisfaction they receive from association with these communities. The psychological damage Blacks have experienced as a result of slavery, Jim Crow segregation and racism will pose significant challenges to developing a strong sense of community.

## The Impact of Social Engineering on Communities

Throughout the relationship between Blacks and Whites, the majority White society has kept Black Americans under various forms of control: physical, legal and symbolic. The majority society, through its primary institutions, has used rudimentary sociological and psychological principles to control Blacks and deprive them of their sense of people-hood. In such a state, Black people could easily be misled into inappropriate behavior, identifying with the oppressor groups and hating their own group. This is not a conspiracy theory, the facts are evident in the marked inequalities between the races and the continued inappropriate behavior patterns of Black Americans. There is no other way to explain why historical inequalities remain unchanged and Black Americans continue to cede and surrender their wealth and resource powers to their competitors while their own family, community, and the race as a whole, remain powerless and impoverished. These are neither innate nor normal behavior characteristics, so let us examine their origins.

Research suggests that aberrant group behaviors among Blacks began in 1710 and were formalized into law when the Virginia colonial government introduced meritorious manumission, a public policy that was used to condition and instill internal controls into the psyche of enslaved Blacks. The practice rewarded Blacks who saw slavery through the eyes of the White society, were willing to work against their own group's best interest and inform on members of their race who were planning to escape and free other Blacks.

This social engineering effectively destroyed most Black people's sense of community, trust and accountability. Though undocumented, many Black Americans believe that soon after its inception, meritorious manumission was merged into what we now call "Willie Lynchism." According to popular belief, Willie Lynch came to Jamestown, Virginia in 1712 offering a mind controlling ideology to destroy Black people's sense of community. A professional slave trainer, Willie Lynch offered the slaveholders a conditioning system that he guaranteed would instill internal controls that would effectively divide Blacks for centuries. He proposed that slave masters create divisions among Blacks and separate them along the lines of gender, age, tribe, culture, class, rank and skin color. To this day, the effects of Willie Lynchism continue to encourage Black individualism, selfishness and self-hatred.

Though slavery and Jim Crow semi-slavery officially ended in 1865 and 1954 respectively, no formal records are known to have been kept that explained the principles and techniques involved in the conditioning process. If our goal is to build functional communities, we can, however, understand the techniques and methods that were used to destroy our sense of community. We can more fully understand what happened if we analyze a similar and better documented mind control experiment that occurred during the Korean War of the 1950s.

## *Meritorious Manumission vs. Brainwashing*

Both American soldiers held in North Korean prisoner of war (POW) camps during the 1950s and enslaved Black people, were psychosocially and physiologically manipulated in parallel ways. The communist North Korean army and its Chinese consorts used brainwashing on American soldiers. Slavery used conditioning. The biggest difference between the two systems was the extreme physical cruelty of slavery. Both systems were designed to tear people apart. In many ways, communist brainwashing was a combination of meritorious manumission and Willie Lynchism. It was a sophisticated form of re-education that operated like group therapy run in reverse. But, unlike group therapy intended to bring people together, Communist brain washing and meritorious manumission were designed to drive people apart from one another.

The larger purpose of these social conditioning systems was to destroy the ability of the subjects to form natural groups and communities, develop normal relationships, support, protect and communicate with members of their own group. Table 2 offers a brief comparative analysis of the brainwashing of military captives in North Korea and China over a three-year period and the meritorious manumission policies (Willie Lynchism) imposed on Blacks for several centuries. The table compares the similarities between the goals, psychological principles, rewards, punishments and resultant behavior changes. The results of the two systems were nearly identical in every respect. But, in each instance the subjects identified with their oppressors and were often unwilling to return to their former communities to be with their own people. The brainwashed POWs who survived were hospitalized and de-programmed. No such therapy has ever been offered to Black Americans.

Table 2: Meritorious Manumission vs. Communist Brainwashing

| A Comparison of Conditioning and Control Techniques | |
|---|---|
| **Meritorious Manumission/ Willie Lynchism** <br><br> **Time Period: 1710-1860s** | **Communist POW Brainwashing** <br><br> **Time Period: 1950-1954** |
| **Subjects**: Nearly 15 million African slaves on plantations throughout the Americas. | **Subjects**: Nearly 7,000 White American soldiers in POW camps in North Korea. |
| **Goal**: To control a large group of captured slaves and make them hard-working, fearful, dependent, docile, submissive and loyal labor tools to build wealth for their captors. | **Goal**: To control a large group of captured POWs using minimum resources; make them non-combative, dependent, and compliant to be used as propaganda tools. |
| **Program**: A system of dehumanizing and physiological conditioning using elementary principles of physical, emotional and intellectual deprivation. Conducted by slave masters with the equivalent of third to fourth grade education. | **Program:** A system of re-education and indoctrination using fundamental principles of psychology in a perverted way. Conducted by communists with masters degrees in the social sciences. |
| **Procedure**: Transported into hostile lands, made a minority and totally dependent; totally deprived of family, hope and basic necessities; rewarded for identifying with slave master. | **Procedure**: Transported into North Korea, isolated from support systems; subjected to various forms of deprivation with rewards and punishments. Divided by military rank. |
| **Reaction of Enslaved Blacks**: Internalized White values and fear of oppressors; eroded group self-interest and abandoned code of conduct; displayed self-hate, exhibited difficulty trusting and cooperating with other Blacks. | **Reaction of Prisoners**: Acquiesced and colluded with captors; compromised on principles; became individualistic, selfish and withdrawn; abandoned code of conduct; unable to organize and trust; built mental prisons within their own minds. |
| **Success Rate**: After 360 years, 36 million descendants of slaves have the shortest life expectancy, low self-esteem, remain divided and non-competitive. They remain fearful and continue to seek White approval and rewards that come with being Sambos and sell outs. | **Success Rate**: Only 2,000 of the original 7,000 American POWs survived; most POW camps had no guards or fences, yet not one American POW escaped in an organized attempt. Survivors remain withdrawn; POWs became turncoats against their own country. |

## *Brainwashed for Life*

Simply put, brainwashing was an intensive program of dehumanization, physical degradation, re-education and indoctrination. The North Korean Communists, much like Willie Lynch, were not simply interested in controlling the POWs while they were in prison camps. They wanted to create humans who would permanently see the world through the eyes of a captor even after they were "free" and "integrated" back into everyday American society. Both systems were enormously successful.

Like Black slaves, the imprisoned soldiers were captured, transported into a hostile country, made a "minority" in their segregated prison communities, and made totally dependent upon their captors for the basic necessities of life. Dependence eventually bloomed into indebtedness. The POWs were grateful to their captors for a few kindnesses, such as occasional extra food, an apple, a piece of candy or an extra blanket. These extras from their oppressors were little different from the welfare, food stamps and public housing subsidies that present day Blacks receive. And, like the White overclass of today, the Korean guards reduced or totally eliminated a benefit when displeased with a POW's behavior. The power exercised by the guards and the powerlessness of the POWs themselves constantly reinforced the cycle of despair and suffering.

Korean brainwashing broke the will of highly trained soldiers so that they had no interest in trying to escape. It destroyed the POW's trust, code of conduct and sense of connection to their captured comrades. Many chose to become turncoats and remained with their captors after release. Meritorious manumission and Willie Lynchism had nearly the identical effect on Black slaves and their descendents. The conditioning broke their will. Only a few thousand of more than five million slaves ever attempted an escape. Out of 252 known slave revolts, a Black informed nearly every time. Ironically, on the eve of the Civil War, over 6,000 Blacks were slaveholders. Many fought with the Confederacy to maintain slavery. Some even elected to stay with the White slave masters after the war was over. The analysis of brainwashing provides insight into why Blacks avoid Blackness and lack accountability to members of our team.

## *Social Integration is Dis-integration*

Throughout the centuries, social engineering, especially integration, has led Blacks to destroy their own group solidarity. Social integration reinforced the practice and destroyed Black communities and sense of community. Increasingly, Blacks are viewing social integration in America as a failure. It is a form of tokenism. It has given Black Americans limited access to resources and institutions within mainstream society. It gave with one hand and took back with the other hand. Blacks now own and control less than they did in 1954 before the integration process began. Blacks gave up their own businesses, educational institutions, political leadership, culture and quasi-communities. By comparison, approximately 90 percent of all the Asians, Arabs and Hispanics in America immigrated within the last 30 years, following the end of the Black civil rights movement, and have economically surpassed Blacks. Each group owns and controls more income, wealth and businesses than 99 percent of Black Americans who have been in America for centuries. The civil rights movement and social integration opened the nation's doors of wealth and power to everyone, except Black people.

Once the majority society consented to integrate Blacks, Whites began a "scorched earth policy," intentionally destroying large urban cities, abandoning them and cannibalizing their industries, businesses and other wealth producing entities. They used the authority of urban renewal policies to drive expressways through the most prosperous Black business districts and communities throughout the nation. The majority society has forced Blacks to bear the burdens associated with the integration process.

Whites frequently complain that Blacks are too race conscious. In fact, their inappropriate behavior patterns indicate they have not been race conscious. When integration destroyed Black business communities, Black consumers commuted to White suburban malls and started spending approximately 95 percent of their annual disposable income outside of their own communities. Black colleges were converted to miniature White colleges. Blacks seeking education, jobs, homes and leadership were forced to turn to the majority White society.

Integration has a built-in unofficial quota system of five to eight percent, sometimes called the tipping point, to ensure that Blacks will always be a powerless, non-controlling minority in White communities, businesses, schools and public offices.[2] Once the Black percent reaches five to eight percent, Whites become fearful of losing their majority status and control over Blacks. They sell their homes, move their businesses and transfer their children to all White schools. Typically, a situation where Whites are the majority and Blacks are the minority is described as "racial balance."

Social integration co-opted Blacks into practicing individualism rather than group solidarity and group competitiveness. Individualism is the perfect ideological weapon to defend the group privilege that each generation of Whites inherits over Blacks. Individualism gives what appears to be a reasonable explanation for Black underachievement. Further, it provides a responsive and neutral justification for opposing any compensatory or preferential treatment for Blacks, while protecting the political and economic group interest of Whites. By ignoring racism, individualism maintains the racial status quo. It argues that emancipation, integration, affirmative action, or even reparations for Blacks, are wrong because government would be called upon to support the rights of a group over the revered rights of individuals. Table 3 shows the placement of Blacks in terms of group competitiveness and consciousness. While White Europeans, Americans and Blacks are individualistic, Asians, Middle Easterners and Latins practice groupism, stressing solidarity, working together for the common good of the family and community.

Table 3: Categories of Competitiveness

| Strongly Individualistic | Strongly Group-oriented |
|---|---|
| England | Japan |
| Great Britain | China |
| Other European nations | Other Asian nations |
| United States/Canada | Arab/Middle-East nations |
| Black America | Latin America/Hispanics |

Table 3 shows that if any group is out of place it is Black America at the bottom of Column 1. Due to social conditioning, Black Americans view the concept of individualism through the eyes of European White society. This puts most Blacks at odds with their own group's interests. All the population groups in Column 1 are considered White, except Black Americans. Black America mistakenly placed a higher value on individual achievement and merit as opposed to group achievement. We surrender our competitive advantages to group-oriented immigrants who enter and dominate Black business areas and out compete Blacks for jobs and educational and social opportunities. Black America will continue to suffer a double loss, losing out to groups identified in both Column 1 and Column 2, as long as there is a gap between our ideology and the reality of our predicament. Our value is misplaced. We should not be in the individualistic column. We will remain outside and underneath the European White societies until we develop a coherent, group-orientation and identity.

When Blacks act as individuals rather than as a group, it is easier for the majority society to control and manipulate them. It also brings comfort to Whites because it lowers their fear of Blacks as a group competitor. Blacks are further misled by our celebrity culture. In our celebrity culture the status assigned to popular Blacks gives the illusion that Blacks are judged and accepted based upon individual achievement rather than the acceptability of the group and community to which they cosmetically belong.

## *Elements of Functional Communities*

Now that we have identified some of the major menaces and impediments to building Black communities, let's begin to design the kind of communities that we want and need. These communities must be built to overcome all the previously mentioned destructive elements. In the following pages, we will present designs for physical and human communities that can reverse the effects of centuries of social conditioning.

The first thing we must do is convert residential neighborhoods into functioning communities that contain three key elements or operating systems:

- First, they should have an *independent economy* that is wholly owned by residents of the community and provides consumer products, services, businesses and employment opportunities.

- Second, they should have an active *code of conduct and group accountability.*
- Third, they should have a form of *governance* that collectively speaks for the residents and is capable of applying political pressure to outside groups.

Let's elaborate more fully on each of these elements:

**Independent economy**: Not one Black neighborhood in America has a Black business economy upon which its members can depend to supply its residents with their daily necessities, products, services or jobs. As stated earlier, the civil rights movement of the 1960s was destructive to urban Black communities in many aspects. Black America would have been much better off had the movement equipped Blacks to be their own job and product producers rather than seekers of the jobs and products of others. If Blacks had become production-oriented rather than consumption-oriented, there is little likelihood that today they would have a hidden national unemployment rate of 34 percent, and live in neighborhoods rather than communities. Today, Black neighborhoods are totally dependent upon Whites and other competing groups to supply the products, services and employment needs of Black neighborhoods.

**Code of conduct and group accountability**: A code of conduct is a standard of behavior that outlines what is right and wrong within and outside of the community. It serves as a competitive tool that promotes group unity and accountability by suggesting either rewards or punishments for its members based upon how their acts help or hurt the members of the group. The burden for establishing and enforcing a code of conduct typically falls upon the shoulders of the community's basic institutions: the church, family and school.

A code of conduct does several things for the community. First, as a system or collection of rules, it prescribes and justifies how Blacks should think, see, and behave with other individuals and groups. These rules can be explicit or implicit, but either way, they act to govern individual behavior that affects a group. A Black *code of conduct* is necessary to keep out the destructive behavior that is so often evident in Black neighborhoods. Moreover, wealth and power can be built only where there is an enforceable code of conduct. A code of conduct defines inappropriate behavior and impedes it. It also rewards behaviors that uplift and strengthen the group. Any group that is characterized by self-hate, a lack of group self-interest, disorganization and other social pathologies must implement a code of conduct in order to build an organized society and maintain an infrastructure that includes schools, health care systems and other human services. Once a code of conduct has been articulated, it should be adopted and communicated through schools, neighborhood organizations, churches and families so that it reaches all the residents. It must not only become a guide to appropriate behavior, but also a guide towards accountability and the development of penalties for inappropriate behavior.

The code of conduct should be carefully taught to Black children, so that each generation will know what is expected of it. Among other things, Black youth need to know how they should treat other members of their family and community; how to conduct themselves at school, in church, or in the community; and how to show respect for themselves, their property, as well as the property of others.

A code of conduct must effectively discourage Sambo behavior that was once known as Uncle Tomism. This kind of behavior is extremely detrimental to community building. It is nearly impossible to eliminate because dominant society rushes to reward it. Samboism is a means of social control that extends all the way back to slavery. The majority society has always needed a few Blacks who would sell out their race for their own personal gains. The practice of Samboism has continued for more than a century after slavery ended because there is still not a prescribed code of conduct that either forbids it or imposes consequences to those who engage in it as a means of selling out their race.

The consequences for Samboism can vary from social sanctions to economic penalties. In some cities, Black activist community organizations post the pictures of Sambos on yard signs and billboards. Others publicly issue Sambo certificates and Hayward Shepherd awards. Hayward Shepherd was a Black man who was killed by John Brown's raiding party for trying to warn the town of Harpers Ferry, Virginia that raiders were there to free the Black slaves.[3] The punishment for violating code and behavior standards must be sure and swift. It is important that every member of the community understands that the community will enforce the code and protect itself.

A code of conduct will be necessary to communicate new team standards. Some Blacks have behaved in their individual self-interest when they perceived disorganization, self-destructive behavior and mixed signals among Blacks to mean that there was no functioning skin-color team. Those who choose to change their behavior, to re-identify with the team, and to take a part in helping the group achieve self-sufficiency and competitiveness, will need a code of conduct as a guide to new behaviors. It can show those who have position and celebrity status in sports, entertainment, corporate America or in government, how to benefit and strengthen the group.

**Social and Political Governance**: Lastly, a functional Black community should have a structure of social and political governance that regulates community institutions and represents the collective interest of the community. All across America, Black neighborhoods are administered and governed by Whites, even in cities where Black elected officials are already in place. Whites set the rules. Blacks are expected to obey. This pattern of domination was achieved with the full knowledge and support of both White and Black societies.

Once Blacks get into a stronger position they should not allow Whites or any other group to represent them in competitive situations. To do so constitutes a conflict of interest. However, for the moment, Whites control all the institutions within Black neighborhoods. They derive the benefits of authority, income, jobs and business opportunities from governing in both White and Black communities. Moreover, they determine what services Black people receive and the products or opportunities that exist within Black neighborhoods. It is now imperative that Blacks put themselves in positions—socially and politically—to represent and be responsible for their own community. This will not be easy.

Even when Blacks are duly and legally elected to public office, they often do not make governing decisions that are in the best interests of their Black constituents. Once in office, they often become sensitive to approval ratings and the need for re-election funds. Since Blacks rarely conduct polls or vote based on criteria other than popularity, and have little money for campaign contributions, Blacks seeking or holding public office find it more advantageous to secure the approval of White society. They believe White dollars will come to them while they are in office as well as when they leave public service. They harbor no such notions about Black dollars.

In the case of Black elected officials, they are restricted from assisting the Black community because they do not control public or private resources. The dominant society makes sure that public resources follow the control of White elected officials. Protecting their own best interests, they do not want the levers of control in Black hands. Most know or suspect that it is easier to ideologically and politically control, and economically exploit disorganized Blacks who lack both physical communities and a strong sense of community. Andrew Hacker, in his book, *Two Nations*, discussed how Whites fear Blacks and hold strong beliefs that political controls should never be surrendered to Black people.[4]

Under this system of White domination, Black elected officials' political power is mostly symbolic. Withholding control of public resources from Black officials is a standard operating procedure. Blacks will not voluntarily be given control, regardless of whether the city's Black population is the minority or the majority. Without tangible resources and power, it is nearly impossible for the properly intentioned Black elected official or the Black community to compete.

## Nationalism and Pluralism

Since nationalism and pluralism allow millions of ethnic immigrants to compete as a group, they have the potential to do the same for Blacks. Devotion to one's own cultural group or nation is called nationalism. Nationalism helps groups build communities, mobilize for power and control resources. It allows cultural groups to function as nations within nations. Black Americans are a nation within a nation, but have never behaved in a manner consistent with this reality. In our pluralistic society many groups are nationalistic. They form their nation of people-hood based on common underlying characteristics, from skin color to language. Nationalism is based upon a sense of community and can make it easier for Blacks to build a cohesive group within the nation. As an excluded nation living on the margins of American society, Blacks have marched, prayed and fought to be accepted into mainstream society. They have wanted to be a part of a nation rather than to *be* a nation.

Blacks need to emerge and begin to compete based upon the reality of where they are. They are an obsolete labor class that is reluctant to build and live in their own communities. Unlike Blacks, European ethnic groups built, worked, learned and thrived in their individual respective ethnic communities up until the end of World War II. Then they proclaimed their Whiteness, abandoned their ethnic communities and assimilated into the majority White society to help fend off the civil rights movement's push for social integration. Thus, today there is solid White unity among Germans, Italians, English, Polish, Greeks, and other ethnic groups on racial matters and Black people. New ethnic immigrants are exercising an old assimilation option. Arabs, Asians, Eastern Europeans and Hispanics are building and maintaining their own ethnic communities again.

**Ethnic Enclaves and Black Nationalism**: First generation ethnic immigrants typically build their own independent communities before assimilating into the larger society during the second generation. They retain their ethnic communities as socioeconomic alternatives. A second generation Chinese, Arab or Hispanic person can always go back to his ethnic community if he feels rejected by other Whites. Whether they practiced separation or assimilation, ethnic immigrants openly demonstrate the advantages of ethno-aggregation and nationalism. Nationalism gives them an internal sense of peoplehood and a cultural base. It also functions as an umbilical cord to their network of communities and their countries of origin. These communities have served the political and economic needs of American ethnic immigrants for centuries.

On the other hand, White America is threatened by any form of competitive Black nationalism. Whites prefer that Blacks remain unchanged, the models of patriotism and democratic principles. They want Black people to be passive and captive consumers who live in Black neighborhoods and remain out of sight and out of mind. Nationalism and pluralism can help Blacks build independent communities as well as promote their own self-interests.

All major population groups in America, except Blacks, practice a form of nationalism, although they do not publicly call it nationalism. As indicated in Figure 8, nationalism is practiced whenever a racial or ethnic group is devoted to and acts on behalf of the interests of its own cultural group or nation. Spanish-speaking groups, under the label of Latinos and Hispanics, practice nationalism by attempting to build a nation within America using the Spanish language to empower them to rights, space and power. Jews, Mormons and the Amish are examples of groups who have used their religion to establish a people-hood and nationalistic identity. Chinatowns, French Towns and Polish Towns are cultural enclaves built on a strong sense of people-hood and nationalism. American Indian tribes are cultural and ethnic groups that feel a sense of people-hood, and pride themselves on being a nation within a nation. More than any group, the majority White society has always been a race-based group with pride in its European nationalism and patriotism.

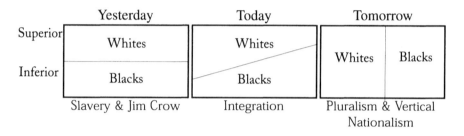

Figure 8. PowerNomics Vision: Tilting the Lines of Power, Wealth & Respect

As stated earlier, Black Americans remain the exception, but not totally by choice. Black Americans are without a sense of people-hood and community and tend to be afraid of Black nationalism and Afro-centrism, simply because the majority White society is also afraid. Though Black Americans, possibly more than any other group, have both the right and justification to be nationalistic, they have consistently elected not to be.

## Aggregation in Urban Cities

A great competitive advantage for Black Americans is the fact that they currently sit on some of the most valuable and best located real estate, whether they are called inner cities or urban ghettos. Since Blacks are the dominant population in a large number of cities, practicing ethno-aggregation and vertical integration can easily convert these areas into prime Black business communities with just a little stretch of the imagination and capital. Most of these areas already have Blacks in political office. Using Black accountability, voters could easily mobilize to remove the politicians who operate from self-interest and a non-Black perspective. Their replacements should be committed new leadership that will mobilize resources and practice majority-win politics. Table 4 shows a partial list of cities that Blacks can convert into communities where Black economic and political empowerment could thrive.

Since Blacks are the dominant population in major cities, they have the political potential to build major industries and establish vertical control. In the cities listed in the third column of Table 4, Blacks make up less than the dominant population and should use ethno-aggregation and vertical integration to build alternative structures or "maroon" towns. This is an appropriate historic name for these communities. When enslaved Blacks escaped from the plantation and into the woods, they joined with other Black runaways and built independent and self-sufficient communities that they called maroon towns. Inside each Black minority cities, Blacks have sufficient resources to build at least one major maroon town, with its own business centers or street malls.

Table 4: Prime Urban Cities for Building a National Economic Network

| Black Majority Cities | % of Population & Income | Black Minority Cities | % of Population & Income |
|---|---|---|---|
| Detroit, MI | 82% w/$10.2 billion | New York, NY | 29% w/$27.2 billion |
| Gary, IN | 95% w/ $7.0 billion | Chicago, IL | 39.1% w/15.6 billion |
| Inglewood, CA | 55% w/ $5.0 billion | Philadelphia, PA | 40% w/$8.2 billion |
| Highland Park, MI | 92% w/ $2.0 billion | Los Angeles, CA | 14% w/$6.9 billion |
| Washington, DC | 77% w/ $5.8 billion | Houston, TX | 29% w/$6.1 billion |
| Atlanta, GA | 67% w/ $3.4 billion | Memphis, TN | 55% w/$4.1 billion |
| Birmingham, AL | 63% w/ $2.3 billion | Dallas, TX | 30% w/$3.6 billion |
| New Orleans, LA | 62% w/ $3.9 billion | Cleveland, OH | 47% w/$3.1 billion |
| Baltimore, MD | 60% w/ $5.6 billion | Cincinnati, OH | 38% w/$1.8 billion |
| Jacksonville, FL* | 30% w/ $2.0 billion | Milwaukee, WI | 31% w/$2.3 billion |
| Jackson, MS | 56% w/ $1.4 billion | St. Louis, MO | 48% w/$2.5 billion |
| Norfolk, VA* | 40% w/ $1.3 billion | Buffalo, NY | 31% w/$1.3 billion |
| Data compiled by author. | | * City boundaries manipulated by consolidation. | |

Also, there are suburban neighborhoods all across America that could be converted into viable, self-sufficient Black communities, instead of simply remaining Black neighborhoods. For example, Prince George's County in Maryland has the honor of being the wealthiest Black neighborhood in America. As a suburb of Washington, D.C., it has attracted Blacks out of the District and now has the highest concentration of the most educated Blacks in America. Yet, it remains simply a residential area where some of this nation's wealthiest Blacks merely eat and sleep. They did not build a community that was self-sufficient and competitive economically.

There are at least 21 Black municipalities that could easily be transformed from residential neighborhoods to functional communities. Most of these municipalities, such as Inglewood and Richmond, California, either have Black majorities or elected bodies where Blacks make up the majority. Other smaller cities, such as Highland Park and Benton Harbor, Michigan, and Gary, Indiana, are approximately 80 percent Black. With visionary leadership and a can-do attitude, Blacks could convert these economically and politically weak neighborhoods into competitive communities.

Rebuilding can begin by staking out competitive space on which to build and operate. When the Black civil rights movement ran its course, urban Blacks exercised new found social freedoms by integrating into previously all-White suburbs, businesses and schools. Upwardly mobile middle-class Blacks abandoned Black cities to establish Black neighborhoods in White suburbs, subsequently surrendering control of their property, institutions and culture.

As Blacks begin to rebuild their physical communities and establish economic control of inner cities, they will surely clash with Whites and ethnic immigrants. Whites are seeking to retake the old urban areas under a new gentrification concept called "regionalization." Regionalization allows Whites to hold onto their suburban territories while their majority legislative bodies push suburban legal boundaries into urban areas and bring them under one regional government controlled by Whites. Under regionalization, Whites seek to control all government, public institutions and properties. They recently discovered that it was a mistake to abandon the urban cities to Blacks following the civil rights movement. Though Whites have cannibalized the cities, the locations themselves and the remaining infrastructures are still valuable. The wealthy and power elite want them back. If Whites are successful in retaking Black neighborhoods and cities, Blacks will be back where they were a century ago. They will own and control nothing. Worse, they will have to compete with new ethnic immigrants as well as Whites for space in cities like Detroit.

Many Black elected officials in Black cities are co-conspirators in regionalization. They invite Whites to reverse the outward migration of the 1960s and come back into the cities. Black elected officials give away their cities' assets—prime property, privatized public services, control over the schools, court systems and public water and sewage plants—to draw Whites back into Black cities. Scant rewards, incentives, or special programs are devised to empower Blacks who live in those communities. Only a few Black public officials are trying to hold onto their neighborhoods and control of government. It is clear by their actions that Whites are determined to regain ownership and control of the power, land and resources in the cities.

The same Whites who work to keep control of Black assets criticize the way Blacks live and would never allow conditions similar to those in Black neighborhoods to exist in their communities. Black America must build and maintain communities to satisfy its own needs, not the economic and political needs of Whites and other groups that want unrestricted access to their neighborhoods. Black neighborhoods should first and foremost be for Black people.

When I articulated this concept on national radio, a White gentleman called in and said he felt White and ethnic immigrants ought to have a right to make their living in Black neighborhoods. This caller missed the point. There is no disagreement that non-Blacks have a right to establish businesses in Black neighborhoods, but Blacks have the same rights that Whites and other groups have to withhold economic support when they choose. Black Americans will get more respect and economic and political power, if they do not support any business or ethnic group that engages in practices adverse to Blacks. No law or public policy can make Blacks spend their money in non-Black-owned businesses. If it were illegal to boycott, then nearly all of White America and its ethnic subgroups would be liable for contravention of the law since they have boycotted and exploited Black neighborhoods and Black businesses for centuries.

## *Boundary Maintenance*

An important task in building new Black communities is establishing and maintaining community boundaries. It is a common sight to see animals mark their territory. Humans operate at a higher level, but they too establish boundary lines then mark them. The majority society closed its communities using markers such as skin color, religion, ethnicity and languages. Community markings also vary with the wealth and political clout of the group. Those with the greater wealth and political clout will typically have more prominent markings. Wealthy communities are marked and closed by signs, gates and security guards. Ethnic communities, such as Chinatowns, are marked symbolically, often by ornate oriental gates. Korea Town and Little Havana are marked and closed by flags and a foreign language. Hispanics claim and mark space and close communities using the Spanish language. As the society becomes increasingly pluralistic, groups stake out, mark and close their turf. That is, every group except Black America.

Black America can build communities, but to keep them and have them achieve their objectives, they ought to be marked and closed. Marking is one of the first practices that we should institute as a part of our code of conduct once our communities are up and doing business. We, must mark our communities the way other groups do. By marking our communities, we send the message that these communities belong to us. Today, there are no positive signs that identify Black neighborhoods and say, "This is ours." When Black Americans begin to mark territory, it does not mean that others are unwelcome any more than when Arabs, Chinese or Hispanics mark their communities. Do the pagodas in Chinatown mean that non-Chinese cannot enter? To the contrary, marked boundaries invite all to come, but primarily as customers and visitors.

Figure 9. Protecting the Hood

Language is an index of culture. It is routinely used by immigrant groups to mark and close their communities. Language is a unifying element, and it allows native speakers to do business within the community while limiting others. It brings status and importance to the people, culture and the community. Visitors to Chinatown, Korea Town, Little Saigon or any other culturally strong communities might feel some discomfort because they do not speak the language.

Others often feel resentful because they feel this is America and everyone should be speaking English, the national language. Public laws in some cities, such as Miami, require that all public announcements be in both English and Spanish. Most of the public notices, business signs, newspapers and advertisements are in Spanish. Immigrant enclaves, like the Hispanic and Asian communities of today, are very much aware that they are marking and closing their communities.

Cubans are an example of a group that used language to mark and close their community and to gain competitive advantages. The first major influx of Cubans began to arrive in this country in the late

1960s. They soon acquired major control of both the private and public sectors of Dade County and Miami Florida. In one of their first acts of power, they enacted a city ordinance that declared Miami a bilingual city. Non-Spanish speaking people had to learn Spanish to interact with Cuban communities. Millions of dollars are now earmarked to print public information in both English and Spanish. Even the *Miami Herald* publishes a daily newspaper that is primarily bilingual. Most business and public jobs require a facility with Spanish. Blacks, who previously held most of the hotel and lower level city jobs, were fired because they did not speak Spanish. Cubans and others demanded bilingual education classes for all students while using the Spanish language to mark and close their communities.

Since Blacks do not have an official language, they cannot use language to mark and close their communities to competing groups. The language disadvantage of Blacks was revealed in the Ebonics issue in Oakland, California toward the end of the 1990s. The local school board had requested federal bilingual funds to teach English to Black children who spoke Ebonics. Not only were they turned down at the federal level, they incurred the wrath of many Blacks and Black leaders who saw no value in recognizing Black language. The Oakland debacle illustrates the bigger problem Blacks face. If they had maintained their communities, built a business structure that provided their people jobs and wealth-building opportunities, their children could have had the same advantages accorded ethnic immigrants. They could have remained in their communities for the rest of their lives, speaking Ebonics or any other language of their choosing. Instead, Black children are required to meet the language standards of immigrant communities, because they are the largest, if not the only group of Americans who regularly abandon their own people and communities to live with other groups in their communities.

Black communities are vulnerable and unmarked. They do not have gates, signs or other markers or barriers. They are wide open to transit traffic and activities from outsiders. Open Black communities are prime targets for those who wish to exploit Blacks economically and politically. Unclosed Black communities are vulnerable to toxic waste and illegal activities, such as drugs, prostitution, fencing and gambling. The Black residents are not sufficiently organized to deal with these illegal activities which are typically controlled by powerful forces outside of Black communities. Open communities cannot control the goods and services within them. Competing groups can enter, confiscate and exploit the host community. They can control Black politicians, start competitive businesses that drain off capital, sell inferior products or commit acts that are injurious to the local residents. A residential neighborhood cannot protect or sustain itself until it becomes a functional community.

## *Levels of a Functional Community*

Once we have put together the elements for a functional community—an independent economy, a code of conduct and a form of government—our team now has a foundation from which to compete politically and economically. We become more familiar with each other and can rally around our collective needs, experiences and goals. We can now begin to move our communities to higher levels of functioning as illustrated in Figure 10 below.

Our paradigm of vertical integration can be applied to community development. Vertical community development establishes a common sense of direction, authority and a collective interest. Members of the community live by a code of conduct based upon principles that dictate how they relate to, care for, respect and support each other. Once people have confidence that others in the community can be relied upon to help and support them, a sense of mutual trust evolves and cooperation can follow. Humans cooperate with people they have learned to trust.

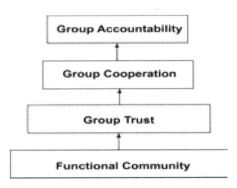

Figure 10.  The Key to Empowerment: Ordering of a Community

Once people are cooperating, they then have the capability to hold members of the group accountable for their behavior. All members of a community cannot be relied upon to live by a code of conduct alone. Some will undermine and sell out the community. They will not contribute to its collective development or support Blackness. A functional community must have a means to protect itself and to hold its members accountable. Other groups have always had formal and informal mechanisms to reward or punish members of the group who intentionally engage in behavior that is inappropriate and injurious to the community. Black America must have some institutional community organizations that will hold members accountable to the code of conduct. With the community developing trust, cooperation and accountability, as indicated in Figure 10, Black people will be able to function as a competitive team in the marketplace.

## *Conclusion*

The success of our national empowerment plan, to a great degree, depends upon our ability to build, mark and close physical communities and develop mind-sets that connect us to one another. Integration destroys communities, it does not build them. Community building is organized around people with common goals who appreciate and recognize each member's contribution to the overall group goals. A competitive community is one that operates upon competitive advantages. Within our national network, we must build competitive communities that contain social, political, economic, religious, educational and geographic assets that act as foundations of power. Communities are repositories for Black assets.

The *PowerNomics* national plan offers research and strategies to build functional communities, but the work of implementing the strategies is necessarily a local function. Some neighborhoods will be able to use out-of-the box thinking and mobilize for change. Others will talk about what they should do and not progress much beyond discussions. Some neighborhoods and communities will never even get to the discussion stage.

Each Black neighborhood should articulate a common set of beliefs and values regarding taking business risks, making a commitment to savings and investment, striving to achieve uniformly high educational standards, abiding by a code of personal and group conduct, and supporting a trust system, a team spirit, ethos and group self-interests. The primary obligation of a community is to equip its members to live and compete successfully in the domestic and global society of today and tomorrow. Those community members who are able to make this work will become the new Black leaders, because they will know how to apply the *PowerNomics* vision in order to achieve Black empowerment.

# CHAPTER FOUR

## *Restructuring Schools for Group Competitiveness*

*When you control a man's thinking you do not have to worry about his actions . . . He will find his proper place and stand in it.*
- Dr. Carter G. Woodson, 1933 [1]

**T**he traditional role of schools for Black children must be changed in order to make them functional and relevant in the lives of Black Americans. Black schools must empower Black children by functioning as extensions of the family, teaching the realities of life, dispensing knowledge and honing skills. It is from these collective school experiences that Black children learn to perceive the world and their place in it as individuals as well as members of a race of people. Schools have yet to perform these tasks. Changing Black schools into what they should be will require major restructuring.

Restructuring Black schools will require more than just tinkering with a few programs. We will need our schools to produce children who are appropriately trained to implement the *PowerNomics* plan in our communities, in our economic development, politics and in our churches. Clearly, it will be necessary to make changes in what and how our children are taught.

The new instructional programs and proposed solutions must be based upon the realistic needs and socioeconomic problems of Black children. If our problem is that our race inculcates values of individualism that hurt our people, then schools must design a solution to that problem. If our problem is that adults in our race feel successful only when they work in White corporations, then our schools must devise a solution and instill new values in the children. At the bottom line, we as Black people must accept full responsibility for the quality of education our Black children receive. There are few, if any, incentives for the majority society to operate Black schools that prepare Black children to compete in the economy. White society has a monopoly of control over the power of schools, and much of that power is hostile to our interests and opposed to our advancement.

## *Black America and Its Schools*

Dr. Carter G. Woodson said in the *Mis-Education of the Negro*, "Blacks are the only group of people who take their most precious possessions, their children, and ask their oppressors to educate them and to mold and shape their minds."[2] Today Blacks are totally dependent upon the majority society to prepare Black children to compete with White children. White control of Black schools presents a conflict of interest for the majority White society whose primary interest is in its own children. As long as Black people continue to wait on White society to educate their children, they will be waiting for a long time.

Black America must educate its children through community-based partnerships between students, teachers, parents, churches and businesses. The same building principles that were useful in rebuilding our communities can be applied to schools, which are essential institutions in functional communities. Schools are also communities in and of themselves, that should be built based upon a strong sense of community, trust, cooperation and group accountability. When teachers, children, and parents work together toward group goals, they naturally evolve into a community of interest that they control.

The design elements for education in the *PowerNomics* plan are very purposeful. This chapter describes how to apply the *PowerNomics* principles of ethno-aggregation and vertical integration to education. This plan is intended to foster a love and respect for educational excellence, and also provide a framework of self-discipline, a sense of community and racial pride. This framework places a premium on cooperation and harmony, and is intended to foster strong and productive alliances between Black families, schools, businesses, public offices, civic institutions and churches as we recreate them through *PowerNomics.* More importantly, *PowerNomics* creates an educational process that is specifically tailored to correct the historical weaknesses of our schools by linking them to a national economic and political empowerment plan.

## *What Does Black America Need From Its Schools?*

Any plan to empower Black America must have the involvement of Black schools to prepare the human or intellectual capital that we need to carry out the plan. Under the right circumstances, education can empower an individual or a group by conveying knowledge, skills, values, culture or attitudes. If we are going to effectively deal with this nation's structural inequality and the inappropriate behavior patterns of some Blacks, then schools must accept the burden of producing the human capital we need to achieve these critical objectives. Otherwise, we will have the blind leading the blind. Nothing underscores racial inequality of power and wealth more than this nation's education system. The question is, how can schools that are underfunded and ill-equipped produce Black children that are competitive with White children? We need an education model that meets and serves the specific needs of Black children. The test of a model is whether it empowers Blacks to compete in political and economic market places. Nothing more, nothing less.

Empowering Black children is more than teaching them math and reading skills. It is more than preparing them for public sector jobs or high-ranking positions in other people's businesses in other people's communities. They must know how to compete for wealth and power rather than poverty and acceptance, to produce rather than consume, and to be job producers rather than job seekers. For schools, preparing Black America to compete means removing the chains of inappropriate behavior and teaching them to see, think, and behave anew. The classroom education must be relevant to the real world outside of the school and Black children should learn more in classrooms than they do on the streets. Black children need schools to teach them how to live a life and earn a living in an increasingly pluralistic and competitive world. Only when schools are able to perform these functions, will they be able to close the learning gap between Blacks and Whites and other ethnic groups.

## *A Look at the Traditional Role of Schools*

Horace Mann, the architect of the common school system, ignored the existence of slavery and racism and described public education as "the great equalizer." Mann was persuaded by the nature of the times to envision schools as institutions for Whites. He felt that schools for the less privileged would provide them opportunities for social and economic advancement. Blacks eventually got access to public schools, but their treatment by the educational enterprise, which ignored their unique experiences and competitive needs, stands as a national disgrace. America's school system traditionally served as a major conduit for racism. It cooperated with social institutions to maintain the structural inequalities that pre-determined Black children's life chances. Today, schools have not fully committed themselves to providing Black children a high quality and relevant education. Instead, social scientists and politicians have devoted half a century to charging Blacks with inferior intelligence and poor educational values. Historical facts debunk these charges as well as the claim that schools fail Black children.

Education is supposed to reward citizens for academic achievements based on the rule that the more education you have, the more wealth and money you gain. However, Figure 11 tracks economic and educational progress and reveals that there is practically no relationship between Black people's level of wealth and income and their level of educational achievements.

When we examine the educational accomplishments of Blacks from the 1860s to the 1960s, we see some astounding accomplishments. Figure 11 also shows that in the early 1860s, approximately 98 percent of America's Black population was illiterate by design. Following the Civil War, nearly 25 million European immigrants came to America with the same illiteracy as the Black ex-slaves. Within the 30 years between emancipation and the Plessy vs. Ferguson decision of 1896, Blacks cut their illiteracy in half, reducing it from 98 percent to 48 percent. Blacks reduced their illiteracy twice as fast as the European immigrants. However, as European immigrants achieved educationally, they moved up in wealth, income, political empowerment, social acceptance and business ownership. Blacks were on the bottom and stayed on the bottom. There was no direct relationship between their astounding educational achievements and benefits. Blacks did not receive increased incomes, upward mobility or political empowerment in accord with their educational achievements. The reason for their lack of forward mobility is simple. Educational achievement by itself cannot override structural racism and make Blacks politically and economically self-sufficient or competitive. This is true because education is a determiner of class but does not transcend or eradicate racial boundaries for Blacks

Figure 11. Educational Gains v. Economic Stagnation

As indicated in Figure 11 above, the spectacular educational accomplishments of Blacks did not translate into the same economic benefits as they did for Jews and other European immigrants before and after World War I. Jewish immigrants were coming into this country with illiteracy rates equal to Blacks. But, since they were not Black, they were accepted into the banking, clothing, entertainment and jewelry industries and professions. As they were being accepted, a national racial backlash moved across the country in opposition to Black people. In the South, members of the majority society burned Black farmers' crops, poisoned their animals, poured kerosene on their farm crops and lynched at least one Black man per day. Their nearly impossible educational achievements did not change Blacks' status in terms of power, wealth and upward mobility.

Even as late as the early 1950s, census data indicated that a White high school graduate earned more than a Black college graduate. A Black person earned only 54 cents for every dollar a White person earned. The largest number of Blacks ever entered college and government service following the Black civil rights movement in the 1960s. Blacks' earned income went as high as 67 cent for every dollar that Whites earned in the mid-1970s before falling back down to 56 cents in the 1980s. Income has remained relatively unchanged. Nearly a half a century after the civil rights movement began, Blacks' earned income is back to where it was in the 1950s. Education has yet to offer the same economic or wealth rewards to Blacks that it does to Whites.

Unfortunately, many Black leaders, just like Whites, tend to believe that the legacies of centuries of slavery, Jim Crow semi-slavery, and benign neglect policies ended in the 1970s. Even with increasing evidence that integration has failed, they continue to believe that integration, in and of itself, wiped the racial slate clean. They believe all ethnic and racial groups started out even in the 1970s and therefore, if Black people are suffering inequalities, they are due to the differences in natural talents. It is naïve of Black and White leadership to believe that four centuries of racial exploitation, oppression, and denial of educational opportunities can be so easily erased.[3]

Wealth and other inequalities continue primarily because the planned inferior education provided to Blacks was never designed to give them countervailing power to offset the racism to which they would be exposed in mainstream society.

## *Education Is Not Enough*

Since education was not designed to eradicate wealth and other inequalities between the races, were the descendent of slaves wrong in wanting an education? No! They were not wrong. It's just that education was not enough. The majority society knew this during Reconstruction when they elected to deny Black ex-slaves "forty acres and a mule" and give them a marginal education instead. Education is an empowerment tool only when it is used in the right sequence. Black people were given no choice but to focus on social and education rights, rather than economic rights. In a capitalistic democracy, however economic achievement and mobility must occur before a group attempts to open up channels of educational opportunities. The educational achievements will then engender a corresponding set of cultural values and a further appreciation for educational achievement. Education allows a group to consolidate and extend its economic gains in the market places. When Jewish immigrants began immigrating into this country in the latter part of the 19th century, they first established an economic base. Fortunately, they entered the country with some skills that were needed in America's emerging industries. They were able to capture these industries based more on cultural experiences and chance than on educational achievements. After succeeding in these industries, they used their acquired wealth, political clout and social acceptance to enter and begin dominating education.

If Blacks are going to eliminate the myths about why they have not achieved, they must understand that structural racism forced Black Americans to lift themselves in reverse, by putting education and social goals before economics. Though Blacks demonstrated spectacular educational achievement and a total willingness to be long suffering, they could not translate those educational achievements into economic gains. There is practically no inherent economic power associated with educational achievement. Black America has encouraged its children to get a "good" education and find a "good" job in a White corporation or some level of government. Most ethnics, especially Jews and Asians, encourage their children to get a good education, develop some on-the-job experience, then use their education to start their own business. There are few Black businesses in which Black children can use their educational skills. As stated earlier, clearly a fundamental change is needed in the role that schools play in the lives of Black people.

## Who are Schools Failing?

One of the most frequently heard complaints in the closing years of the 20th century was that schools were failing. If public schools are failing, they are failing only Whites, Asians, Hispanics and other ethnic immigrants. Schools do not now nor did they ever fail in what they were designed to do for Black children: create a labor class in service to White society. Schools have always been mirrors that reflect the values, goals, needs and priorities of the society and the communities they serve. They have remained almost exclusively controlled by Whites through government policy makers, boards of education and major corporations. These powerful bodies approved curricula, staffing and instructional materials. Regardless of their physical location racial/ethnic makeup, schools across America had to teach their children European-American values. The quality of teaching and the educational outcomes track the racial lines of power and wealth. The academic scores of elementary and secondary schools strongly correlate with parental income, wealth and education. High income students can more easily afford special coaching from parents, professional remedial help and private schools. Schools perpetuate wealth and racial advantages that are inter generational in nature.

Schools produce in their students whatever skills, attitudes or other characteristics public policy makers and business owners need in their present and future workforce. Following the Civil War, for example, the country needed an industrial labor force. President Lincoln signed a national immigration law in the early 1860s that encouraged migration from Europe, Asia and Spanish speaking countries. So, America's first public schools following the Civil War were established to educate the influx of immigrants to become leaders of industry, business owners, professionals and members of the managerial classes. Ignored by Lincoln, Blacks were never educated to be owners, managers or members of the intellectual class. They were educated to be the workforce for those overclasses.

## The PowerNomics Education Plan

The *PowerNomics* education plan calls for a total restructuring of schools in Black neighborhoods. Like an assembly line that is producing an outdated and non-competitive product, the educational assembly lines within Black communities need to be shut down and re-engineered to address the collective needs of the children and their communities. Black children come to schools bearing different burdens, experiences and needs. They are entitled to an education program that addresses who and what they are. The same is true with the Black community. They too have goals and ambitions for their children. Both the needs of the students and the goals of the adults ought to be reflected in a national education plan. This plan should dovetail with what Black America wants to achieve and where it wants to go. Since the primary purpose of education is to be the great equalizer, restructuring the education experiences of Black children to promote their competitiveness in all areas of society is the goal of the *Power-Nomics* plan for self-empowerment.

Once the goals of the education plan have been accepted by Black communities, Black educators have the responsibility of modifying school curriculum, instructional materials, teaching methods, extra-curricular activities, administration, community-based activities, school-parent relationships, and even professional services with the specific intent of bringing educational parity to Black children. The driver of the reform steps that are offered below is a firm belief that Black dominated schools and educators can rise to the challenge and play an essential role in the economic and political reform of Black America by the year 2005.

## Education Reform #1: Halt School Integration

School integration has failed and should be stopped. Even though halting school integration would surely be celebrated by social conservatives, Black America has little choice. The pain of school integration is borne almost completely by Black Americans. The majority White society has not been required to give Blacks anything they did not already have. They profited while Blacks bore the pain. School integration ought to be halted for the following reasons.

First, the original intent of the Clarendon County, S. C. lawsuit in 1953 was for parity in the allocation of education funding. Under a separate but equal public policy, Blacks wanted to stop the local board of education from giving White schools four times as much money as they allocated to Black schools. Blacks were more concerned about the "equal" than the "separate." Second, the U.S. Supreme Court's Brown v. Board of Education ruling that segregated schools were "inherently inferior and unequal," was wrong. They are unequal when they are unequally supported. Instead of integrating and busing Black students into White schools, the Supreme Court should have ordered the board of education to bus more money, better instructional materials, better trained staffs and newer equipment into Black schools. Third, research studies conducted in Norfolk, Va.

(1995) and other school districts revealed that Black children are not performing significantly better in integrated schools than they were in all Black schools. Moreover some schools showed either no progress or, in some instances, academic achievement gaps that were widening rather than closing.[4]

Fourth, integration made Black people guests in America. Integration has been used to justify closing Black schools, firing Black teachers and administrators, busing Black children, assigning massive numbers of Black children to special education classes and depriving Black children of the advantage of being a majority population. Finally in 1991, the U.S. Supreme Court, in its *Board of Education of Oklahoma v. Dowell* decision, ruled that school districts could halt integration efforts. Thus, for the first time in history Black Americans are free to return to local control and fashion their own education plan and policies.

### Education Reform #2: Control Public and Independent Schools

Since 1977, the U.S. Supreme Court has issued a number of rulings that Blacks can now use to regain control of public and private schools within communities that serve their children. These schools must be restructured- the mission, curricula, budgets and teachers- to serve the immediate economic ends of those who control them. Without that control, Blacks cannot direct or use schools for their own purposes.

How does a community get control of its schools? Many majority Black urban areas provide instructive case studies in the types of problems Blacks will encounter as they seek more control over their schools, especially public schools. Detroit is an example. Detroit was a leader in locally controlled schools in the 1960s. The movement that started there spread across the nation. Now Detroit is leading a change in the opposite direction- White control of Black schools and their students. Detroit is a majority Black community with a Black student body, Black mayor, Black-dominated city council and an elected Black school board. Local control should have meant Black local control. However, as is often the case, it did not.

In January 1999, Michigan's White Governor, John Engler, proposed that the Detroit public schools, with a 98 percent Black student enrollment, be taken out of the hands of the elected local school board and transferred to one appointed by the mayor. The governor also proposed that the mayor appoint a representative to the Detroit School Board who would have the power to override and veto any actions. This political maneuver essentially transferred control of the board of education from the electorate to the governor and the mayor of the city. As expected, once this transfer of power took place, the governor appointed a White representative to oversee the predominantly Black board of education.

Whether the schools are predominately White or Black, located in an urban inner city or not, they are always under the control of Whites. So, while parents in non-Black communities are getting more control over their schools, Black communities are losing it. Whites have control of Black schools whether they take over public institutions, or establish under-funded charter schools, a voucher system, or implement similar conservative concepts. While charter schools can be developed to advance *PowerNomics* principles, at present most charter schools are under-funded and lack the support and ancillary services that they need to be successful. They compete with and undermine public schools.

Whether it is vouchers or charter schools, Black parents will try these new education strategies, seeking options for their children and beguiled by the promise of a few dollars, which are insufficient to provide a complete education. Within the next few years, it is not difficult to project that social conservatives, who argue for tax cuts and options that divert funds away from public school, will successfully destroy, or at least severely cripple, the public school system. These growing trends contribute to the loss of control Blacks have over their education systems.

How can Blacks exercise more control over institutions within their own residential neighborhoods as they rebuild them into communities? It will not be through civil rights, equal opportunity or social integration. All have failed Blacks. Control must begin by using Supreme Court decisions to gain control of the money that supports schools. The old adage that "he who pays the piper names the tune," still applies. All states assign substantial powers to local school boards. The bulk of school funding comes from local communities and not from the federal and state governments. Since Black communities pay taxes, they must have the greatest say in how their schools operate. Like White communities, they should control their schools. Otherwise, there is reason to question whether Blacks should collectively withhold payment of those taxes that support a school system that they cannot control locally.

Today, White government agencies and corporations are intensifying their economic control over Black schools and using them to benefit members of the majority society. Across America, corporations are taking over Black schools under the guise of supporting the voucher system, charter schools and privatizing public services. The real prize, however, is the more than $100 billion dollars that is spent annually in urban school districts for building construction, school supplies, textbooks, food services, testing programs, and Internet infrastructure and services. The profit motive remains king in the corporate world, and the Black education systems are the prizes. They are sought-after prizes not necessarily because they have the largest budgets, but rather because their money is an easy target. They do not face significant internal competition from Black people, nor do they encounter cumbersome or restrictive procurement standards.

Corporations use many tactics to pry open the Black community for their own benefit, and the techniques are much the same regardless of the particular area they target. A frequent technique is to hire a credible Black person as the interface. The interface gets a nice salary and the company gets a direct pipeline into the source of profit they seek, which in this case, is the schools. Because Blacks have such a weak sense of community, it is sometimes hard to deconstruct those "opportunities" to find the catch. If Blacks are going to control schools, they must recapture funding. It is the state's responsibility to fund schools, but control is a local decision.

By following the money, Blacks can take conservative programs and use them to their own advantage. They can set up special independent schools. Whether they are charter schools, religious schools or a private academy, they can make this trend a positive one and set up schools to take care of the needs of their own people. Through political activism, Blacks could require that new monetary controls be established that would track the funds allocated for each student. This per-student expenditure should follow the student whether inside or outside the public school system. It should include all other money governmental entities put into the system for management, school supplies, construction and special programs for direct or indirect support of education. Without the additional direct and indirect per student funding, the vouchers would not provide sufficient funds to operate charter schools. The schools would have to charge tuition and seek additional public and private funds. Therefore, any community that seeks to establish a charter, religious or private independent school system must insist that all per student funding follow each student from the public schools into the new school. Otherwise, Blacks should continue to support the public schools.

**Education Reform #3: Cooperative and Group Learning vs. Individualism**

Public and private schools based on the *PowerNomics* plan must teach children to work and learn cooperatively as members of a team. White society credits Anglo-Saxon rugged individualism with development of this nation. Accordingly, they place great importance on educational programs that teach children to compete against each other. Individualism in schools is a form of educational Darwinism, or survival of the fittest and brightest. It is a form of selfishness that encourages a child to be self-centered, to out do and profit at the expense of another child. This is the same ideology that drives this nation's political and economic systems from which Black people have systematically been excluded. If Black children are going to successfully compete, they will have to experience countervailing education practices that play to the strengths of Black people as a community.

One of the biggest weakness in the race is based on the Willie Lynch theory of divide and conquer. Teamwork is left largely to sports. We need less individualism and more togetherness and group cooperation. Instilling the values and advantages of group cohesiveness in most cultures fall upon the shoulders of the basic institutions: the family, school and church. But, since so many Black families are broken and dysfunctional, our schools and churches will have to pick up the slack and do double duty. To reverse some of the inappropriate behavior patterns in our race, it is important that the Black child's early school years be devoted primarily to instilling a strong communal spirit and developing effective cooperative skills.

The nation was founded on the affirmation of individual liberties and rights, while it was holding nearly five million Black slaves hostage as a group. Beyond the rhetoric and myths that admonished Blacks to behave as individuals, they were always treated as a group in practice. Pursuing the individualism myth, left Blacks bereft of group self-interest and group-based support structures. Teaching children to live as individuals is a philosophical design that works best for White children. They can afford to be individuals because they are the majority and everything in the society is designed to support and accommodate the White majority

It is minority groups that are hurt by the concept of individualism in a society in which wealth and power follow the numbers. Understanding vulnerabilities associated with individualism has not escaped many minority sub-categories of the majority society. Jews are a good example. As a religious minority, they stay together as a group. While they encourage Black Americans to seek social integration, they themselves did not seek religious integration. They understand that in a society with constitutionally approved religious pluralism, maintaining a separate religion works to their advantage.

So, instead of social integration, Jewish solidarity should be an instructive model for Blacks. One of the major reasons that Jews have succeeded economically and politically in America is that Jews move as a group. Jewish families and their religious institutions instill a sense of community and groupism in young Jewish children early in life. Years ago, a successful Jewish business man told me that Jewish schools teach cooperative economics. The young students are reportedly taught that "whatever they want to buy in life, somewhere there is a Jewish person who makes or sells it." When successfully taught, this lesson of mutual support and cooperative economics guides Jewish people throughout their adult lives and keeps them united and economically strong at a fundamental level.

In groups, children can educate each other and learn to get along with each other. Research indicates that learning in group activities can provide double benefits. Students in groups functioning as learning communities can master academic subjects collectively, but students in the groups also learn roles. They learn how to be leaders and followers, and how to share and care, depend on and accept each other's contributions to a team effort. Group learning guides students to identify group problems, amass their collective resources and look within themselves for answers. The responsibility rests with educators to develop curricula that make effective use of group teaching and learning methods. Essentially, group teaching and learning can help to concentrate the direction and quality of learning, to foster new patterns of behavior, and to eradicate cross-purpose activities.

In schools that incorporate the *PowerNomics* plan, Black children should learn how to relate to and depend on each other. Achieving a sense of belonging is a driving force behind the popularity of gangs in urban areas. The extra-legal aspects notwithstanding, gangs offer Black children a vehicle for team spirit, togetherness, security, a sense of direction, perceived power and opportunities for gaining wealth otherwise missing from institutions within Black communities. Schools can be forces to redirect the psychological forces that lead to the development of gangs by including opportunities for Black children to compete, group against group, in an approved and guided manner. Groups give children comfort, motivation and instant feedback. Schools can help establish habits of group learning and of appreciating the difference between cooperative group achievements and individual achievement. Students can learn to produce for, buy from, and sell to members of their own communities, while also depending upon them for the necessities of life. They should also learn that in times of difficulty or in solving common problems, they can come together and formulate acceptable, common solutions.

But schools must teach a groupism that supersedes class and income differences. This will be a hard lesson for many upper-middle-income Black children and their parents to learn, because the ethic of individualism is well entrenched within them. Learning group interdependence and interaction begins in the early grades of communal elementary schools. During those years, the early formal socialization of Black children should stress mutual respect, a sense of shared destiny, cultural values, even manners and courteous behavior and build a sense of kinship. These group characteristics will be key if we are to gain group wealth and power. We live in an achievement-oriented society where a group is measured and respected by its competence and competitiveness. The feeling of being loved and respected as a group grows from early group experiences in the family. Both kindergarten and elementary schools are an extension of the family and play a primary role in the socialization process. The old adage that "the way the twig is bent, so the tree will grow" is relevant here.

The early socialization process should teach teamwork to reverse meritorious manumission or the Willie Lynch syndrome of "divide and conquer." The community will be the basic building block for a new Black America, and every Black person should receive his recognition through the success of the group and the community, not for an outstanding solo performance. Competitive businesses, industries, communities, and politicians need socialized young people to benefit the Black community and themselves individually and as part of that community. Teachers, administrators, and ancillary staff need training in the new philosophies, methods and how to revise content to achieve the new group goals.

## Education Reform #4: Retraining Education Teams

Community is the cornerstone of wealth and power and of the *PowerNomics* national plan. In Chapter Three, we learned how to convert our neighborhoods into functional communities. Black America's schools must be communities within a community and carry through that theme, especially in the formative elementary school years. The entire education team will need to be retrained so that they can reform the schools for our purposes.

The instructional programs should teach the keys to community building: a sense of community, trust, cooperation and group accountability, unity, group competitiveness and academics, all in the context of Black heritage and local community goals. A communal philosophy should touch all aspects of the curriculum, defining how learning experiences are structured. For instance, reading and math can be taught in the context of the community's economics, capital and business needs. Schools should establish a direct relationship between the learning experience and ways students could use the information to empower their community and to promote unity.

In Chapter Three we learned that a community code of conduct is essential for a functional community. Learning the code of conduct in school in a formal way will guide the behavior of our children as they learn to relate to each other and to other groups or people inside their sphere and outside. Black children must first learn how to get along with and support other Black children before they can get along with White, Asian or Hispanic children. A code of conduct teaches the child how to respect, appreciate and value Black people, so that those values will be part of the adults they become. It is important that children are socialized early to be part of a group and to accept the responsibilities that group membership brings. Black America has internalized a code of conduct from White society that teaches that growth and stability in the White community is everyone's goal, and that Black America should never be independent, self-sufficient or competitive. Community schools should teach our children that responsible behavior means that every individual act must help strengthen, not weaken, the Black community.

The principle function of the family is to protect young children. The family is the first economic and political entity to which Black children are exposed. Kindergarten and elementary schools are extensions of the home and function as a child's first formal external socialization process. It is at this formative point that we must begin to build community-based education in close alliance with Black parents. In elementary schools, students usually learn how to excel individually, instead of how to use their strengths to benefit their community and their race. Community-focused education exposes children to systematic learning experiences that grow out of and relate to the needs, values and concerns of the community. They should learn that being part of a group does not stop one from competing, but they must also learn the value of doing their best to make their group, their team, competitive. If they learn these lessons in their youth, they will continue to function as a team as they get older.

Parents will also need support because they are products of the very schools that they want to change and because they are also struggling to recognize and reverse the inappropriate code of conduct that was instilled in them. The alliances between schools and families in community-based schools are mutually supportive environments where children grow as individuals while learning to function as an effective member of a defined group.

In these formative years, Black parents and their communities can work together through the schools to devise child-raising strategies to achieve ethno-aggregation and vertical integration. One of the greatest impediments to Black advancement is a lack of unity. Children can be taught ethno-aggregation-to support other Blacks, and depend on their group-in the kindergarten and elementary school years. Later, in their high school years, Black children should be taught the principles of vertical integration, how to move upward as a group and to compete with others outside of their group for control of wealth, resources and power. Learning how to function cooperatively as a member of a group and move vertically within the system reduces Black-on-Black competition and divisiveness.

Community schools can also help parents develop parenting techniques that encourage and reward desired behavior in their children. To foster a strong sense of community, unity and group togetherness at home and in school, children should have opportunities to cooperate with others in getting things done.

Community schools also bear the heavy responsibility of socializing children to be competitive students as well as functional adults. Clearly, this responsibility is not being fulfilled in regular public schools, where nearly 40 percent of all Black children who start first grade drop out before completing high school and many of them spend most of their lives on unemployment, welfare or prison rolls. Whether it is because the children are not in the schools or the schools are dysfunctional, either way, too many Black children are not equipped with the attitudes and skills that they need to function competitively in American society. One of the primary objectives of community-based high schools should be to prepare children for the *real* job markets instead of requiring them to endure instructional programs that have no relevance to the real world.

*PowerNomics* stresses that school, families and communities create alliances that direct students into community service. Out-of-school activities and resources should support and complement school activities. Early communal experiences in elementary school lay the foundation for children to learn the academic and vocational skills they will learn in secondary school.

If Black Americans are going to ever have self-sufficient and competitive communities and acquire group behavior patterns, our schools must, in and of themselves, become communities. It will be teachers, administrators and other staff who will find ways to impart these critical new values and accept the challenge of these new roles, but they will require extensive support and training.

## Education Reform #5: Compensatory Education and Alternative Schools

Too many children cannot read and do not have sufficient academic skills to live a productive life. *PowerNomics* requires an educated, thinking constituency that can read. Black children should stay in school until they have reached an agreed upon level of academic proficiency and can function effectively. There are several strategies that educators may want to explore to accomplish this reform. First, schools may have to run year round. Already school systems are trying this on an experimental basis and are finding that it has many merits and does not generate the opposition from students, parents and teachers originally expected.

Second, the total number of years a child could receive educational services could be increased from 12 to 14 years. During those extra two years, children would receive compensatory training to elevate and fill gaps in their academic skills. These two additional years could be mandatory or voluntary. They could also use this period to learn a trade. Vocational education should be part of our new education design for all children.

### *Vocational Education*

An increasing percentage of the most desirable and highest paying jobs are emerging in the service and blue collar industries. When this fact is considered and paired with the disproportionate number of Black children who fail to finish high school, Black America is presented with an opportunity to gain a competitive advantage.

Black America should design and operate full scale, intellectually demanding apprenticeship and vocational education programs in targeted urban schools across America. These targeted schools should blend academic and job skills options. By combining inside and outside of class apprenticeship experiences and training with basic subject mastery in the classroom, the program can give our Black students an optional way of earning a living and a life.

A *PowerNomics* vocational or industrial education curriculum can be very different in purpose than the vocational education instituted by Booker T. Washington in the late 1800s. Washington's program trained Black students for subordinate roles and jobs for which, in most instances, there were no markets. Black children should now be educated for jobs in Black-owned businesses as well as for jobs where Black people are in authority.

Figure 12. Earning a Living and a Life: Vocational Education

Vocational education programs and apprenticeships should be structured as a *supplement* and not a *substitute* for a core academic curriculum. Black America must look for a model that can make Black children as marketable as possible and use it to develop a vocational and apprenticeship program that can link school and work. Since Black America is beginning to develop countermeasures for structural racism and developing businesses to bring jobs into Black communities, an important issue to address is how to prepare Black children for the work world and train them to fill those jobs. Not all Black children will go to college, but those who don't must be able to earn a living. Even those who go to college should learn vocational skills. The high school reformed for *PowerNomics* is capable of preparing a child for life and the work force.

The *PowerNomics* national plan for education would bring together various segments of the society: parents, churches, school officials, businesses and public office holders. They would work to marry academics and apprenticeship programs in an effort to see that the needs of the students, community and businesses are met. Early in this century, vocational programs in the North and South were used to the detriment of Blacks. In the North, Black children were allowed to elect an array of shop classes, even though Blacks had no outlets for their acquired skills because of closed union shops in skill trades. Blacks did use their Southern vocational program skills within their own segregated communities. White businesses also used skilled Black labor but kept them locked into low level jobs. Thus, White business owners in the South and unions in the North closed out Blacks, and reduced the value of their vocational training.

In educating our children to meet the economic needs of Black communities, the competitive skills they learn to apply in their school groups should translate in later years to group economic competitiveness. The vocational school programs inside *PowerNomics* communities would produce human resources for vertical industries, other community businesses and businesses outside of the community. Schools and businesses should establish apprenticeship and workstudy programs. These internships and work relationships guarantee that the academic program and the business linkages produce on-the-job training relevant to the available job markets inside and outside of Black communities. Black students would then be equipped to leave school with academic as well as vocational skills.

## Education Reform #6: Using Technology

Technological development—computer advances, the Internet, high speed data connections—has rapidly changed the way we conduct most life activities. It is important that our children are exposed to and learn how to use the developing forms of technology so that they will have marketable business and employment opportunities in life. It will be the role of *PowerNomics* based schools, however, to frame technology in the most appropriate way for our goals, as a tool that increases efficiency and information. They will be trained in using computerized technology in processing and research, business and product management, communicating and marketing services and goods, and most importantly, in the creation of new technology. It will be the technology that evolves from our vertical industries that provides wealth creation opportunities for Black America.

However, the traditional relationship between Black people and technology has to change. Technology and Black people have long held an adversarial relationship. Racism has historically kept us shackled until technology arrived and rendered us obsolete. The benefits that can spring from our economic empowerment can allow us to change the historical equation. We may never own any of the Silicon Valley industrial complexes. In fact, a number of Black organizations have pending employment lawsuits against high-tech Silicon Valley firms. We have to learn to be realistic. This nation has anti-discrimination laws, but racial competitiveness guarantees that Whites will break these laws to place income and wealth building opportunities with Whites rather than Blacks.

It is difficult for Black Americans to compete after the fact, on the tail end of technology. As indicated in Chapter Six, once Black America begins to build its own vertical industries, it will need bright, young Black minds to generate new technology within the captured industries. When we are in control of our own industries, we can produce new technology that produces employment and wealth building opportunities. Until then, technology will continue to produce power and wealth for those who own and control it.

## Education Reform #7: New Role for Black Colleges

Now we must reclaim identity and governance of historically Black colleges and restore their original roles. Black colleges were not built to educate "all the children of all the people." They came into existence to educate Black people, to equip them to be a competitive group. Since Black people are far from being economically, politically and educationally competitive, Black colleges have not fulfilled their mission. From Emancipation until the Black civil rights movement, ex-Black slaves sold wood, flowers, pies and ice on the streets to generate enough money to acquire land, buildings, equipment and materials to sustain a network of Black colleges. Black colleges were commissioned to take uneducated Blacks and teach them to be doctors, nurses, teachers and other professionals. We must reclaim our Black colleges and return them to their former glory and mission.

One of Black America's greatest educational setbacks has been the erosion of its historical colleges following the Black civil rights movement of the 1960s. Since integration, Black colleges have been forced more into the mainstream and severely hampered in meeting the educational needs of this nation's Black communities. A study conducted by Walter Allen validated this conclusion. Allen in his study of *Gender and Campus Race Differences in Black Students' Academic Performance, Racial Attitudes, and College Satisfaction* compared Black students at predominantly Black universities with those at predominantly White universities. He concluded that Black schools do a better job in educating Black undergraduates than White universities and provide a more nurturing environment to instill skills, self-confidence, leadership opportunities and a competitive spirit that Black students do not receive at White universities.

As society integrated, state boards of regents and other oversight agencies moved to close down Black colleges or merge them with White colleges. Black colleges found themselves in a dilemma. They were instructed to justify their continued existence by converting their education curriculums and supportive programs to be similar to offerings by White colleges. Once they changed their mission and converted their programs into miniature White colleges, the power structure then argued that they ought to be closed or merged with White colleges because states did not want the double expense of two colleges offering the same educational opportunities.

As required by the integration process, many Black colleges merged into White colleges and disappeared. Never did a White college merge into a Black college and disappear. Within one generation after the integration process began, seven historically Black colleges had become all White and it is projected by some that a similar number will change hands in the near future. When Whites take control and convert the colleges over, they acquire ownership of the land, buildings and other tangible assets, but they do not adopt the original mission to lift the Black race.

The nature of White or integrated colleges impedes their interest in accommodating the interests and unique needs of Black students. Increasingly, Black colleges are prohibited from focusing on racial matters. Black colleges, like their White counterparts, are allowing Black students to become "guests."

Black colleges were once important and viable refuges for Black students and Black professors. Integration sounded a death knell for Black colleges, too. When Black colleges were forced to become miniature White colleges, they lost the justification for their continued existence. Of the Black colleges that remain, the staffs are more than 50 percent non-Black. Many Black college professors abandoned Black colleges to teach at White colleges. Their integration left a vacuum that was filled by Whites and immigrants.

Federal government funds that were historically earmarked for Black colleges are now diluted and shared with White colleges that claim at least a 20 percent Hispanic student enrollment. The private funds donated to the College Fund/United Negro College Fund, which were once exclusively directed to assist Black students, are now "integrated" and available to all minority students. However, education funds that were set-aside for Jewish, Asian, American Indian and Hispanic students have never opened up to needy Black students. Black leadership has not explained to Black America why education funds for this nation's most marginalized student population were integrated to include this nation's more advantaged groups.

Therefore, Blacks need to recapture historical Black colleges for a number of reasons. The first reason is Black colleges were invaluable assets. They should not have been given away just so Blacks could become guests in integrated colleges and universities. Second, since the material conditions have changed very little since the inception of Black colleges, clearly the role and responsibility originally envisioned for Black colleges has not been achieved. Third, predominantly White colleges and universities are either not interested in or are incapable of preparing Black graduates to meet the needs of Black America. And fourth, Black colleges are an essential element in any national plan that proposes to teach Black America to use competitive group politics and group economics.

The loss of Black colleges is a monument to the continued effectiveness of the slave trading practice of the 16th century known as the "doctrine of unequal exchange." As discussed in *Black Labor, White Wealth*,[5] this doctrine developed around the practice of giving African chiefs valueless beads and old firearms in exchange for highly valuable diamonds, gold and Black slaves. Something similar happened with Black colleges. We gave up our Black colleges, brightest professors, students and best athletes, clearly valuable assets, in exchange for the social process of integration, which is not even a tangible asset and has questionable value. By the late 1960s, Black America was trading off its hard education resources—both physical and financial—for social privileges. We are the only "minority" who chose to do so. Jews participate in various inter-denominational activities, but they did not turn over Jewish schools such as Brandies University just to participate or "get along." Catholics also participated in inter-denominational religious groupings but they have not relinquished control of Notre Dame. Women and American Indians have "socially integrated," but they did not turn over their colleges. Apparently, the doctrine of unequal exchange is primarily practiced on Black people.

Black America needs its historical colleges to prepare its young people to become economically and politically independent and competitive. They could provide agricultural extension services, technical business assistance and continuing education programs in targeted Black communities and industries. Black farmers and landowners still need to be in a position to convert their land into productive income streams. Black people still need the resources farmers produce and farmers need access to the markets that exist in urban areas.

Black colleges can help devise a new distribution system that would link farmers and the food that they produce to the communities that need it—first in Black communities then later, into White communities. No matter how many dot-com businesses spring up, people will always need food to eat.

Black colleges should function as research institutions and data centers for guiding Black economic revitalization, reparations and political leadership. They must again become a place where our scholars are able to do research. We will need them to do research on any number of issues, including political independence of Black people, and answer research questions such as: How do we best revitalize urban land and property? How do we rebuild industries?

Black colleges should put our best scholarly minds to work on the question of the best way to organize a reparations movement and to develop a formula to calculate benefits. How much are Black people entitled to? What are the justifications? They should be teaching Black students to take up intelligent political roles, based on a clear understanding of our historical challenges and predicament, to develop public policies and accountability systems that help all Blacks.

To complete the circle of information, Black colleges could establish advisory boards as a mechanism for input from business, political and community leaders. This would link them with national intellectual resources. The purpose of these advisory boards would be to identify trends and industry changes that suggest new directions in academic preparation to lead Black colleges into the future.

They should also have a role in preparing students to take positions in Black vertical industries (See Chapter Six) and establishing a complimentary vocational-technical apprenticeship program that would provide job and business opportunities. Information from such boards should give Black colleges and students valuable lead time to prepare for the future.

## Education Reform #8: Adopt-a-Black School

Across America, billboards and road signs urge us to adopt this highway or that endangered animal. It is now time to post similar signs urging the adoption of our endangered urban Black schools. We need an adopt-a-Black school program that links all segments of our society with targeted Black schools. Urban school boards could establish and coordinate the involvement of various kinds of community-school committees, advisory boards and financial sponsors for school programs. These high profile groups could bring the resources to the schools. For instance, business advisory board and financial sponsors, such as chambers of commerce or other business organizations, could help design the content of high school vocational, technical and apprenticeship programs in neglected schools. A combined academic and vocational program could help raise the academic standards, increase student attendance, reduce discipline problems, develop vocational skills, lift students' self-esteem and offer them recognition for their accomplishments.

Churches, social fraternities and sororities and civic organizations could also adopt-a-Black school. They could also establish and support programs that would serve as a conduit for bringing in additional financial and personnel resources into the schools. These groups could meet regularly with either the school boards or the local school administrators to discuss their progress and needs.

If necessary, schools can be reformed with smaller schools operating within the larger schools. But, all of the schools and programs should be oriented towards the empowerment of the Black students in alignment with the national empowerment plan. This is not a new role for schools. Schools have always produced whatever skills and competencies the society wanted in its children. There simply has not been a societal demand or market for well educated, well prepared and competitive Black children.

## *Conclusion*

Failure to rethink, restructure, retrain, retool and resume control of schools in Black communities will produce yet another crop of non-competitive Black children. Black Americans must respond to new ideological, demographic and political challenges that are emerging. No other group is going to aid Blacks in their need to become more educationally competitive. A solution will not appear out of thin air.

Schools in Black communities must not only teach regular language and computation skills, but under the *PowerNomics* national plan for education, they must diligently search for and use Black history and culture to engage, uplift, motivate and improve Black children's academic competitiveness. These principles and policy recommendations are designed to correct many of the instructional weaknesses within the current system. The most detrimental is that the system is ignoring the educational needs of most Black students while mis-educating the rest.

# Part III

# Empowerment Principles and Practices

# CHAPTER FIVE

## Practicing Group Economics

*The Black race enriched every group on earth.*
*Now it must enrich itself.*

Just three months into the 21st century, two of this nation's most respected sources of economic information laid out the case for Black America to build its own alternative economy and begin practicing group economics. On March 14, 2000, the *Wall Street Journal* ran a two-page story on wealth building in America, from the Civil War to present time. The article detailed the history of boom and bust cycles in the U.S. economy and concluded that the nation is in the midst of the longest period of economic prosperity and expansion in its history. The current economic boom period began in the early 1990s, but the Journal article revealed that whether this nation was in a boom or bust period, Black Americans, unlike any other population group, remained in an economic depression.

A week after the *Wall Street Journal* story, another unexpected source pointed out the economic inequality in our society. In a speech to the Annual Conference of the National Community Reinvestment Coalition, in Washington, D.C., Alan Greenspan, chairman of the Board of Federal Reserve, discussed the economic challenge of eradicating the income and wealth disparities in the society.[1] Greenspan went beyond reporting on the national economy and sounded an alarm to the nation that holds particular concern for Black Americans. He said that despite White America's economic good times, wealth disparities between groups are widening. He said, "I have no illusions that the task of breaking down barriers that produced disparities in income and wealth will be simple." But he warned that this task remains "an important goal because societies cannot thrive, if significant segments perceive their functioning as unjust."

Our national leadership, both Black and White, remain silent to Greenspan's remarks and the *Wall Street Journal* article. For whatever reasons, they avoid the reality that after 400 years Black Americans are still outside of this nation's mainstream economy. Time is running out for Black America to resolve the wealth inequality. If we cannot enter the channels of wealth in the mainstream, we must do the next best thing: take advantage of the fact that we are outside the mainstream economy, and construct a parallel alternative economy within our own Black communities where wealth can be gained.

## *Where Does Wealth Come From?*

Since Black America's primary problem is the lack of wealth, then a primary part of a solution must be for Blacks to gain wealth. We must learn alternative ways wealth is created and how to capitalize on human needs and desires to gain wealth.

But, we must remember that all roads do not lead to wealth. There are two basic methods to achieve wealth: First, it can be created or acquired through redistribution. It is very difficult to earn wealth or to acquire it by working a job. A job is designed to maintain a worker from pay day to pay day and to keep workers one week away from the welfare or unemployment lines. But, what is wealth? In earlier chapters we learned that wealth is the fruit of any labor that is stored and used to satisfy human desires and needs. Wealth can be acquired through inheritance, reparations or profit from someone else's labor. The less a worker is paid for labor, the more wealth the owner of the business or land gains.

Of the available options, increased business ownership and reparations are the best means for Blacks to gain wealth. Businesses can redistribute wealth six to eight times faster than employment. Black Americans are just beginning to seriously seek reparations as a means to gain wealth, even though nearly 97 percent of the majority society opposes the transfer of any form of wealth to Black people. Eventually, the majority society will be forced by the power of the facts to award reparations to Black Americans. However, until White society decides to grant reparations, Blacks must choose from the remaining options and begin creating their own wealth. It will require their best efforts, but it can be done.

Much of the wealth that we need is right before our eyes. If we aggregate, we can see it. If we work together, we can acquire it or create it. We are simply blind to our own wealth potential. The words of a White child talking to his Black friend sums up the essence of the hidden wealth potential of the race. The child said, "I wish I could buy you for what you think you are worth and sell you for what I think you are worth. I could make a fortune."

Throughout history, nearly everyone, except Black people, has seen wealth in the race. Black people have responded by enriching every other group but themselves. It is now time for Black people to create wealth for themselves. The secret to creating wealth is to own and control resources, whether they are natural (land, water, precious minerals and metals), processed (machinery, factories, consumer items, public improvements) or human capital (skilled, literate, labor force). There is no wealth potential in public housing, food stamps, petty crime, drug use, or teenage pregnancy. There is no wealth potential in a job. It is the owner and producer of the job who have the wealth potential. We need activities and mechanisms that produce wealth for Black people and their communities. When a group or community begins to acquire resources and manage them for the economic benefit of the group, they have created an economy, a mechanism to produce income, wealth, jobs, and business opportunities. It is important that we understand this concept of an economy.

John Kenneth Galbraith, in his book, *Almost Everyone's Guide to Economics*,[2] stressed the importance of an economy to any population group. Galbraith points out that those people who do not understand or pretend that they do not know how an economy is built and operates automatically surrender all wealth-building power to those who do understand. Groups with their own economies make wealth-producing decisions in their own best interests. The world is a competitive place and there are few, if any, incentives for other groups to intentionally make decisions in the best interests of Black Americans.

Upon what philosophical base should Black Americans build an economy within their own community? Blacks should use the same philosophical base that the majority society and its ethnic subgroups use: a culture of competition that operates in its own best interests. Those in America's melting pot build their respective economies around *their* needs, *their* cultures, *their* togetherness, and *their* nationalistic goals. Now, Black Americans must build a viable economy to accomplish Black America's goal of producing wealth as a means to be competitive and self-sufficient.

Let's look at a story that demonstrates how an economy and wealth are created. Brian Wesbury, in his book, *The New Era of Wealth*,[3] tells about an imaginary island where 10 villagers earned their living by fishing. Each of the villagers caught two fish each day. The daily Gross Domestic Product of the island was 20 fish, just enough to supply sufficient food for their meals. Clearly, the villagers could not progress because they only produced enough to survive. In this respect they were similar to most Black Americans who have worked jobs or lived off of subsidies and various forms of assistance.

Wesbury explained how the two fishermen in his story fostered an economy by changing their perspective and started to see, think and behave out-side-of-the box. They risked starvation by taking time out from fishing to build a boat and make fishing nets. With their boat and newly designed nets these two fishermen could then catch 20 fish in a day between them. Now two people could produce what it used to take 10 people to do. They now had a fishing industry and could feed everybody on the island. The other eight villagers then had a choice. They could continue to catch two fish a day to live on and enjoy life. Or they could diversify. A few could build businesses that related to the fishing industry, perhaps opening a boat or net repair shop. Others could raise and sell fruits and vegetables or start a bakery. Still others could begin to make sandals and clothing to sell or trade with the two villagers who built and owned the boats and nets. This is how an economy is born and industries follow. Members of the community take calculated risks and begin to build businesses and provide goods and services to members of their group. Later in this chapter and in subsequent chapters, we will suggest ways that Black Americans can be like these island villagers and build an alternative economy.

Without effective and healthy economies, it is impossible for Black people anywhere in the world to compete in producing wealth. The world's total wealth is estimated at $390 trillion.[4] However, Black people, who make up nearly one-fifth of the world's population, own less than one percent of the wealth. In the United States, the wealth has been mal-distributed along a ranking order of skin color and social acceptance. The wealth disparity between Blacks and Whites is so great that two Whites together, Bill Gates ($63 billion) and Lawrence J. Ellison ($50 billion) have a net worth that is greater than the collective net worth of this nation's 36 million Black people.

With Black American households having an estimated $7.2 billion invested in Wall Street stocks and bonds, Gates and Ellison collectively own nearly 13 times more stocks and bonds than all 36 million Black Americans[5]. The wealth disparities between the races are even greater outside of the United States. South Africa has 29 million Black people which makes it a 99 percent Black country. Yet, the DeBeers Corporation, a White-owned company, owns and controls 50 percent of that Black nation's total wealth. The remaining 50 percent of wealth belongs to nearly 2.5 million Whites. The 29 million Black South Africans are left with practically zero wealth in one of the most richly endowed countries on earth. The mal-distributed wealth fixed Black people at the bottom of the world's wealth barrel. Wealth is the great determiner of opportunity. Without wealth, equal opportunity becomes only a dream.

## The Mainstream Economy and the White Majority

In our competitive and race-based society, why would the majority White society want to throw the doors of economic opportunity wide open to Blacks? That is not the nature of competitors who play a game of "I have mine and I am going to get yours." The majority society's economic model extends its economy into Black communities and pursues the Black consumer. To support their economic model, various levels of government and private corporations encourage economic development that is not in the best interests of Black Americans. They routinely offer Black Americans marginal jobs while non-Black businesses exploit the resources, labor and consumer dollars within Black neighborhoods. They offer minimum public assistance in the form of housing, food, home heating and health care subsidies.

In the last two decades, many of the nation's leading think tanks and academicians have come to realize that abandoned urban cities contain a wealth of infrastructure assets, such as waterways, transportation systems and commercial buildings. Whites are buying and renovating property and moving back into the inner cities, spawning an economic rebound. One of the leading proponents of urban economic redevelopment is Michael F. Porter, a professor of business administration at Harvard Business School. During the last 20 years, Porter has written a number of books about competitiveness in business and industry. In his most recent book, *On Competition,* he devoted an entire chapter to "The Competitive Advantages of the Inner City." Porter pointed out the traditional negatives associated with Black communities. But, he also suggested numerous business advantages that can be found in urban cities. His recommendations for inner city business developments are very similar to the traditional social models that give White businessmen opportunities to build wealth and businesses in Black neighborhoods while Blacks get jobs and places to spend their money.[6]

Porter must be given credit, however, for offering an economic model that points out the economic advantages of building businesses within urban Black cities. The major shortcoming of his model from the perspective of *PowerNomics* is that it does not intend to make Black Americans self-sufficient and competitive within their own communities. It is a model of economic growth for non-Blacks within Black neighborhoods. Porter's model has strong moral and ideological overtones. His philosophy is similar to that of Booker T. Washington's admonishment that Whites would be willing to invest and build businesses in inner cities if the residents clean up their crime and improve their work habits. When groups are competing for wealth and resources such admonishments to Black Americans are disingenuous and reflect the structural racism discussed in Chapter One. I have never heard White businessmen say to Asian, Jewish, Hispanic or American Indian communities that if you clean yourselves up, White businessmen will be willing to come into your communities, develop businesses, displace your income and give community members jobs.

Black Americans were brought to this country to be a labor force. Their problem is not the lack of jobs. The lack of jobs is a symptom of their lack of wealth and businesses that produce jobs. Our society does not prioritize creating businesses for Blacks the way it does for other groups. In the Washington, D.C. area there are ongoing efforts by levels of government, schools, banks and businesses to prepare Asians and Hispanics for business careers, but seldom if ever is the focus on Blacks, even though Asians and Hispanics already surpass Blacks in business ownership. The assimilated groups within the majority society came to this country voluntarily in the search of wealth and fortune. According to a front page story in the Washington Post (May 25, 1998), "Any group that does not have an economic structure is heading for trouble. The groups that hold the most control over their financial, human capital, and markets will be the most competitive groups." Porter's economic model would be more of a positive for Blacks, if it encouraged and guided Black entrepreneurs to compete and keep control of their own communities and cities by revitalizing, building, owning and controlling their own businesses. As stated earlier, Porter's economic models contain much that is positive but they are designed to maintain the status quo on wealth and power. They do not address the structural wealth inequality, which is the very difficult knot of the race problem.

## A New Orientation

The new orientation for Black America, within the framework of a national plan, is the practice of group economics. When our ethno-aggregation paradigm is combined with the traditional practice of group economics, it reshapes the concept into ethno-economics. The primary goal of practicing group economics or *PowerNomics* is to draw wealth, income and other resources into Black communities and to make them more economically self-sufficient and competitive. The practice of group economics is not new. To successfully compete, Black entrepreneurs will need some competitive advantages. The action steps proposed later in this chapter are designed to give Black America some of the advantages that Whites and other ethnic groups have in the marketplace. Black people are 400 years behind the majority society and various ethnic groups in structuring their own economy. Our new orientation is built on understanding the cycle of wealth production and getting ahead of the curve, not following it. The principles of wealth building as shown in Figure 12 will repeat themselves just as history does. The wealth cycle will shift from technology to control of resources at some point in the not-too distant future. Before the shift occurs, Blacks can position themselves as the lead rather than the hind dog.

## Technology, Wealth and the New Orientation

Where does technology fit into the new orientation of group economics and the cycle of wealth for Blacks? Many social observers and prognosticators argue that access to computers, the information high-way and other advanced technology is the salvation of Black Americans. There is a subtle suggestion that technology is blind to color. Therefore, in theory it does not matter who owns and controls technology just as long as Black people have access to it they can overcome structural racism. This is blatantly untrue. Black people must not be misled by the computer hype and technology euphoria. Technology is and always has been just as much a political tool as it has been an economic tool. Technological tools are deployed to the advantage of those who own and control them. Like all previous technology, computer-driven technology is not necessarily a friend of Black people. Blacks have never been major owners, producers or controllers of technology. Structural racism holds Blacks in place, as a labor class, until new technology comes along and wipes out that place.

For example, in the early 1900s cotton picking machines that could pick 50 times more cotton per hour forced Black Americans to leave the cotton fields and move North in search of work. Fifty years later, automatic machinery forced most Blacks from the steel mills, automobile and chemical factories of the North onto the welfare, criminal, and unemployment rolls of urban areas. Black Americans never owned or produced the automation technology that displaced and rendered them an obsolete labor force. In telecommunications, the inventions of the radio, the telephone and television did not enrich Black people. They received the benefits of *using* radios, telephones and television, but those who produced and controlled the technology were the ones who became wealthy. In the new *PowerNomics* orientation, technology is important but Blacks can compete best by getting ahead of technology and owning and controlling the industries from which technology evolves. Knowing ahead is getting ahead.

A new orientation to group economics requires understanding the cycle of wealth, illustrated in Figure 13. The cycle began with **natural resources**—minerals and precious metals. Next, it moved to **human labor**, especially Black slave labor, which drove the engines of civilizations around the world. By the mid-1960s, **technology** had become the great wealth builder. Technology did the heavy lifting, moving, cleaning and building. We are currently in the fourth phase, the **information** and **manipulation of symbols**. Information manipulators and distributors have emerged as the greatest wealth builders ever.

They are making untold billions of dollars moving information instead of tangible goods. The next shift will carry us back to the original starting point: **Natural resources** and other tangible goods.

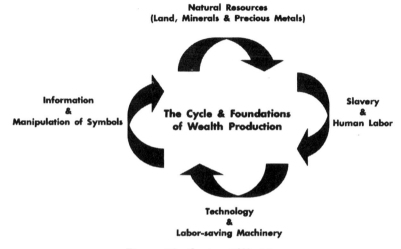

Figure 13. Cycle of Wealth

Since Blacks have yet to capture and benefit from the Technology phase shown at the bottom of the cycle in Figure 13, they could seize a strategically competitive position by advancing directly to the first phase, control of natural resources at the top of the cycle, build vertical industries and practice group economics. Raw resources stimulate labor, which stimulates production, which stimulates income, which stimulates wealth. The foundations of wealth are cyclical. Our global economy is presently in the Information phase of wealth formation. The fourth phase of the wealth creation cycle, Information Manipulation, is virtual. Granted, information technology is extremely valuable, but at some point in the fourth phase it will become a perishable resource, technology will falter and humans will be at risk. The value of technology-driven information will decrease while the value of tangible goods and human labor will increase. Devaluation can be triggered by man-made causes, such as computer viruses, accident or uncontrollable natural disasters. Any of these events could drive the wealth-building cycle back to the beginning —natural resources. The group that controls those resources will be in the driver's seat. Thus, Black America can get ahead by jumping ahead.

In past wealth cycles, society was able to store goods and services from each wealth building phase because they were tangible like the natural resources of land, water and food. They could be stored for prosperity and the enjoyment of future generations. Whether it was from a farm, automobile factory or hospital, it could be stored in warehouses, books and libraries or even in burial tombs. Yet, in our computer-driven world, when computer users are constantly admonished to save back-up copies of their work, what happens when information-based goods and services are destroyed or disappear for any reason? The United States is abandoning its material existence and giving up its resources to other countries. If cyberspace technology fails for whatever reason, there will be a mad scramble to regain the natural resources this nation abandoned. If Blacks are the most vulnerable group of people, why are they following White people down a road of complete dependence on technology? If technology fails and White society becomes disabled, Blacks will become even more vulnerable. With *PowerNomics*, Black America has an opportunity to move into place and establish itself as backup producer and owner of material resources. How Black Americans can acquire material resources to compete today as well as prepare for the negative impact of globalization is discussed in Chapter Six.

When events that shape the next shift in wealth occur, the basis of wealth will move to those who own and control resources. Those who acquired their wealth from information and technology will trade their vast wealth for food, medicine and other essential resources they need to survive and prosper. Black people can make up for lost time by moving now to own and control as many essential material assets as possible and be ready to trade them for other valuables. In the cycle of wealth, material resources always come before technology.

The action steps below are offered to help Black Americans practice group economics within the framework of a new orientation and national plan for Black America. The strategies include establishing controls and privileges within home or community markets; developing product specialization based on culture and consumer patterns, and establishing national and international marketing outlets to achieve economies of scale.

**Economic Action Step #1: Create an alternative economy within Black communities.**

Black America needs an alternative economy to address its business, employment and wealth needs. Our alternative economy should be a small, but competitive business community that exists outside of, but is complimentary to, the mainstream economy. Alternative economies have always existed. In earlier times, most of the alternative economies were the "cottage industries" that sprung up around the manufacturing of certain products by specific identifiable groups. German dairies and Irish distilleries spawned economies that revolved around them. Today, we have many specialized industries such as military installations, university campuses or any number of Chinatowns that function as independent, alternative economies. They run parallel to the mainstream economy and provide jobs, products and services for an identifiable group of people. The issue should no longer be whether Black America should have an alternative economy or business communities, but rather what type. Like all other alternative economies or business communities, Black America needs traditional business communities built upon its group competitive advantages for the specific purpose of building jobs, products and services that satisfy Black consumers' basic needs and desires.

In the best possible world, we should seek to reconstruct traditional business communities where businesspersons took pride in the products they sold. Business owners knew their customers, were their neighbors, and offered the best products and services. In return, merchants expected customers to remain loyal and shop in stores within their own community. Over the last two generations, the commercial mall phenomenon drained off much of the business from local community businesses. But, new ethnic and high-income customers are bringing traditional business communities back. The desire for the old tradition of high quality fresh products fuels today's explosion of boutique shops and organic and natural food stores that are springing up all over the country. Their impact has been so strong that the mega-shopping centers are losing popularity and many developers are moving back to more traditional community shopping centers in urban downtown areas.

Using our concept of vertical integration, and thinking outside of the box, Black business communities can be built in a *vertical chain of obligation.*[7] We have a vertical chain of obligation when a series of obligations exists between various Black businesses and Black customers, when businesses and customers support each other. Application of this vertical concept could build business communities based upon new community understandings, interests, respect and market loyalties similar to those that exist in most ethnic communities.

How does a vertical chain of obligation work in the real world? It establishes the ability to exploit niche markets. An incident between Asian merchants and Black suppliers in Chinatown in Washington, D.C., demonstrates the importance of a vertical chain of obligation as a foundation to an alternative economy. A Black marketing organization approached a group of Asian merchants in an effort to sell them a variety of popular consumer items. After the Black distributors made their sales pitch, they were disappointed when the Asian merchants replied they were not interested in purchasing products that the Black distributors were selling. Determined not to give up on the Asian merchants, and convinced that contiguous boundaries between the Asian and Black communities made them quasi-members of the same community, the Black distributors offered a 25 percent discount from the price that the Asian merchants were paying for the same items.

Again, the Asians told the Black distributors they were not interested. In a collective voice of puzzlement, the Black distributors asked how the merchants could afford to turn down a 25 percent discount. The merchants responded, "You Black people just don't understand. It is not the money, but the fact that we only buy from our own. Only you Blacks will buy from any and everyone." The Asian merchants had made their point. They take pride in and respect the traditional vertical chain of obligation that exists between Asian business people.

We must now recapture the good aspects of traditional business communities as they existed three-quarters of a century ago and continue to exist in many places today. Some are in suburban communities that have grown up near the edge of large urban cities. They are in small and often remote cities and townships off the beaten path throughout the country. They also exist throughout most of Europe, Asia and Latin America.

Black Americans have never had the full alternative economies enjoyed by other groups. However, one of the few good things that came out of Jim Crow segregation was the development of Black quasi-business communities. These quasi-communities were exciting places to shop, work and socialize. Our segregated business communities were limited and could not compare with traditional ethnic communities, but they still provided us with the products, services and entertainment that we wanted. When I was a young boy, growing up in a small town in North Carolina, our quasi-communities were thriving. They had a rhythm, a life of their own. Every Black person shopped at the same groceries stores, drug stores, gas stations, shoe repair shops, coal and ice companies, movie theaters and clothing departments. We shopped in these stores not only because we needed the consumer products, but because we had personal relationships with the owners. On a typical weekend, most members of the community, regardless of their jobs, educational achievements and political persuasions, would come into the business district and shop.

Our *vertical chain of obligation* was in good form. At the main grocery story where I worked, the store owner took pride in the merchandise and prices he offered his customers. Every Black person in this city shopped at the same stores. We did not drive 30 miles to a mall in the suburbs to spend our money. Our local merchants depended on community customers for their business and the customers depended on the store owners for their merchandise and service. We had a sense of community. Members of the community felt some guilt, if they did not patronize the local businesses, just as many of the merchants felt guilty, if they did not extend non-interest bearing credit and charity to those who needed it.

Even though Black quasi-communities have been long dead, ethnic alternative economies continue to defy pure economic theories and market practices. They survive because of the nature of their consumer markets. These ethnic business communities are built on mutual understandings, market loyalties and vertical obligations and give ethnic merchants preferential access to ethnic consumers. Blacks often wonder how immigrant groups can so quickly establish communities and businesses. It is important to understand the strategies they use and to be able to compare behaviors.

The most common tactics that Asian, Hispanic and other ethnic groups use to build alternative economies and achieve competitive advantages in their community marketplaces are listed below. To build an alternative economy, ethnic immigrants:

- Accept low-wage jobs to get a foot in the door so that they can learn a business;
- Are acculturated to take business risks, pool resources and start their own businesses;
- Hire members of their own families or ethnicity in their businesses;
- Harbor a strong group identity and sense of mutual dependency;
- Bank and borrow from their own families, people and community lending institutions;
- Build alternative economies within their communities to supply jobs, services and products for their own people;
- Use satellite businesses in Black communities as platforms to penetrate major markets;
- Conduct business with members of their own group first;
- Use diversity and the minority label to gain access to and compete against Blacks for resources;
- Use language, religion and culture to mark and close their communities;
- Build businesses and industries that use products that can be linked to their country of origin;
- Avoid being identified with Blacks so that they can continue to benefit from dominant society's hatred for Blacks.

Structural racism is a factor that applies to Blacks that does not apply to other racial or ethnic groups. But, many of the ethnic communal behavior patterns can be useful to incorporate into our empowerment plan and action steps.

### Economic Action Step #2: Dominate business ownership and management where Black people are the majority consumer population.

Since social democracies operate on the majority rules principle, learning to dominate businesses in areas anywhere a group is dominant in population should be one of the easiest principles for Black Americans to follow. In Chapter Two, we strongly advocated ethno-aggregation as an empowerment tool. After Blacks have aggregated physically or through a strong sense of community, they should then begin to dominate in business ownership and management.

Figure 14. Building a Black Alternative Economy

Black people are the dominant consumer population in numerous economic sectors, but are conspicuously absent from business ownership. Although human beings are basically the same, Blacks do have different tastes and spending patterns from Whites. These differences in our consumer patterns represent excellent business opportunities for Black entrepreneurs.

Where Blacks are the dominant consumer they have a competitive market advantage. Blacks make purchases that are disproportionate to and exceed White purchases by twice to five times in the following areas: 1) clothes and accessories, 2) watches and jewelry, 3) consumer electronics, 4) hair care products, 5) used cars, 6) theater tickets, 6) intra-city mass transit services, 7) cosmetic products, 8) certain foods, 9) leather goods, 10) children's footwear, 11) athletic shoes, 12) certain brands of cigarettes, and 13) Scotch liquor and certain other alcoholic beverages. If Blacks had an economic part in manufacturing and selling these products, and communities would buy from Black merchants, businesses could be built and sustained around these items. Unfortunately, Whites and other ethnic groups take for granted that Blacks have no options but to go into non-Black communities to buy products. Meanwhile, it does not seem to matter to Blacks that Whites and other groups boycott Black businesses.

Blacks can begin to build an alternative economy by buying from Black businesses the products that they disproportionately consume. Doing so will not only immediately create new market opportunities for Black entrepreneurs, but will also begin to redirect our $500 billion consumer revenue flow back into our own communities. Our neighborhoods are untapped consumer markets in which we can practice group economics. If Black America does not learn to protect its communities, institutions, culture and businesses, the unending influx of immigrants will completely submerge Black America. In time, even the resources that it does own will be used against Black America.

To implement this strategy for an alternative economy, the first step is to study our neighborhoods and determine if and where Black businesses would have a competitive advantage based on Black population, political control, consumer spending patterns, cultural identification or control of resources and markets. We must envision the opportunities that could exist in a vertical order of obligation, then boldly seek to establish industries in those areas.

The nature of racism itself can facilitate building Black businesses and industries within Black communities. Racism is designed to exclude Black people. We can take advantage of this by making excluded Black people and their communities the primary market for businesses. Black people have a separate culture and separate living patterns. Black businesses are already aware of the consumer interests and needs of Black Americans. If they would gather the resources, produce the product, then market their products in every Black community across America, the *PowerNomics* vision will work to condition more people to buy Black first. Thirty-six million Black people represent a prime market for vertical business opportunities.

Let's apply our principles of dominating in business wherever we dominate in population. There is no better example than the Black prison population in America. Though we are reluctant to profit from the suffering of our people who are imprisoned, we have no choice but to offer the best services and products that they could possibly get in prison. Others already profit from Blacks in prison. Crime and incarceration are areas that demonstrate the principle of creating businesses where we dominate as consumers. Black Americans are only 12.4 percent of this nation's population, yet we dominate the prison population. Out of over two million prisoners in the United States, Blacks make up approximately 50 percent of that population. During the years that ought to be the most productive of a young Black man's life, between 20 and 35, nearly 40 percent of all Black men are either in prison, on parole or on probation. Black people ought to dominate in the management and profit-making aspects of the criminal justice system. We can use those profits to help staunch the flow of Black men into the prison system.

Various levels of government spend billions of dollars annually on the purchase of materials, equipment and supplies for prisons, such as sheets, blankets, bedding, shoes and uniforms. The average construction costs for each jail cell is approximately $80,000 plus another $24,000 a year to care for each prisoner. Prison systems spend more than $3 billion annually procuring shaving lotion, soap, and other toiletries for Black prisoners. Additional billions are spent on contracts to private corporations to manage prisons and provide health care. To help cover a small portion of these prison expenses, the federal government appropriated $28 billion in the 1995 Omnibus Crime Bill.[9]

Since Blacks are dominant in the prison population, Black businesses should also dominate in contracts for prison construction, management, suppliers and professional services to prisoners. Black businesses should be allowed to establish prison industries and benefit from cheap prison labor to manufacture products and provide services. Black businesses should provide workforce training to prisoners that they can use once released. Since Black people in Black communities are the victims of most Black crimes, the Black communities, they should benefit from any wealth-building that flows from the prison system. The practice of Blacks dominating where they dominate as consumers and in population should also improve prison conditions and reduce mistreatment of Blacks.

## Economic Action Step #3: Focus on wealth building and restoring the economic intent of the original civil rights laws.

On September 27, 2000, *USA Today* printed an article about racial and ethnic household incomes hitting an all-time high between 1989 and 1999. During that period, the median income of Black Americans was below Asians, Whites and Hispanics. The article indicated the income gap between rich and poor was not getting wider. The article implied that even though Blacks were on the bottom they were not too far below Hispanics, so conditions were improving for everyone. What the article failed to address was why Black Americans were still fixed on the lowest income rung. More specifically, it should have addressed why Asians and Hispanics, 90 percent of whom have been in the United States less than 30 years, can have median incomes that are above and nearly double a Black population that has been here for over 400 years. There will never be a satisfactory answer to these questions as long as researchers and politicians continue to compare Blacks with other groups then conclude that the reason Blacks are still on the bottom is their own fault. Researchers have yet to analyze the race factors that make it possible for poorly educated immigrants to have better life opportunities than better educated Black Americans. According to the National Research Council, Hispanics only need an annual income of $3,000 to live in the same neighborhoods with Blacks who earn $40,000. Comparing Black income and wealth to ethnic income and wealth is like comparing apples to oranges. Black poverty has been fixed over time. It is gratuitous poverty that was given to them by centuries of exploitation and exclusion. Yet, Blacks are consistently lumped in with newly arriving immigrants who brought poverty into the country with them. Their poverty is typically eradicated within one generation. The eighteenth generation of Black poverty is accepted as normal and basically ignored.

Every time Black poverty is pointed out as a problem there is a rush to eradicate the poverty of newly arriving immigrants or to totally eradicate the poverty of poor Whites. Throughout history, the prevailing belief is that you cannot deal with the low-income and poverty of Blacks until you have first done it for all poor Whites. Even Black civil rights leaders accept such a belief and will rush to help poor Whites before helping their own people.

According to Oliver and Shapiro, "Poverty level whites control nearly as many mean net financial assets as the highest-earning blacks, $26,683 to $28,310."[10] Economic data of this nature is publicized constantly. The Black civil rights focus is out of alignment. Why does Black leadership focus on civil rights for everybody except Black people? Why are Black civil rights leaders now urging Black Americans to help poor Whites?

In the absence of leadership, it is imperative that Black Americans become singularly devoted to wealth creation and wealth redistribution in Black communities. This means using all devices, especially local municipal governments and Black organizations, to craft and promote ideologies and programs that enhance wealth building, whether through personal savings or simply by keeping money in Black communities. A refocus of this magnitude must have a firm legal and philosophical basis. We must recapture the early civil rights concept and movement.

As implied earlier, civil rights in the United States isn't what it used to be, nor does it reflect the original laws and legal precedents. Today, the term civil rights applies to the freedom and rights of all members of our society, especially minorities. However, that was not the original intent of the term. When the term civil rights was first used at the close of the Civil War, it referred to freedom and economic rights of Black slaves as ratified in the Civil Rights Laws of 1865 and 1866. The radical Republican sponsors of these laws knew that economic rights were far more critical to newly freed slaves than social and political rights. In 1865, Congressman Thaddeus Stevens framed civil rights as an economic issue, saying that Black people could only be slaves or free. Without at least 40 acres of land, a mule and $100, for an economic base, Blacks would forever be slaves.

The Black civil rights movement of the 1960s developed around the search for social and political rights for everybody, especially for minorities. It lost the focus on Black people and economics. The social achievements of the Black civil rights movement are not without merit. It did help Black Americans socially, but hamstrung Blacks economically by: 1) diverting an economic issue to social and political goals; 2) making Black people consumers instead of producers; 3) focusing on the inequality of income rather than of wealth; 4) encouraging them to be job seekers rather than job producers; 5) espousing altruism for the world rather than group self-interest; and 6) ignoring public policies that made Blacks impoverished guests in America.

Black leadership has a choice. It can lead a national movement back to the original intent of the first civil rights laws, or they can continue to engage in wheel spinning civil rights issues that ignore the

special needs and unique experiences of Black people. It is predict-
able that many Black leaders will not be able to change direction.

### Economic Action Step #4: Counter the "brain drain" with businesses that aggressively attract Black talent from schools, the government and corporate America.

If the mind is a terrible thing to waste, then Black America must stop the brain drain of its best and most talented people out of our Black communities. For centuries, Black parents have worked hard and dreamed of sending their children off to get a "good education" so they could eventually get a "good job" in a White home, business or community. Black parents have been no different from White parents who also worked and dreamed of sending their children off to get a good education so they could get a good job. The greatest difference between the parents is the way they perceive their children will put that good education to use. Whites encourage their children to look within their own communities for business solutions and opportunities. It is almost inconceivable to think of a Jew, Asian or Hispanic telling their children to get a good education, then find a good job in a Black-owned business. Black people do not tell their children that either. It is very difficult to find Whites, Asians, Jews or Hispanics who have worked for Blacks. These groups wisely teach their children to use their training and skills to take care of their own group first.

Since approximately 90 to 95 percent of all Whites and Asians work for their own people within their own communities, Black people become the exception. Only two percent of all working Black Americans work for their own people within their own communities. There is no direct line between a professionally trained Black person and benefits to the Black community. The new industries and communities we build must be places that provide employment and ownership incentives for Blacks who want to use their skills and expertise toward the *PowerNomics* vision for the race.

Our schools, churches, and organizations must join in the effort to instill value for creating employment and wealth-building opportunities within our own communities to end or reverse the brain drain. Black organizations can help reduce the brain drain by fostering and promoting public policy incentives and practices that encourage and provide financial and tax incentives specifically to inner city Black companies that employ Blacks.

Fifty years ago, nearly 98 percent of all employed Blacks worked in White homes, businesses and communities. The story of Black domestic workers illustrates how Blacks have always used their intellectual resources for others. There is a parallel in business. Domestics arrived before sun up to start fires and warm the homes of White families so they'd wake and dress in comfort. Blacks then cooked breakfast, sent the kids off to school, washed, scrubbed, ironed, sewed and cooked dinner for the White families.

After feeding the family, cleaning up the kitchen and putting the children to bed these Black mothers would then return to their homes after dark. Did anyone ever wonder, in all those years, who was taking care of the Black children? Who fed and watched Black children while Black mothers were taking care of White children? I would like to know who is taking care of the Black community and Black businesses today when nearly 98 percent of all employed Blacks continue to work outside of their communities in White businesses or offices. To achieve the *PowerNomics* vision, Black businesses need Black talent and so does the entire Black race.

### Economic Action Step #5: Establish solid "root" businesses within Black communities.

Root businesses are those that are established based on competitive advantages within Black communities. Besides offering consumer products and services, root businesses are critical because they stabilize the community by offering jobs and employment training, and revenues for supportive businesses and charitable organizations. Their identification with and location in the community would give them a competitive advantage as Black behavior becomes more self-directed. Many root businesses already exist within Black communities but few are Black-owned. They are usually owned by Whites or Asians and, when sold, are sold to non-Blacks. To develop Black-owned root businesses, Black communities should establish a system to buy-out existing White and non-Black-owned businesses.

Encouraging businesses to sink their roots deep in their own community is a very common practice in America. Whether it is Sears & Roebuck, Burger King, Kentucky Fried Chicken or Jiffy Lube, business developers routinely construct and operate their first stores within their own communities. The same is true for ethnic immigrants. Asians and Hispanics open and operate businesses in their own enclaves first before venturing into another group's community. After establishing root businesses, ethnic businesses remain ethnic businesses. Asian restaurants and cleaners remain Asian; the Jewish deli remains Jewish; Arab carpet businesses remain identifiably Arab. Where are the root businesses that Blacks established that they passed on from one generation to the next? On the other hand, Asians have even learned how to use government contracts to develop root businesses. Asians are automatically eligible for the Small Business Administration (SBA) set-aside program because of their race.

According to *The Wall Street Journal,* in New York City, Asian's share of SBA contracts has soared from three percent to 64.1 percent within 10 years, while Blacks get less than 18 percent. Though over 90 percent of the Asians have been in this country less than 30 years and have the highest median family income in America, they have devised methods to pass on their certification status to succeeding generations of Asian businesses. While they are accomplishing these feats, Black Americans, who the SBA program was initially designed to help, now get the smallest number of awards of any of the so-called minorities and they are forced to "officially graduate" out of the program by the end of seven years.[11]

Since integration in the 1960s, most Black entrepreneurs seek to "economically pass" by opening their businesses either deep in or on the fringes of White communities to hide their Blackness. Key personnel in these "passing" Black businesses, managers, receptionists and sales representatives, are often non-Black. According to a researcher at the Minority Business Development Agency of the U.S. Department of Commerce, approximately 90 percent of the "successful" Black businesses within the Washington, D.C., metropolitan area were located on the fringes of the Black city or in the surrounding White suburbs, as of 1996.

Black businesses that economically pass are in double jeopardy. Not only must they hide their true identity, but they must also depend on White America for their resources and market opportunities. Because their roots are not with their own people in Black communities, they are vulnerable to White boycotts. Throughout history, Black businesses have often failed because they were boycotted by Whites who resented Blacks' success. Now that integration has failed, Black Americans can begin to show a new attitude and less tolerance for this abuse. They should establish within their own communities an economic base from which to compete and survive, before venturing into anyone else's community or country.

Think for a moment and tell me what is wrong with this picture. When you go into hotels, stores, restaurants, or any other business in Asian, Hispanic, Arab or even White communities, you can count on the management and the working staff to be Asian, Hispanic, Arab or White, the same as the community itself. But in Asian, Hispanic, or White-owned businesses in a Black neighborhood, the staff will still be Arab, Asian, Hispanic or White. Establishing root businesses means that the management and staff in businesses located in Black communities should be predominately Black, regardless of who owns the business. If that is not the case, Blacks must insist on a change if they expect to have an alternative economy that they control.

## Economic Action Step #6: Construct vertical businesses and industries that control all processes from raw resources in markets within and outside of Black communities.

It is physically impossible for Blacks to compete in every kind of business in every community. We will have our greatest impact if we exercise vertical involvement primarily within those businesses in which we have some competitive advantages. Vertically integrated businesses translate into industries. We should seek out key industries and strive to create a monopoly. A monopoly, through vertical integration, locks out competition. Vertical businesses can control markets, resources, research and other complementary activities. The competitive advantage remains whether the businesses are local or national. Black businesses must also be vertically organized in production and horizontal in marketing.

Once a Black business or industry has succeeded in building a vertical industry in one Black community, it should then spread horizontally across the country into other Black communities, until it has control of all its home markets. This vertical movement, followed by horizontal penetration, allows Blacks to establish closed-loop production and marketing networks for the private use of Black businesses. This happens in the mainstream business world everyday. For instance, more than 40 percent of all the United States exports and nearly 50 percent of its imports do not compete in the open market. Instead they move through closed channels. Japan does the same thing. So, if closed-loop production and market channels are good enough for the big boys, why shouldn't we have our channels too?

The challenge to Black people is to build and control their own community markets and the products that pass through them. This means Blacks need a variety of business communities such as manufacturers, suppliers, distributors, technology, marketing and retailers. These business communities can link and serve as conduits for moving products, capital and supportive services. For example, if Blacks built a leather factory in an enterprise and empowerment zone in Baltimore, Maryland, the factory and its supportive businesses could be vertically integrated to serve as a national empowerment model and cluster. Distribution centers for the factory products could be established across the country. Retail outlets could be set up in malls, airports and downtown stores. Our hypothetical leather factory can engender at least three levels of businesses that individually or collectively get together with other Black manufacturers, distributors, and retailers to improve their business operations. This national network of business communities can increase the competitiveness of Blacks in business. (For more information, see the "National Reparations Plan" schematic chart in Appendix B.)

## Economic Action Step #7: Stop the "capital drain" out of Black communities. In other words, "buy Black, but sell to anyone."

Black America has a major problem: the flight of its disposable income into the pockets of racial, ethnic and religious groups around the world. Black people have enriched every group, except themselves. Without a sense of community and a vertical chain of obligation, and no guidelines for how they should spend their money, no product or business loyalty in the marketplace, Black consumers are easily persuaded to be penny-wise and dollar foolish in their spending patterns. They shop for the best price when, for a few pennies more, they can maximize the benefits of their expenditures to include the Black community and race. The few who are concerned about getting

the best return on monies spent or invested use too narrow a definition for measuring return. To achieve the *PowerNomics* vision, return
on investment should be measured in its broadest sense, in personal
economic as well as group socioeconomic terms. For every penny
spent, the Black consumer should know what benefits the group
receives in political, social, educational and economic terms. Not only
does our money go into the pockets of competitors, it comes back
and is used against us. Black consumers ought to value reciprocity
and examine what they receive for the dollars they spend outside
their own community.

Figure 15. The Draining of Black Wealth and Income

Black Americans' spending patterns deprive them of their greatest
potential for power, a flow of financial capital. The statistics we have
used before paint the picture. We spend approximately 95 percent of
our income outside of our communities. Only two percent remains in
Black hands inside the Black Community. We typically take that two
percent down to the local White bank, and deposit it in a traditional
savings account. It is then out of our control and we generally cannot
even leverage it into personal or business loans.

Blacks often express bewilderment over how well Whites live.
They sometimes entertain out-of-town guests by taking them for rides

through White communities to show off the expensive homes and wide array of retail businesses. The question is frequently asked, "How can so many Whites afford to live so well?" The answer is easy. Besides having hundreds of times more wealth than Blacks, they also have the advantage of living off of two incomes: one hundred percent of their own money and 95 percent of Black people's money. While Whites enjoy the economic power of dual incomes, Black Americans struggle to get by on the two percent of their disposable income, which is financially impossible to do without some form of government subsidies.

While our spending patterns are inappropriate for the *PowerNomics* vision, the spending pattern of Whites and ethnic groups demonstrate that they value keeping their disposable incomes within their respective communities. When European immigrants started to arrive into this country following the Civil War, the majority White society ceased purchasing services and goods from Black merchants and Black communities. Previously, Whites transacted business with Black barbers, blacksmiths, caterers and laundries. They initiated conscious boycotts that, for the most part, remain in force until this present day. It would be a rare sight to see a White person drive to a Black-owned business in a Black community to purchase Black manufactured products. While the purchasing patterns of Asians, Arab and Hispanics indicate they too avoid Black businesses, Blacks do not consciously boycott Asian, Arab, or Hispanic businesses.

Our course of action is clear. We should always treat other people and other groups the way they treat us—not better and not worse. In Chapter Three we talked about reciprocity with businesses in building functional communities. It is also important in group economics. If businesses systematically boycott Black businesses, Blacks should develop a systematic way to withhold support from them. If they refuse to hire Black employees, Black merchants should refuse to hire non-Blacks. If they build and operate ethnic businesses in Black neighborhoods, we should build and operate Black businesses in their neighborhoods.

Whatever we do must begin with discipline in our spending patterns. We should identify those companies with whom we spend a disproportionate amount of our money then compare that figure with the amount of money they spend with our Black businesses. This comparative research should be the basis for establishing equitable relationships between White businesses and Black people. Business equality is achieved when the amount Whites spend with us comes close to what we spend with them. When an equitable relationship cannot be established, Blacks should invoke the new rule: *never treat any group better than they treat you.* Blacks should alter their spending patterns accordingly and avoid spending their money in any non-Black-owned business that does not treat us the way we treat them. This single act of 36 million Blacks withholding patronage would probably garner more respect for the Black race than all the marches, riots, and civil rights laws put together. Keeping Black disposable income within Black businesses and community would close the door to the capital drain.

### Economic Action Step #8: Attract semi-finished products into Black communities for value-added manufacturing, processing and assembling.

Attracting semi-finished products into Black communities is a way to practice group economics. Aspiring entrepreneurs need to be mentally conditioned to scour every possible business and community for products that Black businesses can adopt, modify and duplicate. Hundreds of companies build their businesses based on research performed by others or by duplicating products first produced by others. Copyright and patent laws are important to respect and follow, but most commercial products move through a cycle of constant modification and reproduction. Black entrepreneurs can become paralyzed sitting and waiting for the ideal opportunity to invent the single most needed and revolutionary item on earth. It's not likely to happen.

Post-World War II Japan is a good model of this technique. Although they received lots of financial assistance from the United States under the Point Four Plan, and it is easier to recover from a military loss than from centuries of economic exploitation, Japan did pull off an economic miracle within 20 years of World War II.

With limited resources, wealth and manpower, the Japanese traveled the world examining the efforts and products of industries in other nations. They took the ideas back to Japan and learned how to replicate and improve on what they saw in competing nations. They constructed their wealth and industrial base on a "waste-not and want-not" philosophy. They collected every scrap of material and recycled it into new products similar to those produced in other countries. The Japanese purchased products produced by their own industries first, regardless of the cost and quality, because they knew their purchases would give their country's industries a chance to grow and perfect other consumer products.

Acting as a nation within a nation, Black America can use its limited resources to replicate products the very same way Japan did. We have to become more productive and there are numerous good models in existence, but the Japanese economic development model is one of the best for Black America. As Blacks begin to sacrifice to purchase Black-produced products, it should be motivating to know that the measure of progress in a people is not what they consume but what they produce.

**Economic Action Step #9: Promote the competitive advantages of Black communities.**

Urban Black neighborhoods have excellent competitive business advantages. These Black neighborhoods have good strategic locations, work force, market demands, disposable incomes, little business competition, lands and buildings and a great potential for high returns on investments. Until recently, there was little interest in promoting Black urban communities for anything. But, times are changing for the better. As stated earlier, this nation has always had flourishing alternative economies in ethnic communities.

Blacks should similarly build and promote their urban business communities and the numerous business advantages. Inside of every urban Black area there is wealth. It is called infrastructure. It includes assets such as highways, bridges, museums, skyscrapers, expressways, mass transportation, sewage plants, water facilities, and electronic media. Nearly all of the majority Black cities are located on natural waterways. The resident Black populations have disposable income and represent a large labor pool. We can rebuild our neighborhoods into communities by using the competitive advantages of the geographical location, consumer markets, population concentration, human resources and disposable income of Black communities.

CHAPTER FIVE

## Economic Action Step #10: Establish "safe business zones" based upon a code of conduct in Black business communities.

In Chapter Three we discussed how as Black America builds functional communities, it will need to establish safe zones. Safe zones are also important for Black business communities. Without "safe business zones" our business communities cannot bloom and flourish. Of course, in an ideal setting, we want an entire community that is crime free, but that's not realistic. So, let's begin by protecting our new business communities and start enforcing a new code of conduct that spells out acceptable standards of behavior and is promoted and enforced by all segments of the community. The code should include creative means to challenge and punish those who violate these business communities. (See Chapter Three.) Consumers will not become customers, if they or their property are under physical threat. Safe business zones would be areas where these threats would not be allowed to exist.

Increased business and employment opportunities for Black people in the communities should be a positive incentive that reduces neighborhood crime. A major reason people steal is because it pays. In some instances, crime pays so well it is hard to control. But, crime must be brought under control in Black communities and those who violate the new conduct norms should experience consequences. The community can use a variety of techniques to control crime. In the past, community groups have used such techniques as social and economic marginalization. Each community, or at least a critical mass of Blacks, must decide what penalties to levy and enforce through the legal systems and other socioeconomic mechanisms.

As soon as they are formed, Black business communities should declare their independence through an Economic Bill of Rights. Then they should mark their business turf as safe zones in which to do business. The political structures in various cities should endorse an Economic Bill of Rights and allocate resources to build the safe business zones. Working together, governments and the communities can enforce sanctions from within and outside of the community, and strengthen the social bonds between Blacks and government. A special public safety tax can be enacted just to support police protection within the zone. The business owners themselves could pool funds for special security service. But, the best protection would come from

147

an active and committed citizen's group that would simply just say, "no" to crime conducted in their safe business zone.

The safe business zones should be treated in a manner similar to smoke- and drug-free zones with strong enforcement support. Even though increased incarceration will not necessarily reduce crime, legal sanctions should include municipal ordinances and laws that impose additional fines and penalties on those convicted of violating persons or properties within these areas. Crime-free areas would encourage new business development, increase land values, and instill pride in Black communities. Financial compensation from convicted offenders could flow back to the injured communities. Similarly, persons incarcerated for crimes committed in the safe zones should be required to work in some public service capacity in the same community where the crime was committed.

The present high crime rate in Black communities is a gift from the integration process. It emerged with the breakdown in Black communities and Black families. As Blacks grow increasingly disenchanted with integration, now is the time to reclaim our Blackness and Afro-American culture, shore up our splintered families, and build Black business communities around our self-interest and needs. Strict zoning within the safe business zones can anticipate and prevent unnecessary social problems. Land use and other zoning policies in the safe zone should prohibit mixing public services, residential housing and religious structures.

### Economic Action Step #11: Amass "vision" capital and wealth through community-based financial efforts.

Typically, the first question raised by skeptics of Black economic empowerment is, "Where will Blacks get money to establish and operate Black businesses and industries and to practice group economics?" No matter how committed we are to an economically empowered Black America, we must be realistic. Without investment capital, there will be no Black businesses or industries. According to Melvin L. Oliver and Thomas M. Shapiro, in their book, *Black Wealth/White Wealth*,[12] 61 percent of Black households are marginal with the majority of their assets in automobile and home ownership. Our challenge then is to identify creative ways to amass capital to finance our own empowerment.

Now, to the question asked at the beginning of this action step, "Where do Blacks get the money to start businesses and industries?" They get it first from themselves. They begin with their annual disposable incomes. We must begin to save more of the little that we do have. We cannot continue to be this nation's biggest consumer market. Of our $500 billion of annual disposable income, we are nearly 100 percent consumers and zero percent producers.

Consuming is a negative in a capitalistic society. Consuming means to use up or exhaust. Contrary to the rhetoric of marketing agencies, consumer power does not exist in a capitalistic society. Consuming is a weakness. It is the producer of what is consumed who has the power, not the consumer! To amass capital, means Blacks must reduce their consumption and redirect their money into savings for investment purposes.

In this step, we call on our experts in the area of finance and capital development to help us apply the *PowerNomics* principles to develop a national plan for Black access to capital. This must be an organized effort. Our plan should be founded on the belief that to create Black wealth and political power we must amass large amounts of capital. Control and access to capital, which is simply surplus wealth used to produce additional wealth, is a major step towards collective enrichment and community empowerment.

There are three primary sources of large amounts of capital: public markets, traditional financial institutions and private markets. Public stock offerings provide corporate financing through open solicitation to the public at large. However, corporate public offerings must be approved and regulated by the Securities and Exchange Commission (SEC). This is a very important source of equity funds, but it is expensive, technical and time consuming. Most Black Americans are much more familiar with institutional lenders such as banks, credit unions and community development corporations (CDCs). All of these sources should be explored in seeking debt and equity for entrepreneurial projects. It is a statistical pattern, however, that a high proportion of Black borrowers are denied loans. To borrow capital from a traditional lender a borrower must already have capital (surplus wealth), collateral or guarantors. Equity funds are scarce. Just like wealth begets wealth, poverty begets poverty. Blacks must organize and operate their own banks, credit unions, CDCs, savings and loans, venture capital firms and investment clubs. Where they already exist, support them and demand that if they are in your neighborhood, they support your *PowerNomics* community-building efforts.

Reparations is outside the traditional sources of capital, but it is a bill that is owed to Black people and one that we must present to the nation for payment. Reparations for Black people is no longer a far-fetched issue for parlor room discussions. It is now a necessity. Making restitution for damages is rooted in our legal system and has been used by industrialized nations as a mechanism to apologize for and correct institutional wrongs. Reparations payment for centuries of slavery and Jim Crow semi-slavery can take many forms. Government or private corporations can make restitution through such efforts as cash payments, land grants, educational scholarships, tax exempt status and free health care. Cash payments should go into regional development banks from which Black Americans could draw down equity capital for business investments. These banks should be established specifically to allocate those funds as vision capital for Blacks. Funds should be used only for projects that promote the *PowerNomics* vision of a self-sufficient and competitive Black America.

**Economic Action Step #12: Establish international economic alliances and marketing agreements between Black America, Black Africa and Caribbean nations.**

While building its own competitive, yet complementary economic structure, Black America should also play the lead role in constructing international economic alliances and marketing arrangements between the sub-Saharan African countries, the Caribbean and the nation of Brazil. Collectively, these nations and Black Americans, as a nation within a nation, have a total human population of nearly a billion people. Yet, these billion Black people are all economically marginalized. They are forgotten people living in the shadows of all other human groupings as a "Third World of Third World Nations."

As indicated in Table 5, Black people are consistently at the bottom of the barrel. The combined legacies of slavery and colonization left them severely impoverished, politically unstable, and ethnically conflicted to the point that they are vulnerable to and cannot respond to common natural disasters, famine, diseases and the ravishes of poverty. Within the next decade, the greater question will not be whether these poor Black nations can compete but whether they will even physically survive. There is a direct relationship between "pecking order" poverty and powerlessness and major health problems such as AIDS and other "emerging" diseases.

Some scholars predict that up to half of the Blacks in Africa may perish by the year 2013, if the devastation of AIDS, famine, civil war and natural disasters continue on their present course. (See Appendix C.) If this occurs, the natural resources of Black Africa will be up for grabs. This timetable fits in with the cycle of wealth, which by that time would have moved beyond technology to natural resources. At that point, there will be another rush to Africa to claim the resources just as Whites did at the Berlin Conference in 1875.

Black African countries, just like many other Third World nations, tried a variety of tactics to break free of First and Second World domination. Some tried nationalizing Western companies and land rights, setting up commodity and exporting cartels, subsidizing indigenous manufacturing to achieve import substitution, or campaigning for a new world order based upon redistribution of the existing imbalances of wealth. None of these tactics have worked to the degree that these Black countries could industrialize and move out of the Third World category. They failed not because the ideas were bad, but because of opposition from leading industrial democracies, the "have" nations.

The leading industrial democracies protect their vested interests from competition from Third World and developing nations. The First and Second World countries have all the trump cards. They use a variety of institutional devices to keep the smaller nations non-competitive and outside of the major commercial markets. As indicated below, in a global comparison of the wealth and technically trained people within nations, there are grotesque disparities between Black nations and the rest of the world. The wealth and education gap between Black and non-Black countries is too great for them to catch up and compete on their own.

Global success of Black people is contingent upon many "ifs": *if* Black America can build functional business communities with industries; *if* it can establish its own source of economic funding; *if* it can link up a national network of Black consumer markets; and most importantly, *if* it can become the economic and political capital for Diasporan Blacks around the world. If all those *ifs* can be managed, all the Black people of the world would be in a better position to ally with America's Blacks and begin to work together to resolve our institutional dilemma. Only Black Americans are in a position to lead the world's Black population. They have the advantage of being within the United States. There are more skilled and highly trained Blacks here than any other major Black population on earth. But, by every measure of wealth and human capital, Blacks everywhere in the world are on the bottom. Therefore, we must be "on a mission" and come together in an alliance for strength.

Table 5: World Distribution of Wealth and Human Capital

| Per Capita Gross Domestic Product | | Engineers and Scientists per million of population | | World Distribution of Wealth per Country per Capita | |
|---|---|---|---|---|---|
| Switzerland | $36,300 | Japan | 3,548 | Australia | $835,000 |
| Sweden | 32,600 | U.S. | 2,685 | Canada | 704,000 |
| Japan | 29,000 | Europe | 1,632 | Japan | 565,000 |
| Germany | 27,900 | Latin America | 209 | United States | 421,000 |
| Canada | 23,100 | Arabs states | 202 | Russia | 98,000 |
| United States | 23,100 | Asia (sans Japan) | 99 | Mexico | 74,000 |
| Austria | 24,800 | Africa | 53 | Ethiopia | 1,400 |
| Nigeria | 278 | Berundi | 43 | Black Africa | -1,000 |

Black African nations are so far beneath White and Asian nations that their statistics are in the negative column. The wealth gap is so great that it is a miracle that Black Africa can survive, let alone compete. Only a glance at the mal-distribution of wealth disparity in the world should point out the magnitude of the dilemma as well as the impact of 500 years of slavery that denied them the opportunity to own and control wealth-producing resources. The burden of redistributing wealth will fall upon the shoulders of a Black economy to save itself and aid African nations.

Therefore, Black dispersed peoples around the world must unify across geopolitical boundaries and forge economic alliances that allow them to collectively share and control resources, exploit mutual trade opportunities, and compete in the global markets. An economic alliance that allows Blacks across the world to practice group economics must have four elements. It must have: 1) surplus capital, 2) middle-class skills and professional training, 3) control over technology and raw resources, and 4) access to political power. Black Americans are an advantaged group. They have three of the four required elements for an alliance. Even though their group position is less than other non-Black Americans, Blacks have some surplus capital, an educated and skilled professional middle-class, and are politically situated within the most wealthy and powerful nation on earth. They have been marginalized in America by being denied ownership of and control of resources, but they can now play a lead role in an economic alliance that could lift all Black nations. If Black Americans could arrange to link the Black vertical industries and businesses in this country with the raw materials that come out of Africa, Brazil and the Caribbean, and the one billion Black consumers across the world, the alliance would be powerful. No one nation has everything that is needed to become self-sufficient, but we all have something we can bring to make that delicious stew we spoke of earlier, that we can sell to benefit everybody.

The low productivity in Black nations is traceable in major part to the fact that all of the major population groups have economic alliances. The exception is Black people in Africa, America, Brazil and the Caribbean. By grouping our wealth and financial markets we can begin to compete for economic power. The European Whites have a European common market. The Asians have the Asian-Pacific Rim Economic Alliance. The Hispanics and Non-Hispanic Whites have the North American Free Trade Agreement. For maximum political and economic clout, Black America should practice Black nationalism as discussed in Chapter Three and link their various populations and resources around the world. Through vertical integration and ethno-aggregation, Black Americans can exercise greater control over our capital, productivity and markets.

It is important to restate that Black America must play the lead role in shaping and developing economic alliances, especially in African countries. It will not work in reverse. Afrocentricism would be a more useful concept, if it came to mean Afro-American-centric. Blacks in sub-Saharan Africa, Brazil and the Caribbean are not only too politically and economically depressed and unstable, but major democracies will not enable them to become independent enough to compete. They could only compete as an economic alliance behind the safety and stability of Black America. But, time is of the essence, because the wealth and status of Black America is fragile and relative. Black Americans can use the empowerment tools of *PowerNomics* to develop a game plan to bring all the other Black nations around the world into an economic alliance that would allow them to compete worldwide.

## *Conclusion*

The cycle of wealth begins with control of natural resources. The cycle is now in the Information stage. The 12 action steps presented in this chapter reflect the new orientation of practicing group economics and should give Blacks new ideas about how to benefit from the cycle of wealth and take control of their economic future.

Other groups use our neighborhoods and population as resources to enrich themselves. If others can become rich off of us, we must think out-of-the box and redirect our resources to our benefit. This Chapter provided guidance to communities, organizations and individuals who wish to work toward fulfilling the vision of a self-sufficient and competitive Black America.

# CHAPTER SIX

## Industrialization: Using Your New Paradigms

*Building industries is the first step toward
building monopolies.*

In Chapter Five, we stressed the importance of Black Americans constructing traditional business communities and practicing group economics based upon their competitive advantage of being a nation within a nation. The envisioned retail business communities would be a good first step. However, retail outlets would not be enough, especially if they are constructed as stand-alone businesses. They lose the unique advantages of being a part of a new, developing Black community. We need complementary businesses that can produce inter-related products and services to magnify our competitive advantages in the marketplace. The nature of complementary businesses allows them to be vertically integrated into an industrial framework that can attract, hold, and redistribute large amounts of wealth and technological resources.

Black America needs to own and operate industries within its own business communities that are competitive with businesses outside the community. In our use of the term industry, we are referring to certain types, classes or collections of businesses and business activities that are needed to fully provide and satisfy a consumer demand for a finished product. It is not necessary for Black Americans to own and operate every kind of business, nor is it practical. We are a marginalized people who are coming into the business world 400 years late.

## Behind the Industrial Power Curve

Black Americans are in the Stone Age in terms of industrial development. Although slavery begot capitalism, which begot industrialization, which begot a continuous flow of technological advances, Blacks were never the owners or direct beneficiaries of what their labor produced. Throughout the industrial revolutions, Blacks remained cap-

155

tured, but loyal consumers and mere spectators, chained to the lowest rung of the industrial ladder. The closest they ever came to industrializing occurred between 1865 and 1900. During this brief period, about 3.6 percent of Black Americans were engaged in some form of manufacturing. Today, other than as workers, the number of Blacks in manufacturing has shrunk to approximately one percent. Neither White nor Black leaders seem to grasp the importance of industrializing Black America. If Black people do not experience industrialization, a critical developmental process, there is little chance they will ever be able to compete in cyberspace or the evolving new world order. Without industries, there is no mechanism for producing Black-owned and controlled technology.

Whites and ethnic groups were economically advantaged by industry while we were being economically disadvantaged. They have a history of being producers, operating business communities and closing consumer markets to outsiders. But the technological revolution that is evolving offers us a chance to improve our status. We can build special industries and become producers. Our industrial goal should not be to produce everything that Black people need. Our goal should be to build industries that primarily produce products and services over which Black people can establish competitive advantages or monopolies. It is around these group-based advantages and monopolies that we can build both vertical industries and supportive business communities.

## Technology and the Case for Industrialization

There are a number of critical reasons why Black America must have its own industries. The most overarching reason is that owning industries will enable us to become a competitive, independent group. Also, our own industries will enable us to fully utilize our cultural, financial and human resources. No other group is going to do it for us and we should not expect it. Black people have been rendered an obsolete labor class by public polices and technology. Industries are the primary building blocks of wealth. Only industries have the muscle to build solid economic communities and eradicate our noncompetitiveness. Industry will become increasingly consequential to Blacks. Wealth, power and technological readjustments have left market gaps. If Black America does not industrialize now, we run the risk of never being able to do so. This nation is moving onto thin ice and taking Black America with it. The industrial and manufacturing sectors continue to decline because this nation's corporate and political elite have mistakenly convinced themselves that computer technology and computer-based information will be the world's great wealth producers in the foreseeable future.

Like the man who stared too long into the sun, the power elite is blinded by the wonders of technology. Small and large businesses are rushing to build industries around the manipulation of high-tech information, rather than owning the physical resources and traditional brick and mortar industries. They want to join those who have become multi-millionaires overnight by either investing in or building businesses promoting high-tech wizardry. Information-based businesses are held up as the nation's dream models. The dot-com businesses have made so much money that traditional businesses must find ways to keep revenue flowing and keep up with technological developments. But there is not a pot of gold at the end of every rainbow. Many dot-coms are going out of business because they lack the brick and mortar to fulfill their electronic promises.

Despite some developing dark clouds, technology is becoming a religion with its own high priests and miracle workers. Corporate executives and politicians alike gamble that they can make profits and wealth by simply utilizing advancing technology to create intangible specialized information. There is no doubt that great opportunities for profit and wealth exist in high-tech and information, but at the bottom line, neither high profits nor specialized information can replace tangible products, especially those that are essential to life, such as food, water, and clothing. As companies choose information over tangible products to produce and distribute, this nation will soon have no fall back industries, if the technology gamble fails.

## *Technology and Black America*

As the nation moves in this risky direction, it perpetuates the propaganda that what is good for White America is equally good for Black America. Technology has not significantly improved the socio-economic status of Black people anywhere in the world. Technology is advancing while Black people are either standing still or regressing. High-tech advocates refuse to acknowledge the extent to which racial beliefs intrude into the development and use of technology. They argue that market forces will cause the right decisions to be made, yet market forces are racially biased. They respond to those with the greatest economic and political powers.

In the context of globalization and cyberspace, Black America can take some protective steps to insulate itself from some of the risk that this nation is taking. Black America does not have to totally follow the majority society. Black America has options. If it acts like a nation within a nation, it can set its own direction in some matters, a direction that is in its own best interest. Black America can craft its own industrial policy that includes a realistic role for the use of technology. In terms of competitive advantages, Black America would be much better off competing with Third and Fourth World nations rather than going head to head with major White industries in America.

## *Prerequisites for Industrialization*

Black America has the nuts and bolts to industrialize. Many Third world countries that have fewer resources and competitive advantages than Black America have successfully industrialized. Black America has the required educated class, surplus work force, raw and cultural resources, disposable incomes, pools of capital, consumer markets, and most importantly, some of the best infrastructure improvements in the world. Having the physical infrastructure in place allows Black America to start industrializing immediately. White society abandoned the inner city infrastructures more than a half of a century ago. They left Black America the public infrastructure that can serve as empowerment tools to produce wealth and technology.

It bears repeating that within most inner cities there are billions of dollars of wealth in infrastructure, such as expressways, communication systems, water and sewer facilities, buildings, airports, educational institutions and hospitals. Most of the inner city resources are directly under Black political control, but they must be defended. The majority White society realized it abandoned this wealth and is now seeking to retrieve it through such concepts as regionalization, municipal sharing and privatization. With the infrastructure in place, Black

America can build its industries and begin to produce its own technology just like any other nation.

## *Technology and Work*

We discussed technology in previous chapters, but it is also a critical consideration in our discussion of industrialization. Over the course of the last four decades, millions of people have been permanently eliminated from the workforce by technology. Due to economic and political weakness, Blacks were the first to go during the 1960s. Technology made Blacks an obsolete labor force. Every Black person displaced by technology represents a transfer of wealth to the owners of the technology. The owners benefit from the wages they no longer have to pay a Black labor force. Approximately 34 percent of the nation's Black workforce is either unemployed or underemployed. They have suffered from having little or no wages for centuries. The wages that could have gone to enslaved Blacks were transferred to the White slaveholders. In modern times, wealth is transferred to the business owners. Black people are always displaced, yet dominant society continues to introduce technology because it enriches and empowers them.

Now, unlike at any other time in history, computer-driven labor is extracting humans from the work equation. Some displaced workers re-educate themselves and become employed in new careers. Others find temporary and part-time jobs. But, large numbers simply drop out of the workforce, possibly forever. In his book, *The End of Work*,[1] the noted economist Jeremy Rifkin writes about the relationship between technology and the economy. He paints a dire picture. According to Rifkin, the United States has entered a new phase in world history, one in which fewer and fewer workers will be needed to produce the goods and services used in this country. He says, "There is a strong likelihood that by the year 2015, only 25 percent of the people working today will be needed to produce the same amount of goods and services." A part of the problem is the fact that even in an economic boom, about 95 percent of all newly created jobs go to White suburbs and not to Black inner cities. What happens to Black Americans who were unofficially declared an obsolete workforce nearly 40 years ago and today have a hidden national unemployment rate of 34 percent?

Encouraging Black people to prepare for jobs in an expanding service industry is only a partial answer. Developing technology will probably wipe out four jobs for every one service-related job that it creates.

Service-related positions in global markets may be acceptable for White Americans. They have never been a servant class. Moreover, they have sufficient wealth and control of information technology to compete in a competitive global society. But, what will happen to Black Americans, who are already an impoverished, non-producing completely consumptive group that never profited during the 450 years that they were forced to follow White America? How will Black Americans compete and who will protect their markets in a cyber-space or global economy? No race or nation can progress strictly as consumers with "magical" technology. History shows that technology creates just as many problems as it resolves.

## Technology and Industrialization

Technology flows from industry and a group cannot be strong and competitive without ownership and control of some technology. Technology has a multiplier effect on itself. Each new technological advance becomes the foundation for another innovation or advance. Technological competition is destined to intensify as we become more globally interdependent. Black Americans cannot compete in global economics without industries and technology. Now is the time to get a toe hold on some special industries, ones in which we have competitive advantages and can begin to produce our own technology. Otherwise, just as we have never benefitted economically through the progression of low technology, we will not benefit economically from the progression of more complex technology. We must start at the beginning, by identifying and exploiting the competitive industrial advantages of being a Black nation within the richest nation on earth.

## A Model: Japanese Industrialization

If we use the concept of Blacks as a nation within a nation, Japan is an appropriate model for how to industrialize and become a major political and economic power using the concept of vertical integration. Vertical integration as a management concept was first used by the Ford Motor Company and Standard Oil more than a century ago. This business practice allowed a single corporation to own and control all levels of a given industry. The corporation's top-down management controlled everything from suppliers of raw materials to distributors and retailers of finished products for the company. As used in *PowerNomics*, vertical integration is much broader.

The Japanese shifted the use of vertical integration from a single corporation to a nation of businesses, thus they come closer to the *PowerNomics* concept of vertical integration. In addition to the economic feat Japan performed after World War II, which was discussed in Chapter Five, Japan did something else that is important to know. The Japanese linked vertical integration of their businesses with their strong family, cultural and religious values to give them an edge over competing nations. The vertically integrated socio-economic system that they created is called "keiretsu," which is a closed-loop, cohesive group of corporations, suppliers and financial institutions networked around a particular vertically integrated industry. Keiretsu protects Japanese industries, community markets and national economy. Japanese consumers and businessmen feel a strong sense of moral obligation to their keiretsu network. It is their vertical chain of obligation through which they support each other. This unity of purpose reflects an important cultural strength in Japan—the cultural value of first supporting and buying products produced by their own people.

Japan industrialized around its cultural competitive advantages to better compete economically with other nations. Japan's national sense of trust, togetherness and sense of people-hood made it possible for industries in their country to take control of the markets for the goods their industries produce—cameras, watches, toys, VCRs, televisions, radios and small automobiles. Japanese industries grew from small faltering businesses to hugely successful corporations. People who used to laugh at things stamped "Made in Japan," began to see "Made in Japan" as an indicator of quality.

Japan and its keiretsu have many features that Black America can study and adopt. Most important is Japan's closed economic loop that links Japanese businesses and all segments of their community into a solid economic team This is their greatest competitive advantage. Their team commitment and spirit lifted a militarily defeated, impoverished, resource limited, minority population to economic superpower status. Can a similar, but expanded vertical industrial policy do the same for Black Americans? *PowerNomics* principles advocate using a similar vertical linking of businesses to build group wealth and power. The fact that keiretsu has been criticized and that Japan has experienced some economic downturns since the 1990s does not diminish the power of the example for Black America.

## *Rationale and Criteria for Industrializing*

Any particular business sectors that Black Americans select to industrialize their communities must be based upon the strength of Black America's competitive advantages and the potential for vertically integrating the industries. The criteria that we use to determine our competitive advantages were presented in Chapter Five. Some of the competitive factors include high Black consumer demand, cultural identification, control of raw materials and potential to build vertically in whole or in part. Now, let's look at some industries using these factors as criteria. General industries like computers, boating, footwear, cattle or construction industries would not meet our purposes. In a test of industries, we must determine the level of Black consumer demand. Are Blacks culturally attracted to any of these industries? Do Blacks dominate in either the production of raw materials or in spending patterns? Clearly, none of these industries have high competitive advantages for Black Americans. They are horizontal industries and apply to everyone. In the construction industry for instance, Blacks do not dominate the production or purchasing of paint, wood or concrete? Blacks buy homes, but so do most other people in society. If everyone is equally represented, there are no competitive advantages for Blacks and the opportunities are, therefore horizontal, not vertical.

Conversely, professional sports is a far different industry. This industry lends itself to vertical integration and it is an "approved venue" for Blacks. Slavery made athletics a safe area in which Blacks could emotionally and physically vent, compete and dominate. The vertical integration of an industry works best when our competitive advantages are linked to our culture, labor pool, disposable annual income and urban cities in which Blacks have political control. Using our out-of-the-box thinking, we can take negative, historical conditions and convert them into competitive advantages, such as concentrated populations and consumer spending patterns, which can help us to industrialize. (For more details, see Chapter 5, Economic Action Step #9: Promote the competitive advantages of Black communities.)

## How to Industrialize Black America

This following section presents specific strategies Black America can use to build industries, and discusses three strategies that incorporate *PowerNomics* principles useful for guiding the industrialization of Black communities.

## Recapture Sunset Industries

First, Black America's national industrial policy should prioritize the recapture of many of the major "sunset" industries. For the past four decades, this nation has competitively lost or voluntarily given to Second and Third World countries many bread-and-butter industries, such as steel, textiles, footwear, watches, household appliances, toys, and electronic equipment, including radios, boom boxes, televisions, VCRs, and kitchenware. As these industries left the United States, collateral damage resulted. This nation lost hundreds of thousands of supportive businesses and jobs. Government trade and industrial policies, such as the 1994 North American Free Trade Agreement (NAFTA), rewarded corporations that abandoned America and moved to Third World countries. Communities throughout the United States, especially in Black neighborhoods, suffered a double loss. While NAFTA modernizes Mexico's industries and successfully resolves Mexico's socio-economic problems, it is creating new problems for Black Americans. This nation's public policies reduce the quantity of American businesses and jobs, while increasing the number of businesses and jobs within competing nations. Since the 1990s, the NAFTA policy has created 2.6 million jobs in Mexico and boosted Mexico to the second biggest supplier of foreign-made goods to the United States. Yet, the same United States government failed to create an industrial program to help Black America resolve its national 34 percent unemployment, 38 percent poverty, and phenomenal over representation in the penal systems in the very same cities that American industries abandoned. This is blind indifference towards Black America.

Nations such as Mexico want the industries abandoned by the U.S. because they not only resolve many social and economic problems, but industries also bring wealth, jobs, political power and supportive businesses.[2] Most importantly, industries enable the people to become producers. People with industries can produce power and wealth as well as products. The sunset industries that were moved to Third World countries through treaties such as NAFTA could have been retrofitted and relocated into Black communities to provide an industrial base of wealth, business and employment opportunities. If relocated industries do well in Third World countries like Mexico, why wouldn't they do equally as well in Black communities? Since Black Americans are a primary market for the products Third World countries produce, such as shoes and clothing, why can't Blacks build their own clothing and shoe industries, then distribute those products to Black-owned businesses within their own consumer markets and communities? Abandoned industries brought back into operation, just like all other industries, thrive wherever they are needed and supported.

Some towns and businesses in the United States never accepted the myth that declining industries should leave the country. These old industries continue to do well within their established traditional communities. On July 6, 2000, *The Wall Street Journal* reported on one such town, Goshen, Indiana, which retained some of its old industries. The story reported that Goshen does not have many very high-paying tech jobs, but it does have a large number of middle-paying jobs, mostly in manufacturing. The manufacturing sector tends to pay higher wages to skilled and unskilled workers than many other industries. Goshen industries retain jobs and offer competitive salaries to its residents. This is only one community that kept its industries.

If the United States government needs additional models of how to industrialize inner cities, a May 13, 2000 *Washington Post* article offers a suggestion.[3] The Post story was about a national small business incubator program that is providing jobs, businesses, and light industries in rural communities across the United States. According to the article, there are more than 800 small business incubator programs in rural areas. This program was designed to help solve socio-economic problems that inhibit business development, especially in small cities. Since the greatest need for this kind of program is in inner cities, why aren't urban Black Americans exposed to this kind of business development assistance? The article also stated that, "The smaller the town, the less margin for error in vision, planning or financing . . . Most of the jobs the incubators have created pay $10-to-$15 an hour." Those jobs pay two-to-three times the minimum wage. Such opportunities would be welcomed and quickly grabbed by the unemployed and underemployed Blacks in inner cities.

Just like the incubator programs mentioned above, some creative planning would allow for a number of abandoned industries to re-open and operate profitably within Black communities while paying decent wages. For example, most of the athletic footwear and boom boxes in America are produced in the Far East. However, in America, it is impoverished Blacks who buy approximately 40 percent of the expensive Air Jordan, Nike and other athletic shoes and portable radios. Considering Black Americans' socio-economic dilemma, it is worth noting that these consumer items that are primarily targeted to Black Americans provided jobs and business opportunities for workers halfway around the world. Thousands of Asian businessmen became multi-millionaires from profits earned mostly from products sold to Black American consumers. Technology in an urban city factory, combined with public incentives and employee ownership arrangements, can produce an athletic shoe just as inexpensively as low-wage labor in Second and Third World nations.

## Industries Abandoned by the Third World

The second way to industrialize Black America is to capture industries that are now being discarded in the second wave of Third World industrialization. Many Third World countries have a different industrialization problem than they had a couple of generations ago. Nearly a half century ago, they began to acquire discarded industries from the world's more technologically advanced nations. Now their economic prosperity and progression coupled with their higher productivity are forcing them into the race with Second and First world economies. These countries must now either upgrade to a higher order of industrial competitiveness or risk falling back with the "newly developing" countries. Because of their previous success, they will have to move from low-wage, low-end manufacturing to more high-tech, high-paying manufacturing. The second wave of abandoned industries has already started in some Asian countries, where manufacturing corporations like Fujitsu, Motorola and others have relocated to take advantage of low-wage labor forces. Where they have relocated, these manufacturing industries have stimulated further industrial development and the growth of supportive businesses.

Just like the flying geese referred to in Chapter Two, Japan plays the role of lead goose in industrializing, followed by a wave of East Asian and Southeast Asian nations. These successful Asian nations help other Asian nations by either relocating soon-to-be abandoned industries to those countries or by setting up complementary assembly and processing plants in the cousin countries. Japan, for instance, typically produces categories of consumer products that are passed down through a vertical chain of Asian countries and corporations. These Asian countries are an economic alliance flying purposefully toward economic competitiveness.

In this second wave of abandoned industries, Black America ought to be in a position to recapture the discarded industries and produce consumer goods that Blacks consume disproportionately. Japan and China have already passed down the footwear, textiles, clothing and numerous household item industries to countries like the Philippines, Thailand and Vietnam. However, armed with a new empowerment vision and tools, and demands on the United States government, Black America can bring some of these industries back into the United States and compete based upon its own competitive advantages.

Black America's leadership, especially the Congressional Black Caucus, can assist in recapturing these industries by aggressively demanding that the United States government begin to support the industrialization of Black American communities. As Black America begins building its industries, the Congressional Black Caucus should press for legislation and trade laws to protect these Black industries from unfair wage competition in foreign or Third World countries. These trade laws and public policies could be framed as a component of the evolving Black reparations movement.

The Black Caucus and Black Americans as a group should reject anti-protection arguments. The United States protects the cotton, sugar, wheat and oil industries as well as many others. The Japanese government uses keiretsu to protect its industries. They have special trade barriers to protect the leather industry that is owned and operated by the Eta, the Japanese socially despised and economic minority. If Japan can use trade barriers to protect the industries of its official minority, the United States government has ample justification to erect trade barriers and provide subsidies for industries within Black America. Should Black America be deprived of the opportunity or fail to grab these discarded industries during the second wave, they can rest assured that they will be the primary consumer market for products developed by a new round of Third or Fourth World nations. Nearly all of the Fourth World nations are Black countries. Sometimes they are referred to as the Third World of the Third World.

## *How to Build New Vertical Industries*

The third way that Black America can industrialize is to simply survey all existing industries to identify those in which Blacks are playing or could play a dominant role either as a major producer of the raw material or as a major consumer of the finished product. After an industry is identified, the next step is to determine whether it is possible for a Black startup industry to intrude into the larger industry and capture market share based upon Black skin color, culture, population distribution, market loyalties, disposable income, government control or other competitive advantages.

As we industrialize our own communities, our intent should be to own and control a select number of industries and to control them from top to bottom as much as possible—from raw resources and manufacturing to distribution services and retail consumer markets. We want to mark each industry as Black America's territory. Vertical integration of an industry creates the potential to establish a monopoly. A Black-controlled monopoly will help stabilize Black communities by concentrating wealth and political power.

Black-owned-and-operated industries can function much like a closed-loop, geo-economic system, similar to Japan's keiretsu. Within a Black closed-loop system, we can own and control our own resources, production and consumer markets. Each contractor and all employees within the linked system would be expected to buy products and services from within the group itself. Once this happens, we will have transformed our currently overly dependent and subsidized neighborhoods into independent and self-sufficient communities.

## *Capitalizing Startup Industries*

The United States government enacted public policies and used its resources as incentives to relocate businesses out of inner cities across America. The government can now enact new public policies and use similar resources to relocate industries back into Black urban communities. Black America suffers from a lack of access to capital, both as a resource that can be used to manufacture or produce other things and as a pool of surplus wealth that can be used to finance business ventures. To industrialize Black communities, capital in all of its various forms, will be needed. Unfortunately, few Black Americans possess or have access to capital. Consequently, the challenge we face is how to creatively find and aggregate capital to invest in our communities' industrial infrastructure.

To build an industrial infrastructure across Black America, we will need two kinds of capital: debt and equity. In debt capital, we borrow cash, paying the borrowed amount back with interest. Black Americans experience difficulty in securing debt capital from traditional lenders for many reasons, including poor credit worthiness and lack of collateral. Impoverished people are labeled impoverished essentially because they lack capital and collateral. Unlike debt capital, equity capital is cash that investors bring to the table in exchange for some form of ownership interest in a business or, in this particular instance, in an industry. In return for the equity, the investor expects a percentage of profits, dividends and possibly capital gains.

Money is exchanged for equity and interest in businesses and industries through various kinds of public, private and institutional capital sources. The material presented in the following section of the book presents a variety of ways to invest in Black America's empowerment. The capital requirements for industries will vary with each industry and business. Some will require large amounts of capital, especially if the investment entities are vertically integrated into Black communities across the nation. Others will require smaller infusions of capital and can be secured by loans from traditional lenders, family and friends or investment pools. The greatest depository of wealth or capital is the Wall Street stock markets, so let's first look at how that resource can be used for capital formation.

## *Wall Street and the Stock Market*

As mentioned briefly in Chapter Five, the stock market can be an excellent source of capital for our industries. Today there are a few individual publicly traded Black-owned companies. But, an offering can be structured to use the stock market as a national mechanism to attract and aggregate capital to fund Black business initiatives, such as specially selected vertical industries. An offering of this type would be a potent way to apply capital formation activities to the *PowerNomics* principles of ethno-aggregation and vertical integration.

A Wall Street investment structure would give Blacks an opportunity to keep our limited capital inside the race, where it can be used to build a base of wealth for Blacks as a group and individually. Blacks would be able to aggregate their money for the purpose of strengthening our race economically. This investment mechanism can be used to create a capital infrastructure of investment banks, bond and stock markets, trading companies, brokerage firms and investment advisors. It also offers a grand opportunity to those supportive individuals of other races that want to take part in reversing the circumstances of Black America. The few Black-owned publicly traded companies currently listed on Wall Street are designed for the traditional purpose of attracting capital that can be used to expand and operate those individual companies. It would be a new financial concept to use Wall Street to pool Black, White and other dollars for the economic development of Black America.

There are barriers to using Wall Street as a way to aggregate funds. Wall Street is highly regulated by the Securities Exchange Commission (SEC). Preparing an initial public offering (IPO) is expensive, complex, and time consuming. Filing an application involves specialized legal counseling, accounting, and filing fees that could cost hundreds of thousands of dollars. At the same time, additional money, effort and time are required to structure a sound, well-run vertical industry. But, on the positive side, SEC approval to raise capital from the general public would create a financial resource few Blacks have ever had.

It is hard to conceptualize the magnitude of funds that could be aggregated through a Wall Street offering. Let's propose a hypothetical example. If every one of this nation's 36 million Blacks invested $365 or one dollar a day for a year in an offering, it would produce a capital pool of more than $13 billion, greater than the gross revenue of all the Black businesses in America. Just imagine how many Black businesses could be started from a capital investment pool of that size. For perspective, consider that according to *Broadcasting* magazine, Radio One, the largest Black owner of radio stations, has approximately 52 radio stations with an approximate value of $2 billion. Other capital formation mechanisms, such as private placements, involve a limited number of investors, which would restrict the number of Black businesses we could capitalize. An IPO, on the other hand, would allow every Black American who chose to do so to invest and have "a piece of the rock."

When nearly 100 percent of the corporations listed on the stock market and the investors are all White, money invested in Wall Street might help an individual or his family, but it does not translate to helping Black communities. It is important, therefore, to note the difference in the purpose and effect of a stock offering like the one described above and the everyday Wall Street stock offering. The offering above would provide Blacks an opportunity to join with their own people and establish a capital pool that could be used to build competitive Black-owned industries within Black communities. It would also offer a vehicle to others who might wish to support such an effort.

## *The Criteria for Developing Key Industries*

The industries suggested below exploit Black America's strong competitive advantages of population, consumer dominance, cultural niches and patterns as well as ownership and control of raw resources. Nearly all of the suggested industries and stand-alone businesses meet basic competitive advantage criteria, so they are amenable to become vertically integrated and can be located within most urban Black communities. Some are not full industries but substantial segments of an industry. Using competitive strategies allows Black business people to capitalize on these advantages and construct self-supportive, independent and competitive industries.

## Black Business Investment Corporation

When our industrial infrastructure has been established, it will profit from having a national organization that functions like a Black Business Investment Corporation (BBIC). The BBIC should be made up of representatives from major Black industries, local Black elected officials, educators, civic groups and ministers. The role of the BBIC is to: 1) establish and link a national network of Black industries in urban areas; 2) craft and administer industrial policies of Black self-empowerment; 3) amass private and public funds for industrial growth; 4) coordinate linkages between industries, schools, churches and other community-based organizations; 5) function as the chief lobbying and political arm of Black business communities; and 6) aid the industries to incubate and commercialize new technology. To stimulate sales opportunities as well as provide maximum business opportunities, local BBICs can be established to operate as liaisons between the Black industries and Black churches, traditional lenders, families, investment clubs and government agencies. Working collaboratively, national and local organizations can help rebuild and maintain a positive economic environment within Black communities.

## Industrial Models for Black America

Let's discuss some industries that Black America can develop within our own communities based upon the competitive advantage criteria presented earlier. Ideally, we want to own and control every level of an industry through the application of our vertical integration concept. Realistically, this may not always be possible. However, if we use our competitive advantages, we can at least take control of major aspects of targeted industries. In addition to ownership and control, remember that all of our industries must be constructed in or relocated into Black communities. The finished products can be made in one Black community and shipped to other Black communities through a national distribution network. Regardless of the industry, we will need a system of Black distributors, wholesalers and retailers to deliver products to regional and national markets. A Black-owned national distribution system is currently in development.

Each of the suggested vertical industries has been broken down into levels that could generate spin-off supportive businesses. The various levels should interlock to become a complementary vertical industry. Interlocking, from top to bottom, gives the targeted industry its greatest competitive advantage. The schematic chart presented for the leather industry is a graphic view of linked vertical levels. (See Figure 16.) The schematic gives you another way to view vertical integration and the economic potential of an industry.

It is not possible to do a schematic for each industry presented here, but the leather industry is a good example of the use of a schematic as a tool to see the relationship between businesses in a vertical system. Each subsequent section describes some of the competitive advantages that Blacks have in each industry or segment. The suggested industries and businesses are intended to serve as food for Black minds that are hungry for business opportunities. These suggestions are not intended to serve as business plans, but as examples of the way *PowerNomics* principles can be used to industrialize Black America. The industries presented below are:

- Leather production
- Urban hydroponic farming
- Bottled water operations
- Sports industry

## Vertically Integrated Leather Industry

Strategy: Build on Group's Spending Patterns.

Whites abandoned the leather tanning industry over the course of the last century for a number of reasons. Three primary reasons were tough environmental standards for the tanning process, the introduction of synthetic leather, and competition from Third World countries. The leather industry itself has numerous competitive advantages that makes it prime for Blacks to develop as a *PowerNomics* industry. Figure 16 shows the various operating and business levels of the leather industry. The major competitive advantages that Black Americans have in the leather industry are:

- Blacks purchase a disproportionate share of the nation's leather goods and apparel.
- The leather industry lends itself to vertical integration.
- Black consumers are inclined to purchase based on brand loyalty.
- Manufacturing plants in urban inner cities could have access to a ready labor pool.
- Major producers abandoned the industry, leaving it open for strong competition.
- Leather producers are a long way from America, which is the biggest leather-consuming market.
- For a tannery, Haiti, a Black country, has favorable environmental laws, wage scale and close proximity to America.
- North and South America are major producers of animal hides.
- Economic development incentives are available via various government programs.

All levels of government—federal, state, and local—must play non-traditional roles to help Black Americans industrialize and establish a competitive leather industry. Blacks should aggressively demand that the government use its capital, program resources and legislative powers to intervene into the marketplace and create favorable conditions for establishing this Black industry. The book *Black Labor, White Wealth* provides government officials, economists and others legal arguments to provide special assistance to Blacks.

Black America should demand from government the same resources and trade protections provided to many other groups and industries. Most of the world's leather goods come from Asian countries that provide a variety of government assistance for manufacturers. For instance, Japan protects its leather industry by erecting trade barriers against cheaper imports. Thus, Japanese consumers are forced to purchase domestically produced leather goods. What should be of interest to Black Americans is not just the Japanese trade barriers, but who the trade barriers protect. The trade barriers protect the leather industry and the jobs of its workers, who belong to the Eta, a socially despised, excluded and vulnerable minority group. The Japanese Eta are equivalent to Blacks in America. The Eta are systematically excluded from certain jobs and are considered unworthy marriage partners. The same type of government programs and trade barriers

# Vertically-Integrated Leather Manufacturing

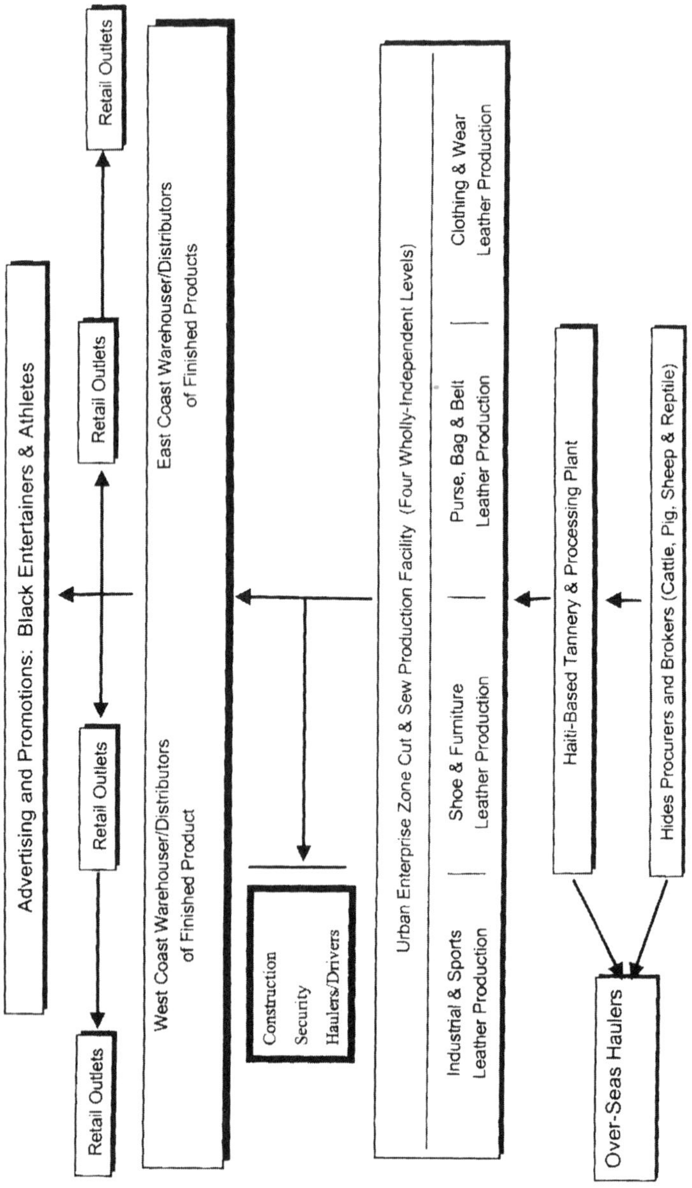

Figure 16. Vertically Integrated Leather Industry

174

that help the leather goods-producing Eta in Japan should be established for Blacks, who are America's despised and excluded people.

## *Natural Resource/Water-Related Industries*

The next two industries relate to using water because it is a vitally important natural resource that is going to grow increasingly scarce. Black urban communities are the core geographical hubs of cities all across America. Since nearly every concentration of Blacks is situated near large bodies of water, and because Blacks live in urban areas in which there are public water plants that are or should be under their political control, then both the competitive advantages and potential industries should be easy to see. However, as a word of warning, there is no assurance that these opportunities will exist very much longer. Using the concepts of regionalization, municipal sharing, and privatization that we discussed earlier, the majority society is aggressively wrestling control of these resources and competitive advantages away from urban Black communities. If Blacks do not use the resources that they control to exploit their competitive advantage, rest assured that competing groups will capture and control these resources and use them to their advantage.

### Urban Hydroponic Farming

Strategy: Build farmers' markets within inner cities.

- Convert abandoned buildings into automatic hydroponic gardens.
- Form farming cooperatives and farmers' markets on unused sites.
- Organize regional warehouses and wholesale distributors.
- Market products through a national network of retail outlets.

Hydroponic organic farming within inner-city communities is about survival at one level and creating wealth and building business opportunities at another. Producing one's own food is empowerment. Hydroponic farming is a water-based industry that can produce high quality food stuffs that can make inner-city Black communities self-sufficient. It addresses the absence of high quality, reasonably priced foods, the scarcity of chain supermarkets and the oversupply of rip-off stores that sell low quality food at astronomical prices in inner cities.

Hydroponic farming in inner cities can capitalize on a number of competitive advantages that Black America has for water-based industries. Nearly every urban Black community borders on large bodies of water or has water plants. White flight, in response to the Black civil rights movement, left prime industrial properties and buildings abandoned that can now be used to do hydroponic farming. These cities are located on some of America's best real estate with nearby public infrastructure. The abandoned buildings we usually perceive as eyesores are eventually demolished, destroying both their financial and cultural values. But they have other uses, if we look at them through the paradigm of ethno-aggregation. Hydroponic farms could be built in large abandoned factories, warehouses and school buildings after they are gutted and cleaned. There are many such abandoned properties in cities with large Black majority populations, such as New York, Detroit, Newark, Buffalo, Philadelphia, Cleveland and Los Angeles. In some cities, under various economic development initiatives could provide funds to assist with building acquisitions and renovations as well as installation of water tanks, electricity and the acquisition of supplies and operating overhead.

Black-owned hydroponic farming could bring to the inner city a growing trend toward organic and natural food. Blacks could raise fresh organic food to meet some of the basic needs of our own communities, while surplus foods could be packaged and distributed to surrounding communities. Hydroponic and organic produce sell for three times the cost of industrial farm grown products. Unlike hydroponic farms, industrial farm products are often of questionable quality and health value. Their products are usually picked unripe and chemically-treated, then shipped long distances to markets. There is also the issue that nearly 75 percent of all Black Americans live in and around 15 large urban areas where grocery stores have less than a two-week food supply, which could be shut off accidently or intentionally. Following the Civil War, 55 percent of America's farmers were Black. Today, the number is less than one percent. Consequently, Black America is nearly totally dependent upon non-Blacks for the quantity and quality of our "daily bread."

176

## *Inner-City Farmers' Markets*

Produce from the hydroponic facilities or any other farming source can be sold to individuals or food cooperatives. Abandoned schools or factories could be converted into marketplaces. The bulk of the organically raised aqua products can be earmarked for regular chain and independent grocery stores or institutions. Black communities should re-establish the old farmers markets that were once available in every large city. Although most of them were razed in the early 1950s, some still exist. Detroit has the Eastern Market and Baltimore has the Lexington Market. Blacks are the major consumers at these markets, but the shops and food stalls are owned and operated by ethnics who have passed ownership down through several generations. As the majority consumer, and on a new mission, Blacks have the capability of changing the game. They can either buy the owners out or open their own vegetable farmers markets around the hydroponic industry. The produce can also be distributed in open-air markets set up on school playgrounds, parks and other community locations. At the bottom line, the hydroponic gardening facilities would provide fresh, healthy, competitively priced food as well as business and employment opportunities within urban communities.

Basic needs for this industry would be land, large abandoned buildings, water, electricity, equipment, water tables, knowledge of hydroponics and access to millions of interested Black customers.

## Vertically Integrated Bottled Water Industry

Strategy: Build businesses around dwindling necessary resources.

- Select majority urban cities with water plants and reservoirs.
- Acquire production plants and equipment for water purification and processing.
- Acquire technical expertise.
- Acquire container suppliers.
- Establish retail commercial office space.
- Acquire fleet of vehicles and establish home delivery services and food markets.

An article in the *Washington Post* on July 17, 2000 summarized the findings of a number of scientists and made the case for the viability of this potential Black industry. The article said, "One of the most severe crises certain to confront Homo Sapiens in the coming decades will be the availability of fresh water." In recent years, various weather systems, droughts, and coastal hurricanes have demonstrated the vulnerability of our water supply systems and increased public demands, especially during emergencies. The growing demands and scarcity of drinking water makes it an excellent potential business for Black Americans.

During the 1990s, the nation and the world suffered unusual water shortages. These shortages will surely worsen as a result of pollution, changing weather conditions and over-population. Nearly half of the world's population lives under severe water stress conditions. Reportedly, the available drinking water in the world will decrease by 25 percent within the next two decades. Drinking water shortages will eventually come to America and when they are do, the price of drinking water will increase dramatically. In Washington, D.C., residents have been advised during the past few years to not drink tap water. During the summer of 1999, both Virginia and Maryland imposed water restrictions due to drought. In North Carolina, drinking water was contaminated by a hurricane.

Whether it is for pure survival or for a profitable business opportunity, there are other competitive advantages that Black Americans can have, if we develop a vertically controlled bottled water industry. As stated earlier, to our advantage we have highly concentrated Black populations near water systems and large bodies of water. Blacks also are the dominant public office holders in the 15 key cities. The industry has low capital and equipment requirements and few regulatory requirements. Finally, Black consumers could control this market with quality and brand loyalty.

What is needed to start a bottled water business? Some of the equipment requirements for a medium-sized plant include: automated distilling and filling equipment, plastic containers, delivery trucks and access to a public water source. Regular public water can be steamed or distilled. The steamed or boiled water is then condensed, collected, bottled and sold as distilled water.

This industry can be divided into several levels. Distilled water can be marketed to grocery stores, commercial offices, airlines and home delivery companies. In the United States, a record 2.7 billion gallons of bottled water were consumed in 1995. Everyone, from street ped-dlers to airlines and hotels, now sell or serve bottled water. In many restaurants, water is served to customers only upon request and many patrons ask for bottled water only. All levels of the bottled water busi-ness can be owned separately or as a vertically integrated industry.

## Vertically Integrated Sports Industry

Strategy: Build on racial and cultural niches.

As stated earier, though Blacks have long dominated certain sports, we have yet to establish and dominate the ownership of sports-related businesses. The sports industry offers at least six levels of business opportunities. Because sports have always been a viable way for a Black person to gain financial success, it is an ideal base upon which to build a vertically integrated order of Black businesses. This industry allows Blacks to combine two *PowerNomics* principles. First, dominate in business wherever we dominate in consumer popu-lation or where we control the raw materials. Second, create an alter-native economy within Black communities. Regarding controlling the raw materials in sports, be mindful that though Blacks make up approximately 80 percent of the basketball players, 75 percent of the boxers, 50 percent of the football players and 48 percent of the base-ball players, the really big money does not go to the ones running or playing with the ball. The big money goes to those who own the industry's raw materials: the owners of the teams, the stadiums and the professional services. Those who manufacture the balls, uniforms and equipment also do well financially.

Over a half century ago, Black fans were proud of the accomplish-ments of Jessie Owens, Joe Louis and Jackie Robinson. How did the successes of the athletes translate to financial opportunities for Black people? The success of Tiger Woods will influence thousands of Blacks to play golf. Why not own golf courses and manufacture golf clubs and other related equipment businesses? The Williams sisters' successes are inspiring more Blacks to play tennis, but why not own and control tennis-related businesses? The same could be said for a basketball success like Michael Jordan. The very same companies that manufacture the basketballs, tennis balls, and golf balls and own sports teams and stadiums will continue to own everything long after our Black sports heroes are just names in the record books.

Think of the socio-economic benefits for the Black athletes and for the race, if the athletes would negotiate for greater Black business opportunities within the sports industry in addition to their personal contracts. They could leverage their celebrity status to demand that Black businesses be involved at every level of the industry. In building a Black alternative economy within Black communities, Black athletes could negotiate for a Black percentage of ownership in the teams, the stadiums, concession contracts, equipment and uniform purchases, and the marketing and promotional budgets. Why can't Black athletes leverage their presence in the various sports to create business opportunities for Blacks in management, insurance coverage, players' pension programs, banking, accounting, legal services and stock sales? The professional sports industry could be vertically integrated just as it once was before integration. This would be a new behavior for Black sports figures and would have a greater chance of success, if they decided to act as a group to champion Black involvement in businesses at every level of the sports industry.

## Additional Industries

Below are additional industries in which Black Americans can have competitive advantages based upon *PowerNomics* principles. Again, as in the industries suggested above, only highlights can be offered in this book. They are presented here in abbreviated form as food for thought.

### Telecommunications and Mass Media

Strategy: Use Black experts to establish a national daily newspaper, a television and radio network and a film distributorship.

In order to achieve the *PowerNomics* vision of a Black America that is self-sufficient and competitive, we must have a national means to communicate, inform and disseminate images of ourselves. Mass media and all other areas of telecommunications could be a base for vertically integrated industries.

We call on the few Black telecommunications owners and the greater number of professionals in the field to adopt the *PowerNomics* vision as their own and apply their skills to develop these industries. We also call on them to take the lead in guiding other Blacks to identify and develop more specific action steps. Blacks from this highly skilled group should be encouraged and supported to become entrepreneurs and special advocates who guide the government to develop policies that increase Black ownership. Current owners and employees in telecommunications and media have the knowledge and understanding to help government and corporations correct the historical inequities that are now built into ownership.

The action steps below should provide beginning points to Blacks interested in building industries in telecommunications.

- In the area of government, Blacks can focus efforts to change the flawed foundation policies that equate Blacks to other minorities. We have made the case for corrective treatment of Blacks. Public policy should spell out the case for other groups generally included in the minority category. The justification is not the same as the case for Blacks.
- We should seek government breakup of the racial monopolies that are established and protected by government and function under government operational authority, such as broadcasting and telephone services. The entities that result from the breakup should be redistributed to correct the historical exclusion of Blacks from ownership.
- Blacks should seek to own local telephone systems that serve predominately Black neighborhoods and cities. This step will take creative arrangements with current local service providers, favorable regulatory policies, or the purchase of local exchanges.
- Blacks can establish a massive Black national news and talk show network that offers Blacks programming, information and a means of communicating. It would also provide a means to build images that we choose, and spread information for and about us.
- Black weekly newspapers can combine to produce a national daily Black newspaper. In addition to expanding the information

base for Black America, this shift can offer operational options to many of the weeklies that are struggling.

- In the area of print media, we can also develop a national book distribution system and a chain of bookstores. This could consolidate publishing industry entities and provide economies of scale as an option for the numerous Black-owned bookstores that are not profitable, but are important institutions in their neighborhoods.

## The Music and Entertainment Industry

Strategy: Build businesses around racial and cultural niches.

Vertical businesses can be built wherever a group has access to the raw resources that are the staples of the industry. In vertical integration, whoever controls the raw resources and markets will reap the profits. They can leverage their position to control middlemen and other support businesses, such as distributors, promoters, marketers, and manufacturers of tangible properties.

Music entertainment represents another industry that lends itself to vertical integration. The music created by people of African descent is the foundation of this nation's popular music as well as the music of Latin America and the Caribbean Islands. Black music in its various forms is a $100 billion industry, of which Black people themselves receive less than one percent.

The mere fact that the raw music products have always radiated out of Black culture, Black churches, Black communities, and Black people themselves makes a vertically integrated music industry an option, if Blacks make a commitment to it. By recapturing our musical heritage, we would be in position to commercialize our cultural assets to build wealth, income, employment, and business opportunities within our communities. We could re-identify with the primary source of our musical inspiration: the Black church. In Black churches, aspiring Black singers and musicians are given a venue for their musical gifts. Again, the church and communities could become breeding grounds for Black musical talent.

Vertical integration would begin at the raw material level, the churches, then extend upward to talent agencies, recording studios, distribution networks and finally to a national chain of retail outlets. By establishing our own production, distribution and retailing economy, we could avoid the economic forces that currently dictate what Black music can be produced and marketed. Most importantly, we could avoid having our musical talent expropriated by Whites who copy Black artists, rename our music, place it in their halls of fame and claim that Black music belongs to the world. During the past several centuries, nearly all forms of Black music were captured and exploited by the majority society. Whites have assimilated folk music, Dixieland, Blues, Jazz and are working on gospel. Some far-sighted Blacks have begun to move to control more of the processes in producing Black music. Where there are efforts underway, we should encourage and support them. Where there are not, we should encourage those who can to try.

## Opportunities through Strategic Alliances

Strategy: Building businesses within "safe harbors" by contracting with an established company.

It is not always necessary for Blacks to reinvent the wheel in order to start a successful business. We can build "safe harbor" businesses by filling gaps within existing mainstream businesses. Strategic alliances linked to a major company are examples of safe harbor business opportunities. Most major corporations believe it is cheaper to contract with an outside company to perform some functions rather than to bear the in-house production expense. For example, some major manufacturers find it cheaper to supply their customers with components and parts rather than a totally assembled piece of merchandise. Putting those parts into a kit is an example of a process that a business might contract out or enter into a strategic alliance with a smaller business to perform. This form of assembling is called "kitting." Large corporations, like Ford Motor Company, IBM and Lucent Technologies award contracts to firms that do nothing but "kit" various kinds of merchandise. A kitting company would need logistical software, large open assembling space and tables, and a labor force.

Other good business opportunities exist simply because in every industry there are production and product gaps. For instance, a textile company would rather buy buttons than to produce them in-house. A person could operate a business producing and marketing buttons, if he or she could get enough textile manufacturers to purchase the buttons. No business, regardless of size, can cover every single aspect of the business. So, the company elects to leave the production gap in place and subcontract with a smaller firm to provide the service or the product to fill the gap. In both strategic alliances and contract opportunities, vertical integration occurs within a plant itself and then links to support services and suppliers. Blacks should seek strategic alliances and contract opportunities with companies that produce products of which Blacks are disproportionate consumers, such as long distance telephone service, sports and recreational equipment, apparel, new and used cars and trucks and food. Every company that receives a sizable portion of its profit from Black consumers should be expected to enter into contracts or strategic alliances with Black-owned companies located in Black communities.

## *Conclusion*

You have now finished the how-to-industrialize chapter. In this chapter, we learned the important role that industrialization played in wealth building and how laws and public policies prohibited Black people from participating in or benefiting from the various industrial revolutions. In order to catch up and compete in the developing technological economies, we must make industrializing Black communities a group priority. We need industries to develop and give us our own technological base. We discussed a number of ways in which Black America can industrialize based on competitive advantages. To give the reader a jump start in building Black industries, we suggested different kinds of industries that could be built around *PowerNomics* principles and the empowerment tools of vertical integration and ethno-aggregation.

This part of the *PowerNomics* plan requires special leadership to focus on the *PowerNomics'* empowerment goals. It is beyond the scope of this chapter or this book to develop detailed business plans. However, the *PowerNomics* Enterprise Corporation has gone further and actually started developing vertical industries. The *PowerNomics* Enterprise Corporation has begun to build a vertically integrated seafood industry.

# CHAPTER SEVEN

## *Practicing Group Politics*

*Transform weakness into power by getting others
to play with cards that your group deals.*

Having examined the historical nature of Black America's wealth and power dilemma and how Blacks can construct an alternative economic structure, we now turn our attention to the next logical step: How to use the political process to redistribute wealth and resource power into our own hands. The strategies for solution arise out of the nature of politics and its role.

Politics as we know it is relatively new. The word and concept first appeared in English around 1529, with the beginning of Black enslavement and the early stages of industrialism. The term "politics" was borrowed from an old French word, *politique,* and it emerged from the struggle to control the increased spoils of power and wealth produced by Black slavery.[1]

Modern social scientists, philosophers and politicians define politics in whatever way suits their purposes or fancies. In espousing their views, they most often define politics as the art of compromise or the art of the possible. However, for our purpose, these definitions are meaningless. They say nothing about the real nature of politics and the rules of the game. In the real world, politics can best be defined as a process that decides who gets what material benefits out of life. Politics is about power. It decides who has food, income, education, shelter, heat and health care. It allows the nation's political elite and overclass to play gatekeeper. They dispense resources on a trickle-down basis. Those who are the closest to them at the top get the lion's share first, while those on the bottom get the least and last. In a competitive society, there is little, if any, incentive to look out for an underdog group. Blacks are the out-group and they can rest assured that the overclass will make all the political decisions in their own best interests rather than the interest of Black Americans.

## *The Rules of the Game*

Black Americans have always been excluded from playing politics by the official rules of the game. Every time we sought to play by the rules, the rules changed or the game ended before we had a chance to play. Therefore, rather than continuing to be like a dog chasing his tail, we need to simply step back and look outside of the box. In the action steps outlined in this chapter, we suggest ways in which we should alter our behavior or change the accepted rules of politics. But, in all instances, we must adhere to the fundamental rule of all politics—quid pro quo. It means something for something, or at a more familiar level, it means "you scratch my back and I'll scratch yours." Those who invest their time, energy and resources in support of a political issue, candidate or political party expect to be compensated in a manner that is equal to their investment.

Figure 17. "It took us 400 years to get this piece of paper!"

In America, this rule of politics applies to everyone except Black people. The primary reason for Black Americans being an exception stems from structural racism and various community pressures and attitudes that set them apart as a political subculture. Political subcultures are typically "minimally integrated" and, out of fear of losing

186

their lowly status, they do not resist being treated as subjects. Lacking population numbers, wealth and leadership, they reject dissent and passively follow the majority society even though they may gain only very small benefits. This is especially true in the case of Black Americans, who traditionally support White candidates and their political parties out of a sense of obligation. History does not show any instances in which Black Americans have been compensated on a quid pro quo basis for the political, cultural or economic contributions they have made.

The worst part of this picture is that Black America has not *demanded* a quid pro quo relationship. In explaining how Cuban refugees in Miami were able to economically and politically surpass and subordinate Blacks in Miami within one decade, a Cuban told me, "We are not like Black people who always march, demonstrate then beg. We demand what we want." Blacks have petitioned for freedom and equality, but never demanded quid pro quo compensation for their political loyalty, labor, patriotism or cultural contributions. Power-Nomics urges Black voters to begin to move towards the politics of patronage for the entire race and not just a few visible Blacks. The practice of political patronage rarely, if ever, presents a problem for non-Black groups, because most politicians and political parties understand that they have to reward their supporters.

Both White and Black candidates for public office, various political parties, and this nation, all get a free ride with Black voters. Black voters are led to believe there are two purposes to vote: 1) to elect the White candidate who is best able to lead and control resources or 2) to elect the Black candidate who is most deserving of a public job and personal recognition. The most we get is personal satisfaction that the candidate we supported won. We play politics just to play. Others play for the benefits of winning or being in the winner's circle. We often support campaign issues that do not benefit us. Blackness is excluded, but we hope that through some miraculous twinge of conscience, once in office the former candidate will offer us some spoils as supporters. We demand nothing and that is basically exactly what we get. We have yet to learn to play politics by the basic rules. We should stay out of any political game that promises that we will get nothing even when our candidate wins. Once we start playing to win, we must always reject candidates who fail to pay their debts to us.

## *Political Accommodation Is Obsolete*

Playing American politics, based upon the needs and interests of other groups, is playing politics just to play. Politics is economic Darwinism. It is rooted in selfish economic aims. Players compete to protect what they have or for further gains. Those who operate from altruistic feelings about "helping everyone" may play the game, but they will not win. Booker T. Washington was a pro-Black leader. Washington's greatest weakness was his dream of being the "Great Accommodator," between Blacks and Whites. He destroyed Black Americans' hopes of being an independent and competitive people by telling Whites at the Atlanta Fair in 1896 that Blacks were "the most patient, faithful, law-abiding, and un-resentful people that the world had ever seen." The White society rewarded Washington and Black Americans for their humble, meek, compassionate and non-competitive attitudes by subjecting them to another 60 years of Jim Crow semi-slavery.

Playing and winning in politics must be based on group self-interest, and not misplaced group loyalty and faithfulness. Black America's political agenda must be just as narrow and exclusive as White politics, Jewish politics, Hispanic politics, gay politics and women's politics. And, just as other competing groups have elected officials who speak strictly for them, Black people ought to have elected officials who speak for Black people and practice the politics of gaining resources for Black people. The issue is not about getting along socially. With more than 9,000 Black elected officials in America, we are now in a position to practice the politics of getting ahead.

Black elected officials cannot challenge the status quo by creating alliances with competing groups. Alliances must be based on common objectives and benefits. Black civil rights organizations cannot help Black Americans by subordinating Black interests and historical needs to ethnic and language groups who are higher in the order of acceptability. Several Hispanic and Korean immigrants told me that they enter this country above Black people and were advised, even before they got here, to avoid association with Blacks. Ethnic immigrants know Blacks were slaves but they do not understand the legacies of slavery that still handicap Black people. What they do understand is that regardless of how low they may fall, they will never sink as low as Black people. Black Americans' humble, non-competitive attitude toward politics and business reinforce the popular image of Blacks as weak and undemanding and allow others to take advantage of them. As the farmer said when asked how he planned to get his crops to market. "It's easy. The willingest jackass will have to pull the heaviest load." For centuries, Black Americans have been the willingest jackass in American politics. Now that role must change.

## *The New Black Political Orientation*

The new Black political orientation must be practicing the politics of gaining resources rather than the politics of morality and establishing civil rights. Those who own and control resources have both rights and might. Therefore, based upon our own group self-interests, we should use the political process to redistribute America's resources, redress historical injustices committed against Black people, and improve the socioeconomic conditions within Black communities so that Black people can have functional communities in which to work and live. We could greatly benefit from practicing group politics predicated on group-based advantages that help us own and control wealth, land, businesses and other resources. Listed below are 12 action steps or strategies to play the game and create political conditions for economic success for Black Americans.

## Political Action Step #1: Promote group self-interest and use political acts to empower Black America.

In any race or contest, a group that has no self-interest cannot successfully compete or win. Black Americans are inextricably bound together by many forces and factors—the presence of racism, African heritage, slavery, emancipation, integration and overall victimization. Yet, as a race, we continue to promote the political agenda of the majority society and its ethnic sub-groups rather than our own. We can neither compete nor win as integrated "do gooders." Racial solidarity is a prerequisite for political empowerment and group-based competitiveness. Black America should prioritize and commit to taking care of itself before seeking to take care of the world.

Carter G. Woodson, in his 1936 book, *The Mis-Education of the Negro*, urged Black people to support their own people first. He said there was nothing wrong with Blacks being kind, generous, concerning, forgiving and compassionate towards all people, but begin with your own people first.[2] Over a half century later, we have still not learned to place our own group interests first. As long as other groups remain primarily interested in their respective groups and placing their interests first, Black people must be equally as protective and interested in our own group.

Some Blacks may perceive any move towards group self-interest as a move towards separation or hate. America's Black overclass (Black elected officials, ministers, business leaders, civil rights representatives and celebrities) are particularly susceptible to this kind of thinking. They fail to understand that directing their resources to aid their own people is normal and natural. A move towards group self-interest would signal a maturation and a readiness to practice group economics and group politics. The pursuit of empowerment is more about self-interest than high-minded principles. Politics based upon turning the other cheek and forming coalitions with rival class, ethnic, and language groups is ultimately doomed to failure for Blacks. Races are won by getting ahead, not helping other participants gain competitive advantages. Believing that "God helps those who help themselves," European immigrants built competitive communities, businesses and political organizations around the needs, interests and goals of their own people. Subsequent non-European ethnic immigrants, religious and gender groups did the same thing. But, in nearly every instance, all of these groups established barriers to exclude Black people.

### Representing All the People

Only Blacks will represent the universe and use non-specific organizational titles that avoid identification with their own people. The NAACP represents the civil rights interest of "colored people and minorities (and poor Whites)," the National Urban League represents the welfare of "poor people and the multicultural (and poor Whites)," and the Rainbow Coalition represents "women, people of the rainbow," (and poor Whites). And, the Nation of Islam is moving to represent all "oppressed people." Who then is representing the political interests of *Black Americans?*

An exchange on a National Public Radio program in 1998 provides a good example of the irrelevance and vulnerability of Black groups that do not have Black issues as a focus and priority. A very high official of one of the oldest Black civil rights organizations described it as one that has always had civil rights at it core, but recognized that in a changing America, Black civil rights cannot be the organization's sole focus. He said, "There are new non-White minorities, people of color, who are demanding a place in the sun. And even though their agenda is not totally like Blacks, we must be prepared to embrace them." He spoke too, about the long history of extensive White involvement in the organization, and that it must fight for all people of color, such as Blacks, Asians and Hispanics, women, senior citizens, homosexuals and even poor Whites.

An Hispanic caller named, Mike, however took issue with the Black leader. Mike asserted that Hispanics were not people of color and requested that the organization not include Hispanics when it spoke of representing people of color. Mike went on to say that he, his family and all his Hispanic friends were White and did not want or need the Black organization to represent them. He said, "Hispanics and Asians have their own organizations so why don't Blacks just look out for their own people?" The Black leader challenged the caller to looked in the mirror and on his driver's license and tell him what he saw. When the Hispanic caller said, "White. I see White." The official of the Black organization responded, "So, we do represent you! White is a color too." Given the dire needs of Black Americans, the question is clearly, is it appropriate behavior for a premier civil rights organization to force itself on people who do not want or need its help while Black Americans go begging?

Our determined but misdirected compassion is one of our greatest impediments to self-empowerment. We fail to concentrate our resources to empower Black Americans. How can Black Americans acquire collective wealth and power resources when our lead organizations dissipate our limited resources on civil rights for everybody? A study of material from a number of ethnic, language, religious, and gender minority organizations revealed that none of these groups include Blacks in their programs, policies and activities. In his book, *Winning Back America*,[3] Mark Green listed all the nation's top minority rights organizations and the only groups that even used the word minority in their program descriptions were the Black civil rights organizations. Ignoring Black people's dilemma by equating them to all so-called aggrieved groups is wrong headed whether it is done by Whites, Blacks or others. Not only does it give the false impression that all people in this nation have had the same experiences as Black people, it also injures and minimizes the impact of centuries of slavery, segregation and ongoing racism.

Worse, it releases White society from its obligations to correct the conditions imposed on Blacks. Organizations whose agendas have evolved into this kind of scattered focus do not put group self-interests first. However, just as their missions became amorphous over the years, they can regroup, reassess their organizational direction, and change once again. If they choose to be part of the effort to maximize Black self-sufficiency and Black economic competitiveness, they can refocus their missions to promote and support Black group self-interest and political empowerment.

## *Know Your Competitors*

To promote its own self-interest, a group should only select for allies those who will support the group and will not benefit from its demise. There is an orchestrated effort to avoid Black issues and to supplant them with Hispanics and other minorities. In 1972, the National Hispanic Party conceived a plan to subordinate Black Americans by the year 2000 by bringing in a layer of minority ethnic groups between Whites and Blacks. The Hispanic empowerment strategy is to track and copy everything that Black Americans do politically and economically, then offer Hispanics as a more socially acceptable alternative to Blacks.

Like Asian, Arab, European, gay, handicapped, and women's organizations, Hispanic organizations do not promote a Black agenda nor do they equate Black and Hispanic interests.

Hispanics and other so-called minorities are competing against Blacks, whether the Black overclass knows it or not. Some Hispanic groups are even more competitive and freely state their intent to totally displace Blacks on the American agenda.[4] In the spring of 1997, C-SPAN aired conference sessions for the Council of La Raza. Several speakers spoke openly and emphatically about how Hispanics would change the issues in this country from Black and White to White and Hispanic. The number of Hispanics in the United States tripled between 1970 and 1990 and will surpass the Black population by 2002. While Hispanics prepare to celebrate becoming this nation's majority-minority population, there is little public discussion on the socioeconomic impact on Black Americans. In a society that maintains a racial hierarchy, discord can be expected as groups compete for resources, especially if one group is shackled by harmful legacies.

Author Michael Lind, in his book *The Next American Nation*, spoke of how Hispanics inherited affirmative action and other programs that were originally designed to help Black Americans because Black leadership failed to protest it. Lind said, "One by one, Hispanic mayors will replace Black mayors; Hispanic contractors will edge out Black contractors; Hispanic quotas in education and hiring will increase; Hispanics will demand their own congressional districts, at the price, if necessary, of the destruction of Black-majority districts." Lind expressed amazement that Black leaders would allow White women and ethnic minorities to replace Blacks. He wondered what Black civil rights leaders would have said in the 1960s, had they known that within one generation, the primary beneficiaries of affirmative action and other civil rights initiatives would be well-to-do White women, Asians and Hispanics? Most of these Hispanics are classified as Whites and lived in Mexico, Cuba, Salvador, Honduras and Guatemala for decades after the end of the civil rights movement. Yet they now displace Blacks. How do today's Black leaders justify their active role in helping women, Hispanics, Asians and other immigrants capitalize on Black issues, then edge out and subordinate Blacks?[5]

## Political Action Step #2: Challenge immigration laws and public policies that have forced Black people to become this nation's only non-immigrant and permanent minority.

Blacks must mobilize at the grassroots level and challenge this nation's immigration policies which forced them to be the only planned, permanent, involuntary minority in a social democracy that operates on the premise that the majority will win and rule and the minority will lose and be ruled. Wealth and power follow the numbers. This country was founded on the principles of liberty, opportunity and reward for achievement, so long as you were White or could reasonably be accepted as White. In the mid-1700s Blacks made up approximately 34 percent of the total population. After the ratification of the U.S. Constitution, one of the first acts of the new Congress was to enact the 1790 naturalization law that restricted citizenship to "free White persons." Immigration laws have controlled Black population numbers. Over the last 200 years, ethnic immigrants have bumped Blacks from employment, business, education and political opportunities and used them as a buffer against hate groups. Layer after layer of ethnic immigrants receive the advantage of the fruits of Black people's labor and consumer markets. Black Americans served as a safety net, assuring every ethnic group that they could never fall any lower than the highest Black person. But, each immigrant group's arrival brought additional harsh conditions for Blacks.

Throughout most of the 19th and 20th centuries, Black leaders were aware of the negative impact immigrants had on Black Americans and petitioned the federal government to halt open immigration until the nation had rendered justice to Black Americans. In the mid-1960s, however, Black leaders made two dramatic reversals that were to have lasting effects on Blacks and from which they would never recover. First, Black leaders abandoned Black people and reversed the commitment of civil rights from Blacks to humanitarian support for all struggling people. Second, they not only dropped their opposition to immigration but began to support it.

In the book, *Immigration Reconsidered*, Lawrence Fuchs, a political scientist who has published widely in immigration and ethnic studies, describes the chain of events. In the mid-1960s, Cuban immigrants were flooding into Miami and displacing Blacks from their service jobs. Though Blacks were economically devastated, Martin Luther King, Jr. decided not to pit Black economic needs against the desires of Cubans to come to this country. He referred to them as "struggling minorities" and the die was cast. Almost all Black leaders bought the social accommodation script.

Fuchs states, "In part, because of King's inspiration, almost every major Black leader in the country, including the mayors of several large cities and leaders of national organizations, signed an advertisement for the International Rescue Committee in 1978, headlined: "Black Americans Urge Admission of the Indo-Chinese Refugees."

Fuchs says that King's altruistic attitude was picked up by such people as Vernon Jordan (past president of the Urban League), Benjamin Hooks (past president of the National Association for the Advancement of Colored People), Jesse Jackson (founder of the Rainbow Coalition), and various members of the Congressional Black Caucus. In the 1970s, Congresswoman Cardiss R. Collins (D-Illinois) declared that "Americans must continue to have an overriding loyalty to mankind as a whole." Congressman Mickey Leland (D-Texas) called on the federal government to help refugees out of our compassionate commitment to human rights." Just as White leaders had done for centuries, Black leaders, across the board, put the needs of other groups before the unmet needs of Black people and forgot about the competitive nature of our society.[6]

Black people suffered a double loss when their leaders reversed their attitudes about immigration. Not only were the needs of Black Americans subordinated, but so were the needs of people of African descent outside of the United States. The leaders did not challenge immigration policies that prohibited immigration from Black countries, committing instead to make them a little more comfortable wherever they were. They were satisfied pushing America to rid Haiti of a despot political regime rather than pushing America to extend the same immigration options to Haitians or Africans that they extended to European, Asian and Latin American nations. Black people remained on the bottom of the pecking order as their leaders helped competing groups come in above them. Like the first immigration law, the 1924 law declared America to be a White nation and had a zero immigration quota for people of African descent. That remained in effect until the mid-1960s, when it increased from zero to one-half of one percent. The new immigration laws ensured that European ethnic groups (later expanded to Asians and Hispanics) remained dominant by setting new quotas based first on the **national origin** of immigrants, then on their **skills and training**, and **family reunification**. In some rare exceptions, foreigners were granted political asylum. Millions of Hispanics and Asians illegally immigrate to America and are regularly granted amnesty. For physical and ideological reasons, people of African descent do not qualify for the special exemptions. They cannot walk across the border, and since Blacks around the world live under similar conditions, it is difficult to prove they are immigrating for political rather than economic reasons. Black Americans cannot reproduce fast enough to keep up with the pace of three to four million immigrants who annually enter this country.

What can the Black masses do at this point in time? Grassroots Blacks can begin by pressuring their leaders to go back and address the needs of Black people. Black leaders can demonstrate their commitment to their own people by challenging the immigration laws, calling for national dialogue and mobilizing Black masses. Black people can relocate their places of residence to become a majority population in specific cities or regions of the country. Blacks would have a population advantage, if they were to relocate or ethno-aggregate in the six Southern states of Florida, Mississippi, Alabama, Georgia, Louisiana and South Carolina. They could become a significant political and economic force and impact regional and national politics. They could control the electoral votes in presidential elections. Once they become the majority population, they must begin to act like the majority.

Many Blacks reacted to immigration by fleeing their former neighborhoods. Blacks living in suburban areas near large urban cities could increase their political and economic impact by relocating back into key communities and cities. Local governments could offer the Black middle-class incentives, such as tax abatements, homestead sites as well as business, employment and political opportunities to encourage them to relocate into Black urban neighborhoods.

Municipal political bodies, especially those in majority Black cities, must publicly define what constitutes a "minority." If Blacks were originally classified as a minority because they were legally and customarily excluded from this nation's political, economic, educational and social resources, what is the justification for classifying ethnic, religious, class, gender and language groups as "minorities" and equating them to Black Americans? When were these groups shut out of the system without alternatives? Less than one percent of them were in this country when Blacks were being enslaved and Jim Crow segregated. Why is the poverty of ethnic groups that came into the country in that condition equated to Black poverty, which stems from 260 years of slavery? These are the kinds of questions that Blacks ought to raise with both Black and White leaders.

**Political Action Step #3: Use vertical integration in politics, like the old political ward system, to deliver services and direct benefits to Black communities.**

A form of vertical integration must be applied to politics in order to position Black Americans to gain access to higher socioeconomic ground. Vertical integration will give Black Americans a vertical structure or channel that allows public officeholders to deliver constituency services directly to Black voters. The old ward type system is needed. Early in history, the word "ward" meant someone who was to be protected. To protect voters, cities were divided into wards that public officials could easily identify and guard. The ward system was a political division of a city as well as a political tool and patronage system.[7]

To a large degree, the ward system became unpopular and was terminated in Northeastern urban cities in the early 1940s in response to the developing Black civil rights movement. For centuries, European ethnic groups used ward politics and political machinery to empower themselves. Both gave the ethnic groups effective mechanisms for maintaining group unity, political spoils, lines of communication, voter involvement, and a device to enforce political accountability. Black America has never had such a political system or machinery.

Immigrants used the ward system to look after their most important needs. In exchange for voting in blocs, they received a variety of services, such as assistance with citizenship papers and patronage in public sector jobs such as policemen, firemen, clerks, and other public jobs. The ward ethnic political machinery in such places as Boston's Italian community provided food, fuel and rent payments, and helped immigrants in times of emergencies, all in return for a unified ethnic votes. Ward politics were vehicles that aided European immigrants in direct exchange for their political loyalties. Immigrants were able to build institutions, savings and loan associations, social clubs, youth clubs, summer camps, sports associations as well as corner grocery stores and other businesses that provided jobs to the community. The old ward machinery served as aggressive affirmative action for European immigrants for more than a century. We can use it today as a model to politically empower Blacks.

Blacks should demand that Black politicians and Black public servants have direct control over political resources for political patronage. Blacks can build a political ward system just as the ethnic immigrants built them to guard their families, communities and race, and as mechanisms to hold their elected officials accountable.

Like the old ethnic wards, Black wards can be built around: 1) maintaining family and community ties, 2) pooling and sharing resources, 3) exercising competitive self-interests in the marketplace and 4) mutual obligation between Black people. Ward systems can create vertical links between public officeholders and Black voters for the delivery of services.

## Political Action Step #4: Support a national network of Black research institutes to collect data, advocate for, and craft group-based, "how-to-win" political strategies.

It is imperative that Black America have scholars and institutions to conduct ethnographic research for the purpose of political and economic empowerment. Black America has played competitive politics with one arm behind its back. Black America has not had the benefit of a national intellectual structure that researches and analyzes issues, and crafts proactive how-to strategies for Black Americans. The majority society has well over 1,200 public policy institutes or think tanks as well as thousands of university-based research institutes, whose sole purpose is to bring concentrated brain power to bear on every conceivable issue. These majority policy institutes have a collective budget of more than a half billion dollars and approximately 6,000 employees.

These public policy institutes vary ideologically from ultra-right conservatism to middle of the road to ultra liberalism. The nation needs and deserves research and viewpoints that are from a Black perspective of life. Black people need research organizations that will develop policy and blueprints to help Black America achieve self-sufficiency and competitiveness. That is the mission of the Harvest Institute, a research organization based in Washington, D.C., and founded by the author. Most Black community-based organizations that could provide political and economic research do not have the financial resource or the ideological commitment. The financial supporters of these organizations would not approve using charitable resources to socially engineer Black people out of their protracted dilemma. The burden falls upon Black Americans to save themselves.

In developing the Black political power tool kit, Black America needs a national network of public policy institutes that want to work toward the *PowerNomics* vision, to form a network. Each participating organization would develop or contribute a particular area of expertise. They would work together to do research, lobby and distribute information to Black America. The network should be totally committed to increasing wealth, income and power resources in Black America. Components of this network can structure themselves as voluntary associations, civic groups, educational or a number of other type organizations. To maximize their effect in communities, the local think tanks should affiliate with Black colleges, business organizations, and churches that also subscribe to the *PowerNomics* vision. Together and separately they could function as a vital part of a national network, using newsletters, the Internet, press releases, conferences, seminars and public hearings to educate, inform and influence Black voters and Black public officials.

The principal goals of the Black American national intellectual network are to:

- Provide research to Black public officials.
- Help the 20 most populated Black communities to develop plans to rebuild communities and to practice group politics and economics.
- Bring about economic and political self-sufficiency and competitiveness.
- Apply the research principles and strategies of the *PowerNomics* national plan and to develop prescriptive solutions for Black America.
- Establish new forms of institutional leadership.
- Link knowledge to power by bringing together scholars, strategists and researchers.
- Establish an electronic information network within Black America.
- Develop public policies and programs to aggregate capital and stimulate vertically integrated Black-owned enterprises within Black communities.
- Promote group accountability, unity and optimism.

**Political Action Step #5: Create a daily national print and electronic news/talk show network that offers Black political perspectives on domestic and international events.**

The economic aspects of this action step were explained in Chapter 6. However, the political purpose is important to isolate and discuss. The saying, "information is power" sounds good. However, information in and of itself is not power. Information represents only the *potential* for power. Just like the power in a light bulb is realized only when it is connected to a circuit, information lacks power until it is connected into a network and used by its owner. If we as Black Americans are serious about acquiring power, we must have a national network for information and news. We need to communicate information, strategies and ideas that connect the group and establish a potential for unity and consistency of message. A Black communication network would increase group power, especially when the information being disseminated is linked successfully with the group's visions and goals.

Black America must be able to communicate with itself because we cannot play group politics or group economics without the capacity to communicate and share information. Mainstream media does not provide information that focuses on what is helpful to Blacks. Just as we must break up the White monopolies over wealth and businesses, we must also break up Whites monopoly on research and information.

Blacks must develop both print and electronic media in order to practice group politics effectively. Few Black newspapers are viable today and most of them are now dependent upon and controlled by White politicians and their business allies. They are used as propaganda tools for the established power overclass. Scattered and financially weak, they are forced to sell out to the highest bidder. To empower Black weeklies they should be nationally linked together, to function as one newspaper. The first step towards building a national print media network is to create a national Black newspaper whose foundation is already in place in the scattered, independent Black weeklies. How would it be done? The remaining 50 or so Black weeklies can be fashioned into one national Black weekly at first, then once established expanded to a daily paper patterned after *USA Today*. *USA Today* assembles content and many of the stories appeared first in other newspapers around the nation. Since many of the stories appeared in local newspapers, they have therefore already been approved for print. A consortium of Black papers could achieve similar kinds of economies of scale. *USA Today's* target audience is a White conservative male. Our Black weekly or daily paper should also target a specific audience, Blacks.

A national Black weekly or daily newspaper would have great value for Black politicians. The paper would give them a national feel for what is happening in and around Black communities and would also serve as a communications mechanism for publicizing political issues of importance to Black people. Having access to all of Black America through one vehicle would be important to our Black officials who, once elected to office, take on a national responsibility to and for Blacks.

A national Black newspaper linked with a radio talk network would attract advertising dollars into Black communities and businesses. Currently, mainstream advertisers operate on the theory that they do not need to buy Black-owned media, because they can reach Blacks on the same media they use to reach everyone else. This is true only to the degree that Blacks lack an alternative information source. A national Black newspaper would change the advertising paradigm and make it more difficult for those who market to Blacks to reach them in ways that keep the dollars flowing through the mainstream economy. The aggregate strength of a national Black weekly or daily would compel White advertisers to use the medium, thereby allowing the newspaper to demand higher advertising rates than individual local Black weeklies. Their aggregate strength also should enable the national newspaper to report Black news without fear of reprisals from advertisers. A powerful component of a national communication network would be a national Black talk radio network that every Black person could tune into around the clock and around the country.

There are more than 300 full-time and part-time Spanish language radio stations and two, soon to be three, television networks. Hispanic media is part of an international effort to build a politically and economically powerful Hispanic nation inside of American society. Media ownership contributes to that plan by:

1. Using the Spanish language to promote the culture, issues and to mark territory.
2. Providing an electronic channel of information for Hispanics.
3. Empowering speakers of Spanish over English[8]

Black America lacks an approved culture and language system. Yet, Black-owned radio and television should serve the same function as Spanish-language radio because Blacks are a scattered people who are out of touch with themselves. But, Blacks will soon lose the only national cable television channel owned by and programmed to Blacks. On November 4, 2000, the owner of BET announced its sale to Viacom, a major White corporation.

The Internet is also now a powerful way to communicate among individuals and groups of people. While not a substitute for the mass media, Blacks must influence policy and devise ways to own and control as much of the new technology as possible. Even more importantly, Blacks must not allow non-Blacks who own these new systems to aggregate Black consumers and exploit and profit from them.

**Political Action Step #6: Establish national political debates, issue forums and conventions for politicians seeking Black votes.**

Black Americans must lock all candidates for public office and current elected officials, into quid pro quo contracts with Black communities. Ever since America's founding, public debates have constituted a major part of the election process. Debates are used as settings for candidates to present themselves and their ideas to the public. They give the public a chance to get to know the candidates and seek their support for issues and projects. However, most debates, from the Lincoln vs. Douglas debate of the 1850s to local modern day town hall debates, avoid any serious discussion of Black issues. For Black America to join the political discourse and to wield political power, we must require all political candidates for high office to participate in Black hosted national and local debates, town hall meetings and other public forums and to respond to questions about their commitment to Black empowerment issues.

This practice would do several things. First, it would make Black America a part of the political process in a meaningful way. Second, it would bring respect to Black people and their voting power. Third, it would allow Blacks to regain some control over politics within individual Black neighborhoods. Fourth, Black America would have a chance to interact with candidates on key issues and extract irrevocable agreements between the candidates and Black America. And last, the publicized national debates would stop candidates for public office from taking Black Americans for granted by saying one thing to Blacks, then saying something totally different to another group or community about the same issue. The biggest benefit of national debates and forums is that they would expose and undermine Blacks who sell influence "as Black leaders" for personal gain and reward. Candidates who have nothing to offer Blacks will not likely come into Black communities. And if they don't come into our communities and participate in the public events, then we will know that they don't deserve our vote.

Every candidate that appears before the Black public forums should present their agenda in terms of what they propose to do *specifically and solely* for Black Americans, not minorities, not women, not *everybody*. What they propose to do should be taken as a contractual commitment. All candidates, whether running for national or local office, should be asked the following questions:

- Do you recognize and understand the nature of the race problem in America?
- Will you take steps to secure long overdue reparations for Black Americans?
- What other wealth, income and business producing programs or public policies do you intend to create to advance Black entrepreneurship?
- What specific amount of money do you pledge to allocate into Black communities during your term in office?
- How many Black millionaires that have the *PowerNomics* vision do you promise to make by the mid-term of your office?

Any candidate or officeholder who does not provide acceptable answers to these or similar questions should not get Black votes. After the election, Blacks should ask newly elected officeholders to return to the public forum and report on their progress in delivering the promised wealth resources. Those who follow through on their promises deserve continued support. Those who do not should either be subjected to voter recalls and other Black voter backlashes. In our effort to correct the wealth and resource disparities between the races, we must accept only those activities that successfully move socioeconomic resources into the Black community. Black voters must never support any candidate who does not promise and deliver equitable financial resources into Black communities.

**Political Action Step #7: Bloc vote based upon quid pro quo agreements between politicians, their parties and Black people.**

The strongest weapon in Black America's political arsenal is the bloc vote. Although it is small, it has great political potency because it is the nation's only bloc vote. No other group, not women, Hispanics, senior citizens or Whites vote as a bloc. These voter groups are not loyal to national political parties and rarely give more than 40 to 45 percent of their vote to any specific political party. Black Americans are the exception. They have the sole distinction of typically aligning 95 percent of their vote with a single national political party. For instance, from 1870 until the late 1930s, nearly 100 percent of this country's Black voters voted as a bloc for the Republican Party. From the late 1940s, until the present time, nearly 100 percent of the country's Black voters vote for Democratic candidates. Over the course of these 40 years, neither of the national political parties nor any White office holders have sponsored a program or public policy strictly and solely designed to address the needs and interests of Black Americans. They have never been paid a quid pro quo for their party loyalty and bloc votes.

A bloc vote and quid pro quo commitments go together like ham and eggs. They support and complement each other. But Black voters do not demand and White politicians do not practice quid pro quo with Black voters. They are paid for their support with tokenism, even by liberal White politicians who hire a few Black staff members, appoint Blacks to powerless boards, and socialize with Blacks when there is racial discord. Since Blacks never seek group-based benefits, how would even a willing politician repay them? Reportedly, President Bill Clinton was amazed that Blacks did not demand benefits for their unflinching support of him. However, as Black America matures politically, the practice of ignoring the needs of Black voters, instead of quid pro quo for Black America is no longer acceptable. Black Americans want to benefit in proportion to their contributions in the political arenas.

We must use quid pro quo agreements to ensure delivery of services and economic resources. We must use these agreements to establish clear distinctions between Blacks having *access* to power and Blacks actually *having* power. Without agreements, only those Black individuals and organizations who benefit from the status quo and hold themselves out as representing Blacks, will receive benefits. At best, the Black masses will receive what little trickles down from broad ambiguous programs designed for everybody.

Figure 18. The Dilemma of the Black Voter: No Quid Pro Quo

Our goal in practicing group politics is to own and control our own power resources. The difference between owning and having access is like a bank clerk whose job allows him access to millions of dollars he cannot use for his own personal benefit. It can be said without any hesitation that the majority White society has no intention of voluntarily relinquishing control of any power resources that could possibly alter their historically advantaged positions. It is our responsibility to change the political relationship by leveraging whatever power we do have.

**Political Action Step #8: Mobilize a reparations movement to place Black Americans in a status equal to American Indians, with legal claims on the expropriation of labor, property and life.**

Black Americans are entitled to monetary compensation from the government and private sector for the myriad of losses that Blacks have suffered, especially as a result of their ancestors being denied the fruits of their labor. Similarly, their descendents are due compensation for the compounded and unjust legacies of slavery and Jim Crow semi-slavery. In terms of benefits to Black America, both integration and affirmative action were dead on arrival. However, the structural inequalities and racial monopolies that they should have eliminated remain active and deleterious. The best recourse for Black America is reparations and it should be made a national issue. It is no longer simply a subject for parlor room discussions but an absolute necessity. It is the most effective mechanism to deliver long overdue economic justice to Black Americans.

Throughout history, our political and legal systems have compensated injured parties including White indentured servants (freedom dues), Southern slaveholders (monetary reparations and approximately one billion acres of land), Japan (billions of dollars in the Point Four Program), Germany (billions of dollars in the Marshall Plan), Japanese Americans (billions of dollars in the reparations for World War II internment), Jews (billions of dollars for the German Holocaust survivors), American Indians (billions of dollars in land, cash, payments and public assistance) and now even cigarette smokers (billions of dollars in damage awards). All of these groups received reparations and monetary compensation for personal injuries and unjust enrich-ment. Black people, victims of the worst Holocaust in history, have not received an apology nor compensation, in part because they failed to mobilize a reparations movement and demand compensation from all nations, governments, wealthy families, churches and corporations that profited from slavery. Although some may be skeptical, Black Americans will be granted reparations. This nation has no other choice but to deliver on its long overdue economic justice to Black Americans. It would be an international embarrassment for this coun-try to espouse democratic principles of fairness and justice and to con-tinue holding Black Americans in the economic ditches created by the laws of the nation. Domestically, should this nation continue to avoid its obligations to Black Americans, it is running the risk of alienating its most loyal and patriotic citizen—Black people.

As the reparations movement grows, Black Americans will search for precedents and models. Most Black reparations organizations look to the Japanese American reparations bill and strategies employed by Jews in their legal actions against Volkswagen and Mercedes Benz. Both of these have merit, but are not the best models for Black Amer-icans who, like American Indians, have a historical, constitutional rela-tionship with this country. Neither Jews nor the Japanese have such a relationship. Moreover, neither group was in this country when the Constitution established "special" relationships with Blacks and Amer-ican Indians. Even though there is still great poverty among Indians, they received many opportunities and advantages because of their special constitutional status. Both federal and state governments, through the Bureau of Indian Affairs and State Indian Commissions, have historically allocated to Indians various forms of compensation such as free land, medical services, housing assistance, economic development funds, tools and equipment, tuition-free education, casino licenses and tax exemptions.

Although initially these benefits were targeted only to Indians con-fined to reservations, within the last half a century they were extended to all who claim to be Indians. Now Indians are getting double bene-fits. They get the benefits of being a citizen living off of the reserva-tion as well as the benefits of being a non-citizen living on the reservation. The benefits did not change when they were declared cit-izens at the turn of the 20th century.

Black people have an even stronger constitutional relationship with this nation than do Indians. Therefore, it should be easier to track American Indians and justify benefits for Black Americans. Other models are insufficient. For instance, neither the Japanese nor Jewish model have a constitutional basis. The Jewish Holocaust did not take place in America and there were no Japanese in America during Black slavery. It should be easier for Blacks to demand reparations by tracking the same path that American Indians took to get their special programs, bureaus, preferences, tax exemptions and other advantages. For centuries, American Indians and their descendants have received reparations while Black Americans have been ignored.

The United States Constitution specifically designated Black people and Indians living on reservations as non-citizens and excluded both groups from certain rights and privileges. Blacks were mentioned four times and Indians twice. The Constitution did not apply to Indians not living on reservations. The path Indians took to reparations that Blacks could track, is summarized below:

- *Indians* filed a "natural rights" claim against the land on behalf of their ancestors.
  *Blacks* should file a "natural law" claim against governments, religions and businesses for death, injury and unjust enrichment on behalf of the victims of slavery and Jim Crow peonage.

- *Indians* sought and received public apologies from state and federal governments.
  *Blacks* should seek public apologies from all levels of government, religions, and business.

- *Indians* convinced Whites to invest resources to preserve and reinvent Indian culture.
  *Blacks* should secure public and private funding for a Black holocaust and cultural museum.

- *Indians* had government economists calculate the value of expropriated "Indian lands."
  *Blacks* should demand that government calculate the value of expropriated Black labor, deaths and property.

- *Indians* drafted their own Civilized Tribes Constitution and formed governing councils.

*Blacks* should adopt a national Black empowerment plan and form a political party.

• *Indians* declared themselves to be a "foreign nation" and developed separate communities.
*Blacks* should declare themselves a nation within a nation and rebuild Black communities.

• *Indians* allowed themselves to be declared "domestic dependent nations" and wards of the government who needed to be protected under the "Doctrine of Trust." The federal government became responsible for their care and well-being as a poor and powerless people.
*Blacks* should seek to be protected under a similar "Doctrine of Trust" that protects and entitles them to double benefits and tax-exemptions.

Herein lies Black America's best model, since they as slaves were also declared subjects and dependent upon the majority White society. Black America is just as dependent today as they ever were. Unlike Blacks, American Indians on and off the reservations have used their historical relationships with the U.S. Constitution to get special benefits. They are a protected class while Black Americans are in an unprotected class. They currently have 237 reservations, but they also have approximately 257 gambling casinos that bring in more revenue than all the 535,000 Black businesses put together. Congress has the authority to award funds to Indians. It also has the authority to award funds to Black ex-slaves, according to the Civil Rights Act of 1866.

On October 18, 2000 *The Washington Post* reported that Congress had exercised its authority to aid Indians when it awarded a New Mexico Indian tribe $23 million and about 4,600 acres to settle lawsuits over land that the tribe claimed under a grant from the king of Spain more than 300 years ago. Again, in a move that would cost taxpayers billions of dollars, Congress on October 27, 2000, urged the Clinton administration to settle a lawsuit over mismanagement of trust accounts for about 500,000 American Indians.[9]

Indians are getting benefits that go back centuries, and Blacks are listening to skeptics tell them they are not entitled to reparations because slavery ended more than a century ago and semi-slavery

209

ended nearly a half century ago. Clearly, any Black reparation movement should track Indians as a model and seek similar nation status.

Black Americans are on the verge of becoming a permanent underclass in American society. Hearings need to be held to specifically document and financially quantify the injury to Black people from centuries of slavery and Jim Crow semi-slavery. The findings should be used to ascertain the many ways that Black people were harmed. The hearings should provide the foundation for corrective actions in economics, education and other areas. They should be used to develop legal theories and policies for reparations. Making restitution for damages is rooted in the legal system and has been used by industrialized nations as a mechanism for apologizing and correcting institutional wrongs. Restitution has been made to nearly every group that has claimed injury except Black people. The hearings should determine the most appropriate forms of reparations and how benefits will be distributed. As much as possible, settlements should track the multiple forms of reparations received by Indians. Organizations should be established for the specific purpose of receiving and administering settlement agreements and assets in a way to make Black America self-sufficient and competitive.

If the civil rights movement was successfully redirected away from Blacks and to everyone, Blacks must expect that there will be efforts by both Blacks and Whites to hijack reparations. Black America must be especially careful not to allow conservatives, liberals, Black leaders or any others who are ill-informed or operating in self-interest to derail or mis-focus reparations efforts. Activities that are imprecise and based on poor or superficial scholarship will confuse the issue and kill the movement. If the reparations movement is derailed, Black America's last hope for economic justice will also be forever thwarted. The only way that the growing number of activities can result in benefits to all Blacks is if the individual efforts are directed to the same outcome—economic justice for descendents of Black slaves and a Black America that is self-sufficient and competitive. Appendix B is a reparations plan in schematic form that can be used to guide Black America toward reparations and economic justice. It will also be helpful to those in the general public working to understand the issue.

## Political Action Step #9: Use electoral voting options to bypass elected officials and political institutions.

One of the biggest political failings of Black America over the last half of a century is that it has been too quiet. The majority society began implementing its benign neglect policy in the early 1970s. This public policy which declared Black Americans an obsolete and abandoned labor force, shifted White society's moral commitments from Blacks to gender, class, ethnic, and language groups. Blacks seem politically paralyzed by this unexpected shift. With Black leadership leading the shift, then later seeking to ally with the new class minorities that they had created, a problem arose.

In any competitive environment, an individual or group that is non-competitive is sure to become extinct. Black Americans are leaderless for all practical purposes. Black Americans must again become active and force those holding public office to be responsible to the needs and concerns of Black people. We need to initiate more direct action, whether we exercise electoral voting options, alter consumer patterns or even use forms of civil disobedience. For example, we used boycotts and civil disobedience reasonably well generations ago. These acts can still grab the public's attention, but, they become wasted efforts when there are no tangible goals and follow up activities. These old tactics would probably be more effective if they were used in combination with some of our voting options and power.

There are a number of special voting rights that are tools we can use to accomplish our political will, such as voter referenda, initiatives, recalls, public hearings, selective withdrawal of patronage, lawsuits, and ballot write-ins. We should employ these special electoral devices to counteract laws, public policies or public officeholders who conflict with our interests.

The laws regarding special rights vary greatly, but all of them are tools we can use to gain some degree of control over our lawmakers and hold them accountable. Through an initiative, for instance, voters can introduce a law; through a referendum, the voters can approve or reject a proposed law; through a recall, the voters can take an elected official out of office before his term expires. Voters can seek injunctive relief through a lawsuit. A dissatisfied constituency can also effect the business revenue and the soft campaign funds political figures receive from corporate donors. These special rights allow any disenchanted citizens to take direct action against government representatives.

Any concerned Black individual or group can file a lawsuit. The same is true for recalls, referenda and initiatives, though they must use approved language on the petitions, meet time requirements and collect a specific number of certifiable signatures of registered voters. Once collected, the petitions are usually presented to a city council or similar body for acceptance. When an initiative has been accepted, neither the mayor nor the governor can veto the initiatives.

Recalls can be a good beginning point to confront elected officials who are unwilling to address or respond to the needs and interests of a Black minority. You do not need to be the majority to get a public official's attention. Only a small number of signatures of registered voters are required to recall an elected official. The recall effort itself and the possibility of creating a run-off election are sometimes enough to convince elected officials to respect and address the concerns of Black voters. If it is not possible to hold the official accountable with a recall, we can shift our focus of accountability to individuals and businesses that supported the candidate. If, for instance, a Black minister or local official persuades the Black community to support a candidate, they should be held responsible for making sure the candidate honors commitments made to the Black community. It is also effective to turn the same attention to the elected official's financial supporters. Applying the rule, Don't treat any person or group better than they treat you," Black voters can orchestrate economic sanctions or withdraw their patronage from companies and their products until they hold the candidate accountable.

Even if Blacks intend to withhold their votes, they should still register to vote because only voting provides access to these special voters rights. Armed with these tools, we can begin to hold lawmakers and their supporters accountable or bypass them to get our issues and concerns into the political marketplace.

In a real sense, however, our country's majority rule voting system is a charade when public policies make Black people a permanent minority. The concept of majority rules is an expedient but misleading and imperfect expression of equality of opportunity. If laws and social customs placed six Whites and one Black in a room and gave them the right to vote on issues and candidates, and if the six Whites agreed to vote as a skin color group only for White candidates and White issues, it is a cruel joke in a democratic society to tell the one Black that he has an equal opportunity to vote and run for office. The six White voters can claim they are fair because the Black has equal voting rights. In reality, if he votes in his own self interest, his vote is null and void because he is a minority of one. The only time he can win is when his interests align with the interests of Whites. The equal opportunity to vote is an exercise in futility when the deck is stacked so that Blacks can never win or prevail. When Blacks are made a permanent minority, the voting system ought to be weighted so that one Black vote carries proportional weight, maybe three to one, over groups that have competing interests and lack the historical past of Blacks. It is an insult and compromises Blacks to vote in a system where they are constantly voting on White issues, concerns and candidates.

The ultimate voting option Black people have is to call for a *boycott* of a national election to dramatize the dilemma of Black voters and the futility they feel when they vote. Worse, with each passing day and each newly arriving legal and illegal immigrant, the Black voting power becomes more and more insignificant. When Blacks are bumped from a majority-minority to a minority-minority in a couple of years by Hispanics, then later by Asians, Black American's votes will become strictly an exercise in futility. Blacks best hope is to act today to dramatize their plight in hopes of changing the immigration laws or weighting their votes. Otherwise, Black Americans can soon forget about voting.

A dramatized boycott of a national election could call attention to the fact that Blacks may be legally able to vote but the political candidates and parties are not willing to address the issues and injustices committed against Black people. And worse, their votes are used as a swing vote to help one political party or the other win an office, but never in exchange for benefits for the race. Once the election is over, they are again forgotten then trotted out for the next close election. An electoral boycott would communicate to Blacks and Whites throughout the United States that Blacks will not play a game in which they can neither win nor benefit. It would communicate to international circles that America is the cradle of democracy for everybody but Black people.

**Political Action Step #10: Compete with the two major political parties by forming a national Black independent party as an alternative voting channel.**

In national politics, there is a long held common belief that regardless of how this nation's political parties treat Black American voters, they accept it because they have no alternative. Black voters are unwanted political pawns. For over a century, one political party rejected Blacks while the other national party tolerated their membership. Blacks were spectators whose sole contribution was limited to a "swing" vote in a close race between White candidates. But, contrary to common belief, Black voters do have somewhere to go. They can join the half of this nation's eligible voters who simply refuse to vote. Or, Black voters can turn the tables on the two national parties and, instead of waiting to be used, rejected or tolerated, Blacks can do the rejecting. Black votes may be irrelevant, but if we apply the principles of ethno-aggregation we can create some alternatives.

Though a divorce proceeding has yet to be announced, the marriage between the Democratic Party and Black America, which was consummated in the 1940s, is on the rocks. The Democratic Party has been unfaithful to Black America. Instead of taking care of its home base of loyal Black voters, the Democratic Party downgraded Black rights and took up with every ethnic, class, gender and language issue group, regardless of their party affiliations. The Democratic Party and Black civil rights leaders brought down an array of minority and women competitors upon the backs of Blacks before they had a chance to catch up from centuries of slavery and Jim Crow segregation. What can the Democratic or Republican parties do for Black people in the 21st century? Contrary to the advice of traditional civil rights liberals who encourage Black voters to stay in a failed marriage and conservatives who advocate that Blacks divide themselves between the two national parties, thus diluting their voting power, Black voters should reject both options. Instead, Black voters must ethno-aggregate and become totally independent, forcing both parties to court them.

## *The Basis for a Black Independent Party*

Black Americans view political partisanship differently from White Americans. Black Americans believe in strong loyalty even with no fixed quid pro quo benefits. White Americans believe in strong quid pro quo benefits with no fixed party loyalties. Whites will shift their party loyalties with the speed of light to get benefits. Blacks have shifted loyalty several times. From 1619 until 1865, Black people were enslaved and did not belong to any national political party. From 1868 until around 1936, most Black Americans belonged to the Republican Party and they were subjected to Jim Crow segregation. From around 1946 until present time, most Black Americans belonged to the Democratic Party and they have been neglected.

Figure 19. Building a Black Independent Party

Quite clearly what counts is not the political party to which we belong but the fact that we have never had enough political power to do anything within those parties. Clearly, there has been no visible and direct connection between Blacks supporting a national political party and receiving benefits from the party. In the mid-1980s, so-called progressive Democrats decided to shift the party away from Black people and the image that Whites had of the Democratic Party, as the party of Blacks. In a move that should have been seen as an affront to Blacks, powerful White Democrats created the Democratic Leadership Council for the specific purpose of moving the Democratic Party away from Black people and to the "center of the political road." The Democratic Party is in a conflicted situation. It is seeking middle-class White votes, while still depending on the Black vote, even though the party is moving in a more conservative, White direction. Both major political parties have demonstrated unwillingness to implement a Black agenda that provides material benefits to Black people, so the choice Blacks should exercise is to pull out of both parties and start an independent, national Black party that practices the group-based politics of gaining resources.

Using *PowerNomics* principles and strategies as the foundation for an independent political framework, Blacks will have a guide to structure their party in their own self interest. When they are not tied to any of the major national parties, there are a number of activities for a Black independent party to consider to gain recognition, respect and political power. First, this will be a vehicle to implement step #9 above, boycott a national election. The new party can use the public platform to recruit membership. Second, Blacks should establish a national planning committee made up of academicians and other Black stakeholders to build upon the base concept of a self-sufficient and competitive Black America. A number of committed Blacks began the framework for a political party at the National Black Political Convention Movement that was held in Gary, Ind. in 1972. This effort did not get off the ground at that time because too many Black attendees believed in the Democratic Party and the integration dream.

Third, while the Black party is building, we must be realistic. Black politicians and leaders will not eagerly jump ship and loose their positions in the political parties, until it is clear that the new Black party is strong. They will need some flexibility, but Black people will seek accountability. There is value in the leaders continuing to affiliate with the major national parties for awhile. They must declare their commitment to Black causes and their intent to join the Black party. They can practice being Black and change direction while negotiating benefits for Black America. When the new party is ready, those who choose should become part of it. Four, after the Black party is operational, Blacks should direct their efforts to register Blacks as independents within a Black party. Fifth, Blacks then inform both the Republican and Democratic parties that they will vote as a solid bloc for their own candidates or party. Or, in the absence of a Black candidate committed to the *PowerNomics* vision for Black America, they will vote for candidates or party that promises to deliver the most. Sixth, Black voters should not identify or announce the candidate they will support for public office until a few days before the election. With that strategy it is not as likely that the bloc vote will be taken for granted. Seventh, Blacks should place candidates for public office on the ballot in all key states. Eighth, Blacks should run strong Black candidates to compete against the other national parties. And finally, Blacks should always vote as a bloc.

A national Black party would give Blacks a strategic and competitive advantage over the established national parties. Black candidates can run and win a national office from an independent party. Voter apathy, both Black and White, is at an all time high. Less than 50 percent of those eligible to vote do in fact, vote. The fastest growing voter categories in America are independent and non-affiliated. A recent poll showed that 36 percent of the electorate in 1992 would have voted for Ross Perot, a candidate for an independent party, if they thought he had a chance to win.

In major elections Black candidates would be major contenders, if Blacks committed to register, turn out and vote at three times our current rate, similar to Jewish voters. Jews are approximately three per cent of the national population, but they come out and vote at a rate that three times greater than any other group. Blacks could have a similar impact if we used the same strategy. Blacks make up approximately 12.4 percent of the population. In national elections, majority White voters split their 80 percent voting populations between the Democrats, Republicans, Reform and Green parties. Normally only 25 percent of Blacks who are eligible actually vote. If all things were equal, each party would receive 20 percent of the votes cast. If all Blacks were members of a National Black party, and if they registered and voted at three times their normal pattern, they would have a major impact on any election. Blacks would get another benefit simply because the existing national parties would be concerned about the potential impact of a Black independent party on an election. They would either court Black voters with more serious intentions of practicing quid pro quo, or they would eliminate some of their existing national parties. Either way, a national Black bloc vote and a Black independent party could serve to highlight our views and give us the benefit of ethno-aggregation in politics.

Once the Black party is established, it should host its own political conventions, especially for the election of the president of the United States. These conventions should be scheduled for the month of June, prior to both the Republican and Democratic conventions, perhaps to commemorate Juneteenth. (Juneteenth celebrations relate to the day Blacks in Texas got the news about the Emancipation Proclamation.) Increasingly Blacks are celebrating that historical event as a national holiday. A convention for an independent party would have the competitive advantage of coming before the other parties, laying a foundation for national issues and setting a political tone. Most Black elected officials and civil rights leaders will be reluctant to identify with or attend any Black party activities because both groups are locked into the Democratic party. With or without them, Black Americans have little choice but to press on in their own best interest.

### Political Action Step #11: Initiate a national leadership renaissance for empowerment-oriented Black leadership.

Black America is in the throes of a full-bloom leadership crisis just when 36 million Black Americans need leadership the most. Black America is poised to slide into political and economic oblivion as a minority-minority in an increasingly pluralistic and competitive society. This is a position of weakness that Black America has to overcome in order to survive and prosper in the 21st Century. Black society must raise up a new and different kind of institutional leadership. This renaissance of leadership must be capable of recognizing the uniqueness of the Black American dilemma, exhibit a strong group identification and maximize the limited resources of Black people, and totally commit to practicing *politics of gaining resources.*

Serving the self-interests of Blacks would be a challenge to many leading and visible Blacks. Since well before the end of slavery, Black leaders played the role of racial diplomats, interpreting Black America's needs and framing the issues for Whites in terms of what is good for everybody. As diplomats, they found it difficult to advocate solely for Blacks. The vacuum in Black leadership is growing in reverse proportion to the deepening socioeconomic crisis of Black America. Though Black America is well on the road to being locked into a permanent underclass by the year 2013, leading Blacks are becoming increasingly irrelevant because they absolutely refuse to practice the politics of resources and race.

Black leadership and their respective organizations are trapped. They have painted themselves into a corner of civil rights and integration. They have been "the hewer of wood and drawer of water" for every aggrieved group for so long that they cannot change roles. Black leadership is being forced to represent all aggrieved groups, even if it is detrimental to their own best interests. Though others practice the politics of gender, ethnicity, culture, class and language, Black leadership is prohibited from practicing the politics of race because nearly all the members of the other groups are classified as "White." Trapped within their own traditions, Black leadership has little choice but to continue minority coalition building and the politics of rights. If practicing the politics of rights reaped great wealth and power benefits, then powerful groups would devote most of their time, energy and resources into this aspect of politics. But, the little attention they do give is solely to contest weak and powerless groups.

There is no question that all Black Americans are indebted to the Black leaders who have fought so hard on behalf of Black America. Throughout this nation's history, most of them struggled and did the best that they could with what they had available to them. But, times have changed. Black Americans' competitors are no longer just White males. They are ethnic, religious, gender, handicapped, language, class and groups concerned about sexual orientation. Black American's competitiveness is weakened by the fact that these groups are allowed to emulate and wrap themselves in Black people's historical experiences so that they can be perceived as being equally as aggrieved as Blacks. This means Blacks must compete for resources where they ought not even have any competitors.

Our new Black leadership will need a group-based vision. It will have to see, without straining, that integration is a tragic failure and is leading Black America into a crisis. It must understand that Blacks are just as impoverished and powerless as ever. But, to make matters worse, Blacks have been stripped of their quasi-communities, businesses, colleges, culture, disposable income and majority minority status in mainstream society, in large measure because of decisions Black leaders made. The Black race is more vulnerable than ever.

Black Americans need the type of committed leadership that they had between 1920 and 1940. During this period, Blacks had great leaders like W. E. B. Du Bois, Carter G. Woodson, Elijah Muhammad, and Marcus Garvey who were proud of being Black and advocated a sense of "public Blackness" for all people of African descent. They did not hide their Black self-interest behind a façade of labels like color-blind, race-neutral, multi-cultural, diversity or minority. They were not like so many Blacks who seek to represent everybody, but their own people.

Most visible Blacks or Blacks aspiring to public office still adhere to the old social etiquette that required Blacks to publicly disavow any group self-interest. The newspapers and magazines are filled with stories about Blacks who espouse a color-blind ideology, but are burdened by race issues. There are stories about Black elected officials who successfully avoided being perceived as a Black candidate who addressed the needs of their Black constituents. Many of the elected officials in these stories are mayors in predominantly Black cities, who boast that they are effectively neutered on race issues. Their indifference to their own people defeats the whole purpose of politics and being elected to hold a public office. How can a Black person justify running for office to represent the majority White society? It was Black people who have lacked political representation and access to public resources and public office for more than 360 years. When Whites make up 99 percent of all public elected officials in America, why would Black elected officials conclude that the majority White society had a greater need for representation than under-represented Blacks?

Blacks holding public office should use the power of the office to address the wealth and resource power inequalities that exist between the races, problems that White office holders do not usually address. Everything else is secondary. If Black socioeconomic issues are not addressed by Black officials or any other Black person who is in a position to assist, then who does have the responsibility in a representative democracy? The primary responsibility of a Black person in a leadership position should be to represent and reflect a cosmetic commitment to his group. Otherwise, the only benefit Black voters can gain from electing a Black person to office is simply the emotional thrill of having a person with Black skin holding public office.

## Political Action Step #12: Adopt a public code of conduct for group accountability.

In politics, the temptation is strong to promise things that cannot be delivered or to sacrifice a constituency group for selfish reasons. Black Americans must devise a group code of conduct, role models and the means to hold people accountable for how they treat Black people. Elected officials should be the first group of whom Blacks demand accountability. It is especially important for them to hold responsible those Blacks who demonstrate more concern for the broader society and its institutions than for the collective interests of Black people. Listed below are some of the strategies Black groups have employed to hold public figures accountable for doing injury to the group:

- Denounced Blacks who displayed inappropriate behavior, staged public protests and labeled them "Sambos."
- Ostracized Blacks who demonstrated inappropriate behavior and imposed social, political and economic sanctions on them.
- Publicized the inappropriate behavior. Some community activists circulated flyers and placed pictures of the offending Blacks on yard signs, posters and walls of shame.
- Presented Hayward Shepherd awards to those who practiced inappropriate behavior. Hayward Shepherd was a Black man who tried to warn the town of Harpers Ferry of John Brown's arrival in town to free the Black slaves. Brown's raiders killed him, but Whites honored Shepherd with a monument.
- Opposed contract awards, jobs, political appointments or public recognition to those who exhibited inappropriate behavior patterns.

Whether or not a community adopts any of the above measures, Blacks should establish organizations that protect the race and hold members accountable for their behavior. Holding people accountable to the Black community will be tough. It is not for the faint of heart.

Blacks must develop a pattern of exacting consequences on those who betray or attempt to profit by imposing pain and suffering on other Black people. This is the only guaranteed way to stop inappropriate political behavior.

## *Conclusion*

Politics is competition for essential resources. Those who play politics to get along, will usually end up "being gotten." The *PowerNomics* political principles direct Blacks to rebuild communities, maintain population numbers, develop competitive human capital, secure resources to support an alternative economy and ensures social justice.

For Blacks to benefit from our bloc vote we must demand that candidates react to Black issues and problems and not convert them to "minority" problems. We should demand that Black leaders be Black and that all those who seek Black votes recognize and respect us as a group to which this nation owes a debt. Politics is played based on group self-interest, not altruism. In our new politics, everybody must be held accountable via an array of rewards and penalties.

# CHAPTER EIGHT

## A New and Expanded Role for Churches

*Man was admonished not to covet his neighbor's wife!*
*Nothing was said about coveting a neighbor's wealth.*

Throughout recorded history, God's words and teachings have been used, and even distorted, to teach that it is wrong to want and have wealth and power. The most often cited scripture was Matthew 19:24 that said, "It is easier for a camel to go through the eye of a needle, than for a rich man to enter into the kingdom of God." This scripture is not anti-wealth. The scripture challenges those who do acquire wealth and power to use it to help those who do not have it. Therefore, it is wealth inequalities and not wealth itself that the scriptures oppose. In accord with scriptural admonishments, the *Power-Nomics* national plan is about acquiring wealth and power then using it to improve the lives of people who have been long denied the joys of a decent quality of life.

This chapter calls for a new and expanded role for those of Black America's 65,000 churches that choose the *PowerNomics* vision. Just as established religions played a central role in institutionalizing Black slavery, modern organized religion can be instrumental in carrying out Biblical instructions and correcting the wealth and power inequities between the races. The Black church community is the only Black institution that successfully survived centuries of slavery, Jim Crow semi-slavery and government-directed benign neglect. With that survival record, they are the most qualified institution to bring wealth and prosperity to an impoverished Black race.

God must surely have intended for Black people to be wealthy and recognized as a special people. Otherwise, why would He have honored them by making them the first humans, established the Garden of Eden in Africa, and made Africa the most resource rich land mass on earth? Why else would the color Black be the dominant and base of all other colors? Though Black people were put upon and enslaved by all nations, religions and ethnic groups, clearly this was not God's original intent. The holy scriptures admonish us to aid the impoverished and despised people of the earth. What group of people are more impoverished and despised around the world than Black people? Surely Black people are some of the most religious people on earth. It is on the basis of this special spirituality that we now challenge Black churches to expand their traditional role and to use the fullness of their status and visibility to come to the aid of Black America. In this chapter, when we use the word "church" it means all Black religious denominations and organizations, and the term "ministers" refers to the leaders of these organizations.

## Black Churches: Our Oldest Economic Institution

The Black church is the only institution over which Blacks have had some reasonable amount of control. They are the oldest and largest Black-owned economic enterprises, holding the highest concentration of Black wealth and social power. These realities alone qualify and position Black churches to play a pivotal role in Black America's building alternative economic structures within its own communities.

For centuries, both Black ministers and their churches performed an important societal function. They were always visible manifestations of Black consciousness, values and spirituality, the one area in which Black people have had our greatest degree of freedom. Despite legalized slavery and Jim Crow semi-slavery, Black churches instilled Black family values and a community code of conduct, guided our emotionalism and spiritual upliftment, cultivated and contained our culture and refined and passed on our musical and artistic talents. Within the community itself, our churches have been very productive. They have trained our civic and political leaders, fought for justice, freedom as well as developed our first mutual aid societies, insurance companies, newspapers and numerous other businesses. With a present annual revenue flow of approximately $50 billion dollars, Black churches remain Black America's largest and oldest mechanism for aggregating wealth and creating businesses. But a 1983 survey of more than 1800 Black clergymen found that only about half supported use of the church to achieve Black political and social change.

CHAPTER EIGHT

## *A Growing Danger*

We are now in a critical post-integration period. Black churches, like Black people, are at risk. The flight of the Black middle-class from inner cities to the suburbs weakened Black churches and left them with smaller congregations, a weaker financial base and a lesser Black orientation. This weakening of the role of Black churches is occurring at the same time that Blacks are losing faith in social integration. Black churches are the last standing truly Black institutions. Just as Black Americans lost their communities, schools, role models, baseball teams and music to social integration, there is great fear that Black churches have also been lost. For centuries, Black people looked to their ministers for knowledge, guidance and insight in spiritual as well as worldly matters. With integrated congregations and ministerial alliances, Black ministers can no loner openly use Black churches to address the needs and concerns of Black people.

## *The Original Role of Black Churches*

Black churches were one of the first tools slave masters used to socially engineer Black people. A slave's exposure to organized religion in this country was limited to accompanying the slave master to Sunday morning services as an attendant or driver. While Colonial laws of 1672 discouraged slaveholders from baptizing Black slaves, Christianity was used to benefit the White masters. In general, slave masters hoped Christianity would encourage slaves to be "Christ-like," render them submissive and obedient, justify Black bondage, and instill internal controls over the hearts and minds of Black slaves. These internal controls were accompanied by self-serving interpretations of the Bible, alleging that Blacks were a cursed people. Many Blacks became so convinced that the world was so full of sin and sorrow, that the sooner they were dead, the better off they would be.

From their inception in the early 1800s, they had the responsibility to focus the aspirations of Black people on "the next life." The Scriptures were used to promote Black inferiority and justify slavery. Once the White power elite selected or approved a Black person to administer to the Black masses, they admonished the ministers to teach that: 1) when the Holy Bible referred to the "slave and master," it was referring to the Black race and the White master here on earth; 2) Blacks were supposed to be hard working, trustworthy, obedient, and humble; and 3) they were to accept their lot in life, postpone worldly pleasures, and look forward to their pie in the sky after death. Essentially, Black churches and Black ministers were approved to induce Blacks into colluding in their own exploitation and subordination.

## On the Positive Side

The use of Biblical scriptures to control and render Black people passive, pliable and accepting has never worked with all Blacks. Instead of using the Bible to teach Blacks to be all forgiving, long-suffering, with a turn the other cheek attitude, some independent Black ministers used the scriptures to embolden Blacks to oppose and escape slavery. They feigned compliance with social policies and instead, preached coded sermons that gave hope to Black slaves. They helped the Black masses by fashioning a different sense of reality within the Christian religion by teaching them to identify with the plight of Jews in the Bible and providing resources to escape slavery. Following the Civil War, many Black ministers, especially those in the African Methodist Episcopal (AME) churches, aggressively asserted their spiritual independence. In the mid 1860s, over 100 ex-slaves walked into St. Paul's AME church in Raleigh, N.C. and demanded that the church help the five million newly freed slaves who were poor, hungry, ignorant, homeless and defenseless. Black churches responded to this and similar demands across the South and provided food and clothing. Within a decade, they used the churches to start banks, newspapers, benevolent societies, insurance companies, burial societies and other Black businesses. Black churches eventually became the repositories of Black culture, music, wealth, and leadership. Most importantly, Black ministers began to use their churches as training grounds for community and business leaders.

## Out-of-the-Box Religious Teaching

Many looked to the Old Testament and identified with Biblical characters such as Moses, Joshua and Samson in their struggles to free their people. They saw aspects of these stories that Whites did not teach. The story of Samson in the Book of Judges provides a particularly inspiring and non-traditional role model for Black religious leaders. The model of Samson obligates Black leaders to be more protective of their Black followers just as Samson was of his fellow Jews.

The story of Samson and Delilah was not just a morality story of a man's betrayal by a woman or about Samson being punished for giving in to the weakness of the flesh. It was a story of a man who God brought into the world with unique strengths and powers. As an instrument of God, Samson loved and championed the causes of his people. But, Samson was not a priest or a man of the cloth. He never saw himself as being perfect. He gambled, drank wine, chased women, and committed violent acts. Samson was a Dannite commissioned to provoke the Philistines and, when necessary, to stand up to them. He was not sent to the Earth to get along with the enemies of his people.

The story of Samson is about unconventional, out-of-the box thinking. The lesson in the story of Samson is that, even when blind, he remained committed to fighting his people's enemies regardless of personal sacrifices he had to make. Today, as in Samson's time, the system that is oppressing Black people stands upon two pillars: 1) a structural economic and political inequality between the races, and 2) the learned inappropriate behavior patterns of Black people. The lesson of the story of Samson is more about commitment than it is about betrayal.

## The Hour Is Late

A great number of societal factors, including the breakdown of the family, deterioration of Black communities, lack of moral standards, increased crime and integration negatively impact Black churches. Integration is one of the most detrimental. Why? Because, to a large degree, integration triggered many of the current social pathologies that are crippling Black communities. Churches also had to respond to changing neighborhoods. Some churches welcomed the newcomers and abandoned their own Blackness. Others welcomed the newcomers into the Blackness of their church and maintained their cultural heritage and orientation. Some White ministers moved into Black neighborhoods and set up churches with Black members. The integration process has already compromised away our music, colleges, businesses, sports teams and communities. By compromising away our Blackness, whether it is inside or outside of the church, we lose our common past and a common future aspiration. We become a people who are blind to reality.

A couple of years ago, while speaking at a community forum in a local high school auditorium in Ohio, a member of the planning committee advised me that a Black minister of one of the city's largest Black churches would not be attending the program. He anticipated that the program would focus on Black issues and "Black rights," and as a minister, his concern was "human rights" not "Black rights." It seems that by focusing on human rights rather than Black rights, the minister implied that Blacks are less than human. Ironically, the first time the phrase "human rights" was made a public issue, was in the 1850s in response to Harriet Beecher Stowe's book, *Uncle Tom's Cabin*. It was later that human rights, like the concepts of minority and race, was expanded and watered-down to include nearly everybody but Black people. Unfortunately, this minister is not unique. There are hundreds of Black ministers who have similar attitudes and avoid Black rights and Black people.

Though the racial inequalities created by slavery and Jim Crow segregation continue to exist, apparently many ministers feel some obligation to protect White society's feelings by avoiding racial matters. Some do not. There are two notable exceptions. On the West Coast, Dr. Frederick K.C. Price, Pastor of Crenshaw Christian Center in Los Angeles delivered a phenomenal year-long series of lectures on *Race, Religion and Racism*, which he later published as a book by the same name. Dr. Price approached the problems of race in the church with scholarship, integrity and in an effort to educate. He chastised various religions on their institutionalized racism. On the East Coast, in Washington, D.C., Dr. Earl Trent, the pastor of Florida Avenue Baptist Church is equally committed. Dr. Trent teaches about the role of Blacks in the Bible, but he also focuses on economic development within the church. He works to save his people and his community. The church is buying property and building Black-owned businesses.

But, many Black ministers are afraid to be Black. They are often dependent upon non-Blacks for supplemental incomes, political appointments and government grants. To protect their relationship with the majority society, they avoid anything that is identifiably Black and willingly sell out their people, whether for extra income or special recognition from Whites or simply out of ignorance. Whatever the reason, the harm to Blacks cannot be erased. A case in point is a business alliance formed by five of the nation's largest Black churches in the late 1990s called the Revelation Corporation of America. According to reports, a White businessman from Memphis helped the churches create the alliance. Predominantly White-owned businesses would sell their products to Black Americans at a discount through these churches. Both the White-owned businesses as well at the businessman who helped establish the alliance stood to make substantial profits. Black ministers earned about 12 percent commission for steering consumer dollars out of Black communities and into the coffers of White and other non-Black businesses. This economic model is not in the self interest of Blacks. It directed dollars away from Black businesses, and to White and Korean-owned businesses. This alliance followed the historical pattern of using Black consumer dollars to make Whites and others wealthy, dropping a few crumbs to Blacks along the way. Alliances of this type allowed Whites and Korean businessmen to take over the Black funeral home industry, just as they engineered the recent takeover of the Black hair care industry and Black music industry. It is inappropriate for Black churches and Black ministers to allow themselves to be used as "hunt dogs" by those who want to exploit Black consumers.

## Expanding the Role of Black Churches

As this nation enters the 21st century, Black America needs unconventional, out-of-the box thinking from its Black ministers and their respective churches on ways they can expand the traditional role of the Black church to include an emphasis of Black empowerment. The annual revenue flow in Black Churches is twice as large as the total revenue of all of Black-owned businesses. *PowerNomics* calls on Black ministers to use their respective churches to do what they did over a century ago—commit themselves to improve the quality of life for Black people by reducing the racial, wealth and power inequality. Those who choose this commitment should join together in a demonstration of ethno-aggregation, step forward, and like Samson, place their collective hands upon the great pillars that support the inequalities and push until they overcome the corrupted spiritual, economic and political structure that has entrapped Black people. Churches can act as a catalyst for change and function as a social glue that holds Black America together, while teaching how to economically and politically compete as a group.

What should Black churches do? First, they should begin espousing a new Black spirituality that promotes community building, both in terms of physical structures and in the sense of people-hood. As active community builders, Black churches can influence nearly every aspect of Black life. They can reach out and apply *PowerNomics* principles to rebuild the physical communities, local economies, public and private school systems, and most importantly, give Black people an expanded base for their spirituality. The distinction between Blacks as "religious" versus Blacks as "spiritual" is important. Black people can be spiritual even without belonging to a particular church. Those who are spiritual may not regularly attend a church, but do believe in the existence of God, and feel religion is important in their lives. Many would be attracted to church affiliation by religious institutions that are reformed and more committed to the Black community.

The challenge for Black churches is to prepare Black people to compete and prosper here on Earth. Not all Black churches will be able to accept this challenge.

Since wealth and power follow the numbers, Black America needs its churches to expand their philosophical and program boundaries to include as many Black people as possible, whether members or not. Churches that choose to accept the challenge will retain their religious leadership but expand it to include civic activities and challenge America's structural inequalities. The following 10 principles offer guidance to Black churches committed to expanding their traditional role and encouraging Black Americans toward self-sufficiency based on competitive self-interests.

### Action Step #1: Incorporate a new focus around Blacks, the Original People

With the exception of Black people, all races of mankind claim and practice their own religion. Other population groups enjoy the decided advantage of ascribing to religious philosophies, doctrines, and cultures that link them, in a positive way, to an omnipotent being. Black people suffer the double disadvantage of having been given various religions, such as Islam, Christianity, Judaism and Hinduism, then subsequently relegated to and perceived as guest worshippers in the religion. This should never have happened. Black people hold a special place in Biblical history and we miss the boat when failing to claim that special place. It is difficult, if not impossible, to be respected and appreciated when religions of which you are a part, teach Black inferiority and condemnation.

Now is the time for Black churches in America to use their spiritual and cultural inheritance to promote the interests of Black Americans. Black ministers can use our spiritual history and reclaim our rightful place as "the first humans on earth." Just as Jewish people claim to be, the "chosen people," and American Indians claim to be "Native Americans," Black people can lay claim to being both religiously and biologically the "first humans" or the "original people" on earth.

Moreover, Africa is "the birthplace of all mankind." These ancestral claims are important because they set precedents and demonstrate that Black people have an historical importance and deserve respect that is not reflected in today's society. Recent DNA studies found a genetic link between the priests of the tribe of Levi and a group of Blacks in the Middle East whose religious practices and oral traditions had tied them to the Levites for centuries. We are the *ancestors* of all people—Whites, Asians, American Indians and Hispanics. When Black churches and Black ministers illuminate and teach these racial and religious truths, they make important contributions to truth and to reversing erroneous church teachings.

## Action Step #2: Develop and instill a group code of conduct

For the sake of group stability and functionality, every group or society should have an organization whose primary responsibility is the promotion of its social cohesiveness, values, norms, conformity and way of life. Black churches in aggregate are the logical institution to assume the responsibility to develop and instill a code of conduct in Black America. This group code of conduct should be based on two assumptions, which can best be taught by Black churches. First, to overcome Willie Lynchism and build unity, Black churches should teach their members that God has assigned them to a skin color team. And when the team loses, everyone on the team will lose regardless of their education, income or social status. Second, churches can teach Blacks to love and support the group to which they belong and never treat other people better than they treat their own people. Such group commitments would lay a solid foundation of acceptable behavior upon which Blacks can begin to empower ourselves through group economics and group politics.

White America and other ethnic groups have a code of conduct that defines the role and place of Black people. Without our own code of conduct that teaches us how to support, love and care for members of our own group, we would have no recourse but to continue to accept the majority society's code of conduct, which is not in our best interests. The majority society's code of conduct accommodates its needs. It is based on European beliefs and values, especially in White culture, superiority and individualism. Their code of conduct advantages them while our lack of a code of conduct disadvantages us. Their religious institutions develop, promulgate and enforce codes of behavior. As we build communities, our churches are the most appropriate institution to develop a code of conduct specific to our race and our communities. The code of conduct should require us to fully respect and support one another for common goals of the race.

With a code of conduct, we have a way to judge when we are working against our own best interests. This is especially true in regards to inappropriate behavior patterns. The Black churches are the ideal institutions to develop and promulgate standards of behavior. They are in contact with a great number of Black Americans, and for the first time, we could have an orchestrated effort to recondition our behavior and teach us how we should interact with other members of our primary group and communities.

The code should include a mechanism that rewards those who help and punishes those who mislead the race. If we do not offer rewards and recognition, our leaders will seek it from other groups. The code of conduct should incorporate the group's need to hold individuals, organizations and others accountable for the effects of their behavior on the group. Before the birth of Jesus Christ, mankind had the Ten Commandments. Since that time every society has established governments and enacted laws primarily to protect the dominant group and to make their communities safe. Most of those laws are not designed for the benefit of a Black minority.

Black churches may be able to devise a code of conduct, but are there examples of other cultures that have orchestrated a change in group behavior? Let's look at a society that has many of the values that we would like to have in our communities, once they are built. The Japanese and other Asian communities are group-oriented cultures that offer instructive models for ways to structure a code of conduct that binds a group together while promoting group competitiveness and tranquil communities. Their group-based values are rooted in Confucianism, which is more of a code of conduct than a religion. Confucianism is a system of ethics and education that stresses love of family and ancestor worship. As a part of the Asian code of conduct, Confucianism is taught in their schools and churches in most Asian communities. Black Americans could benefit from the aspect of Asian culture that supports group self-interest, and places a high value on group competitiveness.

Japan is particularly instructive because it made a purposeful cultural transition. Prior to World War II, Japan was a state-oriented society, and not a group-or family-oriented society. Their emotional and physical loyalties were totally devoted to the national government. Even more than White Americans, they were very individualistic with blind patriotism and a militaristic mind-set. With their defeat in World War II, the Japanese discarded many of those characteristics and replaced them with philosophies of Confucianism. Their new orientation sought to make Japanese society a cohesive group of families, friends and communities. They conceived new ideologies that taught them how to respect each other and work together for the common good of the group. This ethical code of conduct was articulated by the religious community and incorporated into the public policy of all of Japan's institutions. It shortly became standard operating procedures for "the state." If a code of conduct can have such a powerful impact that it turned the Japanese society away from individualism and blind patriotism, then it has potential for Blacks to build a sense of togetherness and to instill values of respect, trust, support and care for each other.

## Action Step #3: Build a Black alliance across religious denominations

It is self-defeating shades of Willie Lynchism for Blacks to build self-contained economic and political bases that do not transcend church property lines or denominational lines. Black ministers should remember that Black people were not enslaved and segregated because of their religious denominations or because of the church they attended. They were subordinated and exploited because of their group skin color. Therefore, any efforts to aid Black people should place skin color before religious denomination. Black religious organizations that subscribe to the *PowerNomics* goals of a self-sufficient and competitive Black community should form together into a national network or alliance. Black people have lost their historical religious identity and are scattered across nearly every religious denomination or sect. Black people's original religion was ancestor worship, just as in the Asian and Egyptian societies. All other religious denominations were given to Black people by White masters and overseers. The goal of the alliance should be group unity in dealing with racial problems even while there are differences in religious dogma.

The body could also serve to more fully develop a national empowerment plan for religion. One of the first elements it should look at is a sensitive but crucial issue of deficits in Black America - the lack of a national mechanism to make contacts and raise funds to support critical issues and events for Black people.

Here is a wish list of causes that a religious alliance could support with fund raising:

**Fund raiser #1** should be a legal fund. This fund would develop and file legal actions in the various court systems to achieve *PowerNomics* goals through complaints, challenges or lawsuits that address the lost legal and economic rights of Black Americans and other critical issues. Heading the list would be legal efforts to reclaim the 14th Amendment, reverse the Dred Scott decision, and initiate reparations lawsuits to recover some financial remuneration from thousands of government and private entities that have deprived Blacks of our rights, wealth and lives.

**Fund raiser #2** should be a land tax certificate program and land bank. The primary purposes of land program would be to:

- Halt the loss of Black-owned land through public auctions or failure or inability to pay public property taxes.
- Create a Black land bank through which Blacks could either save, buy or sell their lands and keep land within the Black race. The bank would monitor tax rolls, especially in the South, and either purchase the tax certificates on delinquent taxes or lend the money to Black land owners to pay taxes. The property inventory would be available to Blacks seeking to develop either urban or rural agricultural lands.

**Fund raiser #3** would provide educational funds, through either scholarships or grants to Black youth seeking post-high school education and training. The primary purposes of the education program ought to be to:

- Link formal religion and spirituality with educational achievement by providing educational options that reflect the *PowerNomics* Vision from nursery school through graduate school.
- Provide funds to Black youth who want to direct their efforts to achieve the *PowerNomics* vision for Black America and specialize in skill areas such as business, economic research, computer sciences, math, engineering and physics for post-secondary education or vocational internships that will help develop group economics or politics.

Funding programs similar to these above would bring Black churches and their ministers back into the Black empowerment equation. How much money should and could a Black religious alliance systematically raise? The design of the fund by the alliance would reflect the degree of commitment by the church and its members. If we look at a simplistic example of ethnic aggregation resources, however, we can get some sense of scope. There are 10 million Blacks who attend church regularly. If just 25 percent of them elected to support the *PowerNomics* vision and contributed $1.00 a week, the alliance could raise approximately $130 million dollars per year. This would be a massive amount of economic clout for a modest investment. A dollar a week is less than what we would spend on one evening at the movies or for a music CD. Ethno aggregation across denomination lines would give the religious alliance a meaningful and powerful role, cover the costs of the important programs and signal to the world that Black America is taking care of its own.

A national Black religious alliance could also serve as a major distribution network for Black products and services. As distribution outlets, Black America's 65,000 churches could draw income and compete with most of our language, ethnic and gender networks.

## Action Step #4: Teach Black Economic Prosperity

Since Black ministers have long held a monopoly on Black American spirituality, they should use it to economically enhance the quality of life for an impoverished Black America. Black churches have a long history of abetting the conditioning of Blacks to believe that there is something virtuous and noble about being poor, downtrodden or the impoverished underdog. Biblical scriptures condemned the "love of money." It does not condemn money. When Jews began migrating to this country in the latter part of the 19th century, nearly all of them were poor and impoverished. Their synagogues became the source of group unity. When Jewish children were young, the synagogues and the families taught the value of seeking out and buying from those in their own group. The synagogues taught their families the importance of gaining wealth, religious tithing, understanding and practicing capitalism, building Jewish-owned and controlled schools, supporting the family and community, and using wealth to protect their homelands. Today, as a group, Jews are wealthy and politically powerful.

Through preaching and teaching, churches could establish a value within their respective congregations for a moral obligation to acquire sufficient wealth and power to support our families, our church, our race and ourselves. The parable of the master and the slave in *Matthew 25:14* is instructive. The scripture tells the story of a master who gave each of his three slaves a different amount of money before going on a journey. He instructed them to protect his money. When he returned from his trip, he called each slave to report how well he had done with his money. The first two slaves reported they had sizably increased the original amount they had been given. The third slave, however, reported that out of fear, he had buried his money and failed to produce a profit. The master was furious. He took back what he had given that slave and cast him out. The lesson for Black

America is that Blacks should take whatever money or wealth they have been given by God and increase it. If we are to follow Biblical responsibilities, we must have wealth. Churches can teach a Biblical view of wealth and it must be used to do what God intended.

Expanding the role of Black churches begins with teaching Black America to acquire wealth and power, and how to use it appropriately. Poor people cannot help poor people. The amount of financial support received by the church is directly related to the financial condition of church members. Without it, the ministers cannot raise enough money to keep the church solvent and perform their religious work.

In the context of our vertical integration paradigm, Black churches and the cultural gifts they produce—music, songs, and dance—can provide the basis for alternative economic structures. We can produce and sell Black consumer products within Black America that are primarily designed for Black consumers, but can also be sold to the mainstream consumer. Look at the history of Black music and song. As stated earlier, Blacks have produced a wide range of musical forms, from Dixieland and jazz to rhythm n' blues and gospel, all of which have had popular appeal for centuries. Black music represents an important acculturation of Blackness into the majority society and the world. It illustrates the way Blacks, as a group, can surge outward and compete in the larger society, while simultaneously retaining our own culture, people-hood, and Blackness. While Black music can be the base of commercial products to jump-start a vertical industry, the same thing can happen with other products. In all instances, the Black church can aggregate and distribute products derived from Black cultural gifts and strengths. But, if we whiten our churches and our culture, we run the risk of losing a major mechanism for addressing the unique problems, history, and socioeconomic needs of Black people.

## Action Step #5: Operate the church as an educational and instructional center

Black churches could serve as community centers for health services, employment opportunities, leadership and business training, especially for the growing Black underclass who feel abandoned and confused about what its role is in today's America. Churches should ally with families and schools to share this social burden. This burden falls primarily on the shoulders of the church because nearly all other institutions within Black neighborhoods are dysfunctional, and various levels of government have disavowed any responsibility to aid this segment of the Black community.

It would be helpful if Black churches would teach to enlighten rather than preach to excite. All too often, our Black congregations go to church simply to get excited and to walk away feeling good. Most Blacks need more in their daily lives. They need to be knowledgeable of the skills that would allow them to negotiate the economic and political world outside of the church. Churches could develop educational programs to educate Black youth and adults by teaching them economic principles and capitalism from the pulpit and in Sunday schools. Black children should be taught the nature of a capitalistic democracy and the role of group economics. Churches can do this in the context of their dogma. In the early years, children ought to be trained to support their own people first. They should see those principles in operation in church activities. Teaching these values to Black children is not teaching them to dislike any other group. The issue is who Black people are for and not who they are against.

Once these principles are taught in the nursery schools they should follow through in high schools, independent and religious school policies, or special trade or apprentice programs that complement the regular public schools. A supportive group spirit of unity must be instilled in Black children in their early years. As they grow, they'll know how to respect themselves and each other and how to stay in their communities to seek out Black businesses for goods and services.

Religious or church charter schools could offer Black children intensive, specialized training that would support community building or vertical integration in economics or politics. They could offer courses of study such as environmental sciences, business and industrial management, community-based wealth building and productivity, personal investing and saving, marine sciences, computer sciences and bionics. At another level, churches should also focus on educating and instructing adults in the skills they need for building and supporting new *PowerNomics* communities. Churches could help parents and other adults learn how to be self-sufficient and competitive by building Black communities, practicing ethno-aggregation and vertical integration, and commercializing Black culture through business development and inculcating a code of conduct.

Many Black churches in such cities as Washington, D.C., New York, Detroit and Los Angeles are well into developing church-owned business projects. The most frequent projects are the ones that provide social services such as nursery schools, nursing homes, senior citizens homes, low-income housing, florist shops and food service programs for seniors. They have made a start. Others have progressed a little further and have begun to invest in more substantial business projects. They are beginning to build commercial office space for professional services and retail outlets. One church in Michigan invested its money in a potato chip plant, a meat processing factory and cookie companies. Profits from the operation of these businesses flow into the church's coffers and enabled the church to purchase additional land upon which they built a chartered school for the local Black community.

## Action Step #6: Use the church to attract and hold wealth

Black communities have long suffered a scarcity of wealth and income-producing resources needed to be competitive. We are getting beaten: first by competitors who impede wealth and income from entering Black communities, and also by internal agents who abet the flight of wealth and income resources out of Black communities. Black America has not had a benefactor with the potential to reverse the outflow of resources from Black communities. Black churches, however, have the potential power to stop the capital drain from the Black communities. Black ministers and their respective churches have enormous socioeconomic potential for power because they can attract and hold wealth.

Black America reportedly has $500 billion in annual disposable income. To understand the power of that statistic, imagine the capabilities Black religious organizations would have if just 10 percent of that money, approximately $50 billion, were given to churches in a one lump sum payment. Even though it is not a lump sum payment that is in fact what Black churches take-in annually, this amount of money represents three times the gross receipts of Black America's nearly

500,000 businesses. If this $50 billion in tithes and other contributions were kept within the Black community and made to pass through the hands of eight to twelve Blacks, it would nearly equate to *the total annual disposable income of Black America*. Money of this magnitude could easily foster economic growth if Black churches conducted the majority of their business with Black companies. Today, unfortunately that is not the case. Nearly 99 percent of money spent by Black churches passes into the White community through mortgage payments, insurance premiums, printing expenses, maintenance, utilities and so forth. Nearly every collected penny is deposited into a White bank. Once a church pays off a mortgage, a new building fund is usually initiated, to construct or purchase another building as the church tracks White flight into the suburbs.

Black ministers and their churches could attract and hold wealth by establishing faith-based businesses such as mortgage and insurance companies, church-owned lending institutions, paper supply and printing companies, funeral homes, travel agencies, and choir robe manufacturing companies. They can increase the wealth ownership of Black people by exposing their congregation to wealth-building opportunities in Black communities in general, and by offering entrepreneurial and business development training, financial planning and business networking.

The role that Black churches should play in a *PowerNomics* national plan should be just the opposite of the Revelation Corporation example we looked at earlier. The Revelation program aggregated Black dollars to enrich others and aided Koreans and Whites to take over the Black funeral home business, paying commissions to Black ministers for referrals. On the other hand, when Black churches use their collective resources to attract dollars into Black-owned businesses and Black communities, they become ethno-aggregation agents. They could help keep dollars in the Black community with promotional campaigns to both educate and reward Blacks for making our dollars bounce eight to twelve times in Black hands before leaving the Black community.

## Action Step #7: Establish church-based lending programs

Every Monday morning, Black churches typically deposit approximately $1 billion in White-owned banks across America. In most instances, these are the very same banks from which Black people, as well as Black churches and Black businesses, have a difficult time securing loans. These deposits represent three times the amount of money produced and deposited by Black businesses in Black or White banks. Churches could establish banks, savings and loans, credit unions, or loan funds designed to provide business and personal loans to Black businesses. This would provide capital pools for our aspiring business people while the church-owned lending entities profit from the interest and fees on the loans.

Black churches are needed also as key players in the industrialization of Black communities. They should participate in and help administer the Black Business Investment Corporations (BBICs) proposed in Chapter Six. The proposed BBICs would be direct links between the developing industries, related supportive businesses and the Black communities. The Black churches could benefit by being involved in the leadership and also could profit from the interest paid on loans to a large number of Black businesses within the vertically integrated industries. Churches would be members along with other key groups, such as traditional lenders, civic organizations, business executives, academics, elected officials and investment club representatives. Smaller church-sponsored capital pools could also be created. Church investment clubs, for instance, could also function as alternative sources of business financing. Smaller churches should be encouraged to join in and pool their lending capital together with larger religious institutions.

At some point in the future, after we have some experience under our belts, the free loan concept used by Jewish lenders could be a model for distressed Black communities. Administered through associations, these loans do not require interest payments. The concept embodies civic and religious traditions that combine social service commitments to economic development for the poorest people. The loans are made in the belief that a loan is preferable to charity. Black churches, especially the larger ones, could start modified versions of Jewish free loan associations.

## Action Step #8: Provide social and community services

God commanded his followers to take care of the poor, not to become the poor. In America, Blacks are so disproportionately poor that being Black is almost synonymous with being poor. Even as the entire Black community begins to lift up, those who are economically and socially depressed will need increased social services from Black churches. If a Black minister builds the biggest church in the world with the largest congregation, it contributes nothing if the church does not render social and community services to Black people. It is important that Black churches expand their ministries into the communities and engage in projects that lighten some of the suffering of all Black Americans.

Like Jews, Chinese, Arabs and other ethnic groups in America, we should begin to take care of our own as we begin to build a strong sense of community. Either within our own programs or in cooperation with community organizations, Black churches are encouraged to refashion established public policies and programs. *PowerNomics* principles should be incorporated into them so that they address the needs and predicaments of Black Americans. With limited funds and lots of commitment, we could craft programs that run parallel to traditional public welfare systems, such as food assistance and stamp programs, farmers' cooperatives, rent subsidy programs and mortgage buy-downs. We need a network of churches that would eventually provide sufficient services for all of our Black inner cities.

As religious schools mature and incorporate vocational work experiences into the curriculum, churches could aid the local high schools by creating work opportunities for student enterprises within the congregation or the local business community. They could even take on the role of guiding students who want to save money for neighborhood businesses in support of the vertical industries within public housing or other neighborhoods. A creative housing director could seek alliances with local churches to cooperatively establish business development funds. Farmers' markets, repair shops, janitorial, landscaping and delivery services are examples of the types of businesses that could be started with joint support among creative and enterprising churches, schools, government or community businesses.

## Action Step #9: Establish a network of protective organizations

Based upon the historical treatment of Black people in this country and around the world, Black Americans need a national organization or network of secret societies whose sole purpose would be to protect Black people from physical and political-economic abuse. The need for such organizations are included under religion because the majority society's organizations, whether the Ku Klux Klan, The Knights of the Camellia, Black Horse Brigade, or simply the ultra-right wing Moral Majority all had direct church links. They all laid claims to some religious dogma to justify the society's commitments to protecting their people and way of life. On the government side, the majority society uses agencies such as the FBI, to maintain the status quo for the power elite. As an outside group in the current status quo, Blacks need to establish organizations similar to those established by Jews such as the American Jewish Congress. The mission of this organization is: 1) to safeguard the welfare and security of Jews in the United States, Israel and throughout the world; 2) to strengthen the basic principles of pluralism as the best defense against anti-Semitism and other forms of bigotry; and 3) to enhance the quality of American Jewish life. Note that these organizations are very specific about who they are supporting and protecting. They say nothing about "all denominations" or "minority religions." Unlike Black civil rights organizations, Jewish organizations make no pretense about their priority for their own group.

After more than four centuries of slavery and Jim Crow semi-slavery, Black Americans have both the justification and motivation for such security organizations, even more so than Jews. Every population has not only a right but an obligation to protect itself. Therefore, Black America should have a national organization or network of organizations to: 1) function as a research and policy organization that analyzes and interprets political and economic issues for Black America; 2) overtly provide information and advocate for key Black communities through the United States, Caribbean Islands, Brazil and Sub-Sahara African nations; 3) monitor and raise the awareness of Black Americans about the activities of anti-Black and terrorist groups; 4) challenge immigration laws that are closed and make Black Americans a permanent minority; 5) encourage political dialogue and economic alliances between all Dispersed African Blacks; 6) challenge the dissemination of slavery and Jim Crow semi-slavery revisionism in print and electronic media; and 7) identify and expose liberal and conservative Sambos whose activities endanger Black people. Similar defense organizations ought to be established in all Black nations; and 8) Black America needs a monitoring organization that tracks right wing conservative organizations and reports their activities to every level of Black America. The suggested organizations ought to be religious-based and supported by the combined efforts of Black churches and Black businesses.

## *Conclusion*

Churches in America helped to establish a foundation that supported slavery. Black churches were established to keep Blacks pacified and under control. But, like those early independent ministers who used their churches to help their people escape slavery, *PowerNomics* calls on those religious organizations to be agents of change to empower Black America today. Many religions are represented in Black communities and there is a role for all of them. *PowerNomics* does not ask that religious differences be set aside, it asks instead that we work together on common ground to establish and strengthen communities. In so doing, we strengthen ourselves and the Black religious organizations to which we belong.

The many roles for churches presented here are suggestions based upon our need, history and analysis of issues. Church leaders have to work together to fine tune these suggestions and shape them so that they are practical. Some are functions in which churches should take the lead. Other functions are ones in which the churches should work cooperatively with other institutions. Not all churches will venture from their comfortable niches to work toward this vision, but there will be many rewards for those who do.

# *Epilogue*

*PowerNomics* is a missing link between the historical analysis of the problems facing Black America and the strategies needed to resolve those problems. My drive to understand why Black people live such difficult lives and are betrayed and mistreated by all elements of society is personal. God has assigned me to a skin color team, but I do not like to be on a losing team. I want Black people all over the earth to live healthy, comfortable and enjoyable lives. Black people are so marginalized that most of them spend every waking hour of their lives, aware of their Blackness, always on guard and alert for the traps, pitfalls and threats they must avoid to survive and perhaps get a few steps ahead. After 19 generations, Black people deserve to enjoy life and they deserve justice. To fashion solutions that lead to those outcomes, I researched and analyzed historical facts and current events to identify those factors that are injurious to Blacks, then I drew from my background and experience to design *Power-Nomics.*

As a practical matter, *PowerNomics* starts where we are as a society. I know that Black people have made this country strong. I also understand that racism is so embedded in our system that, rightly or wrongly, we will have to change our own reality and our actions will only work if they are race specific. Some from other races will help, but no other group will take up our cause. But, this *is* our country and this is where we must make our stand.

I hope the reader understands that for Blacks to challenge the concepts of immigration, minority, diversity and multi-cultural does not mean that we are against other groups. It does mean that we expect concentric circles of justice and that the people who built this country, Black people, should be at the center of the circle. We are the nation's oldest and most patriotic population group. Ninety-nine percent of all Black people were here before 99 percent of all other population groups arrived. What is owed to us has never been acknowledged nor paid. We are the people who built the foundation of the greatest country on earth. We should receive the benefits of our work and that of our ancestors, before those benefits are extended to newcomers.

*PowerNomics* was written with the fervent desire that with a plan, Black people who see the problem will work together toward a new vision and change reality for themselves and their children. Now that the plan has been presented, those who want purposeful change will have to make a substantial intellectual investment. Purposeful change will require reading, critical thinking and careful evaluation.

We must understand the underlying reasons for the problem in order to design solutions that will take us where we need to go. Those who make that intellectual investment and accept the challenge of change will become the new leaders. This book was not written for those who do not see the problem. *PowerNomics* is offered as a start, a beginning point for those who are ready to begin.

Black people will have to be careful. There will come those who want to maintain the status quo and will try to lead Blacks the wrong way. They may adopt some of the *PowerNomics* principles or use the language, concepts and suggested activities to promote a color-blind or race-neutral society or to extend the concept to "everybody." They will intentionally seek to mislead, confuse and sidetrack Black people just as some did during the civil rights movement. They will use the same words but attach their own meaning, objectives and target populations. Black people will have to be intellectually vigilant to recognize the tricksters. Some will be White and some will be Blacks who do not choose to be Black and do not accept the vision of an empowered Black America. Some will be conservative and others will be liberal. Their intent will be the same—to thwart change.

Writing this book was my moral responsibility and commitment to help resolve this nation's long standing racial problem. This book was written out of love for my people and the hope that Black people will change their own reality. Those who read this book have a choice to be moved to action or entertained. May you glean something positive from this book and put it to good use.

It is important to note that *PowerNomics* is a term that is trademarked. The *PowerNomics Corporation of America, Inc.* will allow only those whose efforts reflect the specific set of principles presented in this book to use the term *PowerNomics*.

# APPENDIX A

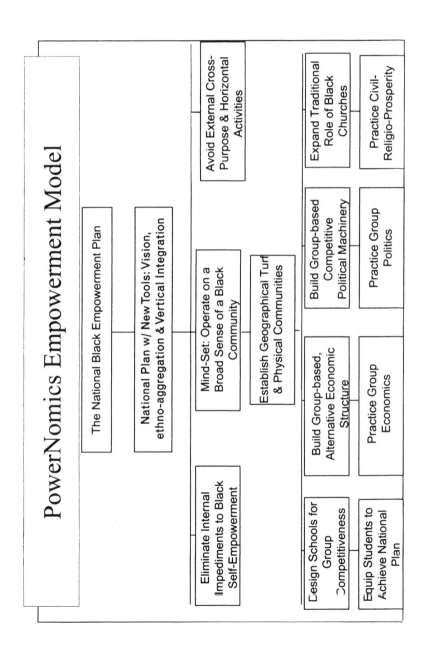

## PowerNomics Empowerment Model

- The National Black Empowerment Plan
- National Plan w/ New Tools: Vision, ethno-aggregation & Vertical Integration
- Eliminate Internal Impediments to Black Self-Empowerment
- Mind-Set: Operate on a Broad Sense of a Black Community
- Avoid External Cross-Purpose & Horizontal Activities
- Establish Geographical Turf & Physical Communities
- Build Group-based Competitive Political Machinery
- Expand Traditional Role of Black Churches
- Practice Group Politics
- Practice Civil-Religio-Prosperity
- Design Schools for Group Competitiveness
- Build Group-based, Alternative Economic Structure
- Equip Students to Achieve National Plan
- Practice Group Economics

# APPENDIX B

*The National Reparations Plan*

## Schema to Secure Black Reparations

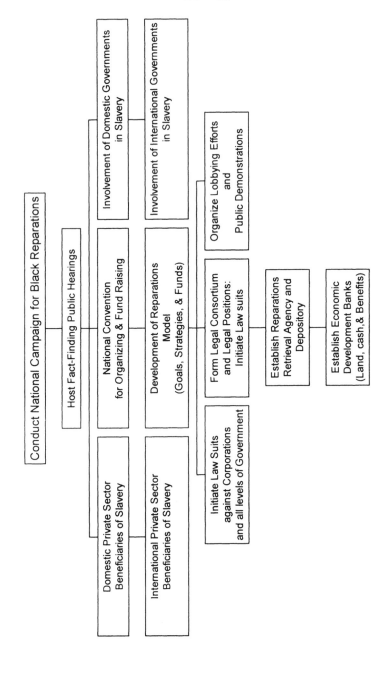

# APPENDIX C

## *AIDS and Wealth*

There is a direct relationship between "pecking order" poverty and powerlessness and major health problems such as AIDS and other "emerging" diseases. On their present course, with the devastation of AIDS, famine, civil war and natural disasters, some scholars predict that up to half of Blacks in Africa may perish by the year 2013.

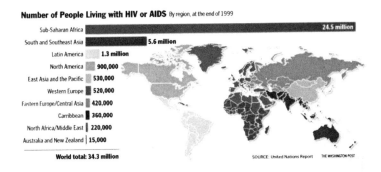

**Number of People Living with HIV or AIDS** By region, at the end of 1999

| Region | |
|---|---|
| Sub-Saharan Africa | 24.5 million |
| South and Southeast Asia | 5.6 million |
| Latin America | 1.3 million |
| North America | 900,000 |
| East Asia and the Pacific | 530,000 |
| Western Europe | 520,000 |
| Eastern Europe/Central Asia | 420,000 |
| Carribbean | 360,000 |
| North Africa/Middle East | 220,000 |
| Australia and New Zealand | 15,000 |

**World total: 34.3 million**

SOURCE: United Nations Report    THE WASHINGTON POST

**Reprinted by permission of the *Washington Post*, 2000**

Number of People Living with HIV or AIDS—Year 2000

# *APPENDIX D*

## *PowerNomics Assessment Checklist*

Working toward the *PowerNomics* vision of a self-sufficient and competitive Black America requires behavior changes, new accountability and unity of purpose. Most of the efforts by Blacks and others who target Blacks do not now lead to that end.

You can use the checklist below as a template to help assess the extent to which any particular program, policy, or activity proposed or targeted to Blacks, meets the criteria of *PowerNomics*. If the answer to the question in the left column is "no", the issue/leader/program being assessed will not lead to the *PowerNomics* vision. Use the last column to note the comparisons between the issue/leader/program and the *PowerNomics* vision and principles.

| Question | Yes | No | Comments |
|---|---|---|---|
| 1. Do the issues/programs/leaders focus on Black Rights and economic integration instead of social integration and civil rights? | | | |
| 2. Do the issues/programs/leaders acknowledge that Blacks are the only group that does not have a single community in America and without communities they cannot build group wealth? | | | |
| 3. Are the issues/programs/leaders responding to a national political and economic empowerment plan for Black Americans? | | | |
| 4. Do the social and economic issues/programs that Blacks are asked to support create vertical movement instead of horizontal activity at cross-purposes to Black development? | | | |
| 5. Do the issues/programs result in making the Black community and its sense of community stronger? | | | |
| 6. Do the issues/programs/leaders aggregate Black dollars to make Black people, not others, wealthy? | | | |
| 7. Do the issues/program/leaders circulate Blacks' annual $500 billion of disposable dollars in Black businesses within their own community? | | | |

| Question | Yes | No | Comments |
|---|---|---|---|
| 8. Does the person/program/organization seeking support from Black Americans demonstrate commitment to quid pro quo support for Black reparations? | | | |
| 9. Does the issue/program/leader understand and acknowledge that structural racism and inappropriate behavior are the major two impediments to Black empowerment? | | | |
| 10. Does the issue/program/leader acknowledge the unique history of Blacks and refer to them as distinct from other minority groups? | | | |
| 11. In coalition building do programs/issues/leaders who advance immigrants, multi-cultural, cultural diversity, and minorities demonstrate and support Blacks becoming a self-sufficient and competitive group? | | | |
| 12. Do politicians and candidates who proclaim to be color-blind deliver the same financial and other favors to Blacks as they do to Hispanics, American Indians and other minority groups?<br><br>Did you check? | | | |
| 13. Do the issues/programs/policies Blacks are asked to support aid Black communities to capture or build industries? | | | |
| 14. Does your school's curriculum equip Black children to earn both a life and a living at the completion of high school? | | | |
| 15. Do the schools in your community address racial realities and prepare children to appreciate and respect the Black community? | | | |
| 16. Does your community have a public forum for interviewing political candidates, asking them what they will do for Black people directly, and mechanisms for holding them accountable? | | | |
| 17. Does your minister teach a theology of economics and Black prosperity here on earth? | | | |
| 18. Does your church draw money into Black communities then hold it to invest in Black businesses and industries? | | | |

APPENDIX D

| Question | Yes | No | Comments |
|---|---|---|---|
| 19. Do the issues/programs/leaders develop wealth capital and business opportunities so that Blacks can be job producers instead of job seekers? | | | |
| 20. Do issues/programs/leaders direct their efforts to developing Black communities instead of neighborhoods? | | | |

# *NOTES AND REFERENCES*

### Acknowledgements

1. Woodson, Carter Godwin. *The Mis-Education of the Negro.* (Trenton, N.J.:Africa World Press, Inc., 1933)

### Introduction

1. Goldhagen, Daniel Jonah. *Hitler's Willing Executioners.* (New York: Alfred A. Knoph, 1996)

### Chapter 1: Racism, Monopolies and Inappropriate Behavior

1. Lerner, Gerda. *Why History Matters.* (New York: Oxford University Press, 1997) 184.

2. Jacobson, Matthew Frye. *Whiteness of a Different Color.* (Mass.: Harvard University Press, 1998) 108-111.

3. Hacker, Andrew. *Money: Who Has How Much and Why.* (New York: Charles Scribner Books, 1997) 29.

4. Steinberg, Stephen. *The Ethnic Myth: Race, Ethnicity, and Class in America.* (Boston: Beacon Press, 1989) 217.

5. Geisst, Charles R. *Monopolies In America.* (New York: Oxford University Press, 2000) 6.

6. Hacker, Andrew. *Two Nations: Black and White, Separate, Hostile, Unequal.* (New York: Charles Scribner's Books, 1992) 16.

7. Kennon, Patrick E. *The Twilight of Democracy.* (New York: Doubleday, 1995) 7.

8. Steinberg, 180.

9. Lebergott, Stanley. *The Americans: An Economic Record.* (New York: W.W. Norton and Company, 1984) 212.

10. Jacobson, 29.

11. Woodward, C. Vann. *American Counterpoint: Slavery and Racism in the North/South Dialogue.* (New York: Oxford University Press, 1971) 88.

12. Kivel, Paul. *Uprooting Racism: How White People Can Work for Racial Justice.* (Phila: New Society Publishers, 1996) 25.

13. Phillips, Kevin. *The Politics of Rich and Poor.* (New York: Random House, 1990) 10.

14. Brouwer, Steve. *Sharing the Pie: A Citizen's Guide to Wealth and Power in America.* (New York: Henry Holt and Co., 1998) 21.

15. James, Jennifer. *Thinking in the Future Tense.* (New York: A Touchstone Book, 1996.) 212.

16. Lind, Michael. *Up From Conservatism: Why the Right is Wrong for America.* (New York: The Free Press, 1996) 190.

17. Fox, Geoffrey. *Hispanic Nation: Culture, Politics, and the Construction of Identity.* (New Jersey: Birch Lane Press Book. 1996) 178.

18. Steinhorn, Leonard and Barbara Diggs-Brown. *By the Color of Our Skin.* (New York: A Plume Book, 2000) 238.

19. Frederickson, George M. *The Arrogance of Race.* (Conn: Wesleyan University Press, 1988, 102.

## Chapter 2: Keys to Empowerment

1. Anderson, Claud. *Black Labor, White Wealth: The Search for Power and Economic Justice.* (Maryland: PowerNomics Corporation of America, Inc., 1994) 100.

2. Steinberg, Stephen. *The Ethnic Myth: Race, Ethnicity, and Class in America.* (Boston: Beacon Press, 1989) 105.

3. Wheeler, Tom. *Leadership Lessons from the Civil War.* (New York: Doubleday, 1999) 23.

4. Flores, William V. and Rina Benmayor. *Latino Cultural Citizenship: Claiming Identity, Space and Rights.* (Boston: Beacon Press, 1997) 1.

5. Fox, Geoffrey. *Hispanic Nation: Culture, Politics, and the Construction of Identity.* (New Jersey: Birch Lane Press Book. 1996) 178.

6. Gates, Jeff. *The Ownership Solution: Toward a Shared Capitalism for the 21st Century.* (Mass: Addison-Wesley, 1998) 68.

7. Steinhorn, Leonard and Barbara Diggs-Brown. *By the Color of Our Skin.* (New York: A Plume Book, 2000) 19.

## Chapter 3: How to Build Competitive Communities

1. Material was selected from two books.
Fox, Geoffrey. *Hispanic Nation: Culture, Politics, and the Construction of Identity.* (New Jersey: Birch Lane Press Book. 1996) and Flores, William V. and Rina Benmayor. *Latino Cultural Citizenship: Claiming Identity, Space and Rights.* (Boston: Beacon Press, 1997).

2. Anderson, Claud. *Black Labor, White Wealth: A Search for Power and Economic Justice.* (Maryland: PowerNomics Corporation, 1994) 203.

3. Anderson, Claud. *Dirty Little Secrets About Black History, Its Heroes and Other Troublemakers.* (Maryland: PowerNomics Corporation, 1998) 102.

4. Hacker, Andrew. *Two Nations: Black and White, Separate, Hostile, Unequal.* (New York: Charles Scribner's Books, 1992) 206.

## Chapter 4: How to Design Schools for Group Competitiveness

1. Woodson, Carter Godwin. *The Mis-Education of the Negro.* (Trenton, N.J.: Africa World Press, Inc., 1933) xiii.

2. Woodson, xiii.

3. Fisher, Claude S., Michael Hout, et al. *Inequality by Design: Cracking the Bell Curve Myth.* (New Jersey: Princeton University Press, 1996) 175.

4. Orfield, Gary and Susan E. Eaton. *Dismantling Desegregation.* (New York: The New Press, 1996) xiii.

5. Anderson, Claud. *Black Labor, White Wealth: The Search for Power and Economic Justice.* (Maryland: PowerNomics Corporation of America, 1994) 112

## Chapter 5: Practicing Group Economics

1. Remarks by Alan Greenspan, Chairman of the Federal Reserve Board, before the Annual Conference of the National Community Reinvestment Coalition, Washington, D.C. March 22, 2000. Title of speech, "Economic Challenges in the New Century".

2. Galbraith, John Kenneth. *Almost Everyone's Guide to Economics.* (Boston: Houghton Mifflin Company, 1978) 2.

3. Wesbury, Brian S. *The New Era of Wealth: How Investors Can Profit from the Five Economic Trends Shaping the Future.* (New York: McGraw Hill, 2000) 46.

4. Gates, Jeff. *The Ownership Solution: Toward a Shared Capitalism for the 21st Century*. (Mass: Addison-Wesley, 1998).

5. "Target Market News," May, 1999. *Target Market News*, Inc. (Chicago, Illinois) 4.

6. Porter, Michael E. *On Competition*. (Boston: A Harvard Business Review Book, 1995) 377.

7. Luttwak, Edward. *Turbo-Capitalism: Winners and Losers in The Global Economy*. (New York: Harper Collins Publishers, 1998) 106-107.

8. "The Buying Power of Black America," *Target Market Report*, 1998 edition. (Chicago, Illinois.)

9. "California Prison Study Finds Wide Racial Disparities," Tuesday, February 13, 1996, *Washington Post*, page A3.

10. Oliver L. Melvin and Thomas M. Shapiro. *Black Wealth: White Wealth*. (New York: Routledge, 1997) 101.

11. "Who Benefits: Asian-Americans Gain Sharply in Big Program of Affirmative Action," *The Wall Street Journal*, September 9, 1997. A1.

12. Oliver and Shapiro, 61.

## Chapter 6: Vertical Industrializing for Group Economics

1. Rifkin, Jeremy. *The End of Work*. (New York: A. Jeremy P. Putnam's Sons, 1995) 69.

2. "Mexicans Reap NAFTA's Benefits," *The Washington Post*, September 17, 2000. A22.

3. "A Town Builds Its Own Boom," *The Washington Post*, May 13, 2000, A3

**Chapter 7: Practicing Group Politics**

1. Davidson, James Dale and Lord William Rees-Mogg. *Sovereign Individual.* (New York: Simon & Schuster, 1997) 83.

2. Woodson, Carter Godwin. *The Mis-Education of the Negro.* (Trenton, N.J.: Africa World Press, Inc., 1993).

3. Green, Mark. *Winning Back America.* (New York: Bantam Books, 1982) 242.

4. Flores, William V. and Rina Benmayor. *Latino Cultural Citizenship: Claiming Identity, Space and Rights.* (Boston: Beacon Press, 1997)

5. Lind, Michael. *The Next American Generation.* New York: (The Free Press, 1995) 135.

6. Edited by Yans-McLaughlin, Virginia. *Immigration Reconsidered: History, Sociology, and Politics.* (New York: Oxford University Press, 1990) 297-298. The quotes were taken from Chapter 10, "The Reaction of Black Americans to Immigration" which was authored by Lawrence H. Fuchs.

7. *Microsoft Encarta Encyclopedia*, "Political Machine," 1999.

8. Fox, Geoffrey. *Hispanic Nation: Culture, Politics, and the Construction of Identity.* (New Jersey: Birch Lane Press Book. 1996)

9. "Administration Urges to Settle Indian Suit," *The Washington Post*, October 27, 2000, A9.

# INDEX

## A

academic achievement.
accountability, group, 74–75, 86, 87, 221–222
affirmative action, 14–15, 17, 193
AIDS
  number of people with worldwide, 249
  and wealth, 151, 249
*Almost Everyone's Guide to Economics*, 121
American Indians
  ethnic identity and rights of, 45
  as "Native Americans," 231
  reparations for, 206–210
  treatment of, 15
American Jewish Congress, 243
Anderson, Claud, xiv-xv, 49, 112, 173
Arab immigrants, 46–47
Asians
  behavior patterns in adversity, 29
  as quasi- Whites, 11
  as cultural model of success, 37–38
  establishing "root" businesses, 140
  and vertical chain of obligation, 130

## B

behavior patterns among Blacks
  code of conduct, 74–76, 104–105, 147–148
  group accountability, 74–75, 86, 87
  and group self-interest, 189–190
  hard work ethic, 38
  *See also* inappropriate behavior patterns
Benmayor, Rina, 40
Black Business Investment Corps., 171, 241
Black churches
  as an economic institution, 224
  expanding role of, 229–244
  growing danger to, 225
  historical role of, 225–227
  out-of-the-box religious teaching, 226–227
  as positive influence on Black culture, 226
  *See also* church-based action plan
Black codes, 13
Black colleges, 110–114
Black competitiveness

and community building, 63–88
  first impediment, 7–9
  major impediments to, 7, 8
  second impediment, 7–8, 25–30
  third impediment, 7–8, 30
Black elected officials, 76–77, 188
  crisis in leadership, xvi, 218–219
  leadership renaissance, 218–221
  questions for candidates, 203
Black immigrants, bias against, 11, 16, 194
Black Independent Party, 214–218
Black "inferiority" myth, 4, 38, 92
  churches role in, 225–226
  Scriptural basis for, 225–226
  *See also* White "superiority" myth
*Black Labor, White Wealth*, 112, 173
Black leadership. *See* Black elected officials
Black ministers, and racial issues, 228–229
Black music industry, 182–183, 237
Black-owned businesses
  and an independent economy, 73, 74
  and Arab immigrant competition, 46–47
  in Black neighborhoods, 65
  economic action steps, 129–154
  and horizontal social integration, 57–59
  television outlets, 21
  White vs. Black wealth ownership, 18–19
  *See also* economic action steps
*Black Labor, White Wealth*, xiv-xv
Black scientists and engineers, 42
Black underclass, vs. White overclass, 2–3, 96
*Black Wealth/White Wealth*, 136, 148
Blacker-than-thou militant, 26
Blackness
  avoiding, 28–29, 70
  Black leaders pride in, 220
  compromised by integration, 227–228
Blacks
  contributions of, 9
  as the "original people," 230–231
  population in U.S., 17, 194
Blacks in prison, 134–135
*Board of Educ. of Oklahoma v. Dowell*, 98
bottled water industry, 177–179
boycotting
  of businesses, 82, 141

259